"Jacobs has produced a useful accounting of the major events and themes of our national past..... [he] has chosen his filmic texts well... the films on his list explore critical themes and crucial issues in American history... Jacobs... [uses] his films to seek out the deeper and broader questions that engage the serious historian... Jacobs employs the judgments of major academic historians, including Bernard Bailyn, Gordon Wood, Eric Foner, and James McPherson, to inform his own... a solid and usable narrative of the first three centuries of American history... Jacobs' historical judgments... are sound...Throughout, the issue of race is treated with insight and sensitivity... Jacobs is careful not to claim too much for his films. He makes careful note of the instances in which they substitute fiction for fact." - *Film and History Journal*, **Jerald Podair, Professor of History and American Studies at Lawrence University, Wisconsin**

"An enthusiastic and detailed... film-centered approach to United States history that will engage the casual reader and provide inspiration to educators... Jacobs is passionate and knowledgeable about his subject, qualities that drive the book's spirited, informative approach to history... This history book... uses... movies... as focal points for a comprehensive journey through the history of the United States. Each movie serves as the symbol of an era... By going outside the mainstream--for instance, choosing Little Big Man (1970) rather than a John Wayne classic to anchor the discussion of westward expansion--the book takes its historical analysis in intriguing and unexpected directions." - **Kirkus Review**

"Jacobs' book would be a perfect addition to a faculty library... its use extends far beyond merely being a useful scaffolding tool... As students increasingly rely on film as a major, and sometimes only, source of historical information, it has become incumbent upon History teachers to ensure students have the skills necessary to decode film as an historical source... Any chapter is worth a course on its own, but the coherence of a course based around the ten provides a wonderful discussion starter for students... Each chapter here places a specific film in its historical context, and examines its historical accuracy. There is material to support follow up investigation after viewing the film, a timeline of the period under discussion, and an examination of further viewing options that teachers will certainly find useful... It can be used for content, general American history, and perhaps best of all, some serious historiographical discussion, which can only enhance the development of classroom skills." - **Bernie Howitt, History Teachers' Association of NSW, Australia, newletter**

A History of the U.S.

in 20 Movies

An All-Movie History Course

Volume One
the First Ten Movies

M.W. Jacobs

Escallonia Press
www. escalloniapress.com

This, my heart, my life for Nancy

A History of the U.S. in 20 Movies: an All-Movie History Course
Copyright © 2015 M. W. Jacobs

ISBN-13: 978-0692313930
ISBN-10: 0692313931

Table of Contents

Introduction

After more than a century of commercial filmmaking, there is a vast library of movies based on history. Some rank among the finest achievements of Hollywood and some are at the other end of the spectrum, but there are more than enough, from just watchable to great, to impart an accurate overview of U.S. history. Of course, the movies must be assembled right and each given context, missing information provided and inaccuracies corrected.

This book will teach you history by explaining interesting movies, all of which are available on Netflix or Amazon. This book will walk you through each movie using virtually every appropriate detail, providing historical context, explaining historical references, pointing out pertinent cinematic devices, and even occasionally tossing-in a tidbit of Hollywood history. Almost without noticing, you are going to absorb an accurate overview, an outline, a satellite photo image of the contours of the story of America. Like an introductory course, this book will help provide the indispensable foundation for more detailed knowledge in the future. Of course, the book can also be used piecemeal for brushing-up on a particular period in an entertaining way.

In essence, this is an illustrated lecture, using a variation of the technique used by PBS and the History Channel: reenactments intercut with expert talking heads. Except here, the movies are the reenactments and *A History of the U.S. in 20 Movies* is the expert talking head. The movies and this book entertain by emphasizing history as human drama, which is what we go to movies for and what movies go to history for. The dates, the statistics, the treaties, etc. are here in abundance, but they are presented in a way that enhances the narrative.

If Hollywood has been cavalier about historical accuracy, it has also at times compensated with scrupulous accuracy in everything that didn't affect the box office formula. But even in films that have no box office calculation, there can be unavoidable historical distortions; for example, the HBO miniseries *John Adams* (2008). If John Adams didn't actually arrive at the Lexington-Concord battlefield until days after the battle, is more lost than gained having him arrive in the movie immediately after the battle, when there is still musket smoke in the air, the wounded groaning where they fell, and mothers wailing over the corpses of their sons? To cinematically illustrate an important point or event, filmmakers might have characters witness or even participate in events in a movie that they didn't in life. I will explain historical distortions like this when they are important enough, but I won't overwhelm or distract you with all of them.

There is one movie per chapter and three sections in each chapter. The first section, "Before," prepares you by providing background and explaining the beginning of the movie, while avoiding spoilers. The second section, "After," explains the whole movie, completes the history, and generally adds whatever might be missing from the movie that is indispensable for the fullest understanding of the subject of the movie and/or the period in which it is set. The third section, "Recommendations," describes other relevant movies and documentaries that complement the one chosen, including the one or two other films that in some cases might just as well have been used in place of the one chosen. At escalloniapress.com, there are also free chapter-by-chapter recommendations of books - novels as well as histories, memoirs, and biographies - that are not already mentioned in the text. Some of the books are classics but most are the best of the newest among the relevant. Each chapter in *A History of the U.S. in 20 Movies* also includes easy-to-read timelines with explained historical high points.

Over two hundred and fifty films are referenced in both volumes one and two (making this book also a resource for teachers). Incidentally, there may be good films not mentioned because they weren't available on DVD at the time of writing. There also may be some mentioned that are no longer available as you are reading this. Availability is often erratic, especially with lesser-known films. There are also different edits so a scene mentioned here may not be in the version of the film you see.

I have honed that two hundred and fifty films to an indispensable core twenty. That is the least intimidating and the bare minimum that provides enough references for a thorough overview of U.S. history. The standards for choosing a film were: 1) it had to have an historically important subject, and/or (2) at least be rich in references to its period, and (3) it had to be at least "watchable." Taking into account the subjectivity variable in esthetic judgment, I didn't hold out for great or even good, but a bottom line of simply "watchable." However, many of the films here are Emmy or Oscar winners and some are based on Pulitzer Prize winning books or plays. If the choice was between two or more films equal in usable historical references for the same period, I chose the esthetically superior.

Though *12 Years a Slave* (2013) is esthetically superior to *Amistad* (1997), the latter touches on so many more important subthemes that I chose *Amistad* for slavery. Same with *Glory* (1989), which is superior esthetically to *Gettysburg*, but the latter deals with the pivotal battle of the Civil War and features more of the war's major players. *Amistad* and *Gettysburg* are at least watchable, though plenty of those rich in history are not. A good example is *Midway* (1976).

It was the pivotal battle of World War II in the Pacific and deserves a movie. The true story is full of the fictional devices that make history so fascinating and exciting: tactical brilliance, desperate gambles, lucky breaks, etc. The film has a cast of top stars and makes a laudable pioneering effort to include the internment of Japanese-Americans. But the stars wrestle lines of clumsy exposition that sound like lecture notes and the special effects are so bad that they include stock footage from silent movies. So, the Battle of Midway will get paragraphs instead of a movie. Ideally for a project like this, we would have a rich satisfying movie on each important high point of American history. And we do for some. But in some cases, we have nothing whatsoever, and in others, we have excellent films about footnote events that nevertheless exemplify important themes.

An example of the latter is *Matewan* (1987) (a favorite of U.S. history teachers). It's about a small and seemingly unimportant coal miners' strike in West Virginia in 1920. But *Matewan* is esthetically top tier and extraordinarily rich in historical references, providing teaching opportunities on the history of labor, on immigration, racism, and even the Spanish American War and World War I.

Some of the films included in this book are historically significant themselves, such as *Little Big Man* (1970), and I'll explain why for each. Here's one of those tidbits of Hollywood history: in his masterpiece *The Red Badge of Courage* (1951), based on the famous Civil War novel of the same name, John Huston has the most famous coward in American literature played by the most highly decorated American soldier of World War II. Audie Murphy had a long and prolific screen-acting career that included playing himself in a hit movie about his own war experiences.

Like PBS and the History Channel, this book is popular history, for curious laymen and students. It is about narrative not sources, so there is no bibliography or endnotes. Still, this is evidence-based history with no quarter given to comforting myths. As a consequence, in some chapters, there are revelations based on the latest research from the most distinguished sources, which are cited in the text.

Some of the sources for this book were the best history textbooks available, from which I taught for nearly twenty years. Of course, textbooks can be slanted toward school boards that are guided by prejudice more than evidence. The distortions of textbooks are widely known thanks to *Lies My Teacher Told Me: Everything Your American History Textbook Got Wrong* (1995) by James W. Loewen, and of course that great corrective, *A People's History of the United States* (1980) by Howard Zinn. So the textbooks have been supplemented by the very best of the most recent popular histories, most of which will appear in the literary Recommendations section at www.escalloniapress.com.

There are revelations here even for history teachers. Was the Confederacy defending states' rights or slavery? Tens of millions believe strongly on one side or the other but the most recent study is conclusive. The debate is over. Virtually every Hollywood western climaxed with a quickdraw showdown but what do historians say about its role in the real Old West? What was the largest armed uprising inside the U.S. after the Civil War? (It included the American Air Force participating in the bombing of American citizens.) Few history teachers could answer correctly, yet this occurred as a direct result of the events in one of our movies.

The two most basic elements of a nation are land and people. In these first ten movies, we will focus on where the land and the people came from that make up this particular nation. War is emphasized in these first ten movies because of the death and devastation, the resolution of issues, and the political realignment that results. In the second ten chapters, the presidency is emphasized, not just because of its power and influence but also because presidents are often a nexus for the major issues of their period. I welcome suggestions and corrections. Leave them at www.escalloniapress.com.

I have the ultimate qualification for commenting on the movies, one that nearly all "professional film critics" lack: I wrote, directed, produced, and edited a feature film (available on You Tube as "Twisted Tales from Edgar Allan Poe"). It was low budget and independently produced and made during the advent of the home video market in the early Eighties. In the late Eighties, I worked for George Lucas' special effects division, Industrial Light and Magic. Then I became a history teacher, and for nearly twenty years, I searched for the most effective way to teach the subject that polls perennially rank as students' least favorite. You are reading the results of that search.

Chapter One – The New World

Before

Boy meets girl. It's a core Hollywood plot formula, and in our first film, by legendary writer-director Terence Malick, the boy and the girl are also the touch points of the Old and New Worlds. It's the story of English adventurer and explorer Captain John Smith and Powhatan Indian princess Pocahontas, a story that passed from history into the iconography of American popular culture even before there was a USA. Subject of numerous paintings, the story was eventually Disneyfied in a 2003 animated feature. Peggy Lee summarized the story well in her 1958 jazz classic, "Fever."

> "Captain Smith and Pocahontas
> Had a very mad affair.
> When her daddy tried to kill him
> She said, 'Daddy, oh, don't you dare …
> He gives me fever'."

How much of their story is myth and how much history is still being debated by scholars and we'll wade into that debate. Whatever happened, it answered a need as a founding myth: the Romeo and Juliet of the New World, the imaginary royal wedding of the two worlds.

Terence Malick planned his version of the American foundation myth for over twenty-five years, and he finally got it into theaters just short of the 400-year anniversary of the establishment of Jamestown, Virginia, where the lovers met and most of the story is set. Such is his reputation in Hollywood that Malick was given a 50 million dollar budget and total artistic control. Prior to becoming a filmmaker, he translated a book by German philosopher Martin Heidegger and then graduated from Harvard summa cum laude and Phi Beta Kappa; then he was a Rhodes scholar; then he taught philosophy at Massachusetts Institute of Technology. He did all this while still in his twenties.

The New World strains for authenticity, which is great for our purposes. It was shot on location at the Chickahominy River, a tributary of the James River not far from the site of the historic events. The film crew created reconstructions of the Jamestown settlement and of the Powhatan village based on archaeological evidence and consultation with historians. They got a linguistics professor from the University of North Carolina to come up with a form of the extinct Powhatan language. They even sought historic varieties of Indian corn and tobacco rather than just plant contemporary strains.

The epigram at the beginning of the movie is from John Smith, "How much they err, that think everyone which has been at Virginia understands or knows what Virginia is." This cues us that this story is going to be about a mystery or at least different visions of reality. We next get an epigram from the New World when Pocahontas intones in a voice-over, "Come, Spirit. Help us sing the story of our land. You are our mother. We, your field of corn. We rise from out of the soul of you." We hear this while the camera skims the briny primordial soup in which multicellular life evolved. Her invocation, "Come spirit. Help us sing ..." echoes the traditional "Sing Muse..." that begins classical epics, and even more important, it highlights the intense spirituality of these so-called "heathen savages," or "naturals" as the Englishmen call them in the movie.

Malick uses the opening credits to preview the story, animating maps and drawings of the period. There are drawings of ocean-going ships, maps in which rivers are filled-in by animation as they are explored, then images of shipwreck, and indigenous people around a fire. Of course, there is a detailed drawing of war and slaughter, which incidentally was completely imaginary, this particular drawing having been created in Salzburg, Austria. This animated montage (a series of images with a common theme) ends with a drawing of a suspended fish which becomes a segue into the movie when it is immediately followed by a suspended fish in the opening cinematography.

Pocahontas then continues her prayer to the Great Mother, "the great river that never runs dry." And during her prayer, lest we forget that it is sex that makes that river flow, we watch Pocahontas and two other beautiful young women swimming naked through the primordial soup to strains from the prelude of Wagner's "Das Rheingold." Then the aliens arrive.

H.G. Wells intended his science fiction classic *War of the Worlds* (1898), about invading space aliens, to be an allegory about indigenous peoples' reaction to the conquering Europeans. Throughout the momentous first meeting of Europeans and Indians at Jamestown, Malick maintains an appropriately charged atmosphere of unearthly visitation, from the natives' first sighting of the English ships to the first face-to-face meeting in an insect-infested meadow where a native leader slaps Captain Newport, the English leader, on the chest to test his solidity.

The first time in *The New World* that we see the three English ships (echoes of Columbus' three), we also see a title, "Virginia / 1607." At this time, Virginia (named after the "virgin" queen, Elizabeth I) is what the English called the entire New World. With the permission of Elizabeth's successor, King James

I, a private company, the Virginia Company, has sent the three ships to colonize Virginia.

During this era, English nationalism blossomed under the threat of Spanish invasion, assisted by militant Protestantism and the leadership of Queen Elizabeth. The major colonial powers in the Americas were Spain and Portugal, but soon enough the English, the French, the Dutch, and even the Swedish would join them. There were three distinct forms of European colonization in the New World: empires of conquest, commerce, and settlement. Spain regarded the Indians as a usable labor force, while France treated the Indians primarily as trading partners. The English, in contrast, adopted a policy known as plantation settlement: the removal of the indigenous population and its replacement with native English and Scots. This English pattern of colonization was based on the conquest and settling of Ireland, as the Spanish pattern was based on their experiences resettling areas of Spain from which they drove out the Moors.

On the sparsely populated eastern seaboard of the present-day U.S., an area the Spanish dismissed as not worth the effort, the English were not faced with conquering and ruling established empires like the Spanish were with the Aztecs and the Incas. The English just had to survive harsh conditions. Spanish colonialism was the exclusive provenance of the crown, with the English it was business, involving "joint stock companies" which combined the investments of shareholders. The joint-stock company was supposed to make a profit from the natives to whom it brought the benefits of civilization. There were about 15,000 of the latter in eastern Virginia when the English first landed.

Jamestown was the first *permanent* English colony in the New World but not the *first* English colony in the New World. That was at Roanoke Island in what is now North Carolina. It earned the name "Lost Colony" when supply ships delayed by England's battle against the Spanish Armada, arrived at the colony to find 118 men, women, and children had vanished. To this day, we don't know what happened.

The Virginia Company charged the Jamestown colonists with fulfilling three objectives: find gold, find the Northwest Passage (a short cut to Asia and its trade goods that would make rich everyone associated with the venture), and find survivors and/or descendants of the Lost Colony. When the ships of the Virginia Company reached Virginia, they had been sailing for an unusually long five months, passing through the Caribbean. In the movie, we see the crew getting their first close look at the part of the New World that will be English. We also see our hero, Captain John Smith, emerging like a cave dweller, in chains below decks. Then the Englishmen land and we see an armored soldier, weapon at the ready, wading into a vast lush meadow in a state of untrammeled purity, a symbol of the entire expedition.

Captain John Smith was a classic Hollywood swashbuckler come to life. It's a wonder Errol Flynn never played him. Smith was twenty-eight when he arrived at Jamestown, and by his own account, he had already gone to sea at sixteen, fought as a mercenary for the French against the Spanish, fought for Dutch independence against the Spanish, and in Transylvania, killed and beheaded three Turkish commanders; for which, he was knighted by a Transylvanian prince and given a coat of arms with three Turk's heads. Later, Smith was captured and sold into slavery and eventually owned by a Greek noblewoman who fell in love with him. He escaped and made his way back to England. This is only the broadest outline of his adventures. They have strained belief from his time to ours and garnered many detractors.

But during the 1950s, a linguist and former intelligence officer, Philip L. Barbour, scoured Eastern European archives, ignored by Smith's detractors, and corroborated a huge number of details in Smith's writings. Barbour's *The Three Worlds of Captain John Smith* (1964) forever lay to rest any suspicion that Smith invented his adventures from whole cloth.

When we are formally introduced to Smith in the movie, it is with a drum roll and a camera shot of him beside a hangman's noose, and we learn he has been accused of "mutinous remarks." It's true he was scheduled to be hanged, but he wasn't saved by the good graces of Captain Newport as in the movie. Sealed orders when opened indicated that he had been officially chosen by the Virginia Company as one of the leaders of the colony and that's what saved him. "The Warres of Europe, Asia, and Affrica taught me how to subdue the wilde Salvages... in America," Smith later wrote. The value of such a man for a remote outpost vulnerable to attack by the Spanish, French, and/or Indians must have been obvious to the Virginia Company.

His "mutinous remarks" show Smith to have been a rebel as well as an adventurer. Colin Farrell as Smith shows the certified rebel's slight nod and slighter smirk the first two times that he is addressed by the authority figure, Captain Newport. The latter is played by two-time Emmy winner and one time Oscar winner, Christopher Plummer. Immediately after his reprieve, Smith wanders in the New World savoring the wonders of nature and showing us that, besides being rebellious, he is also sensitive. That quick insert shot of the swaying noose is meant to remind us that he has just narrowly escaped death, so the whole world is transcendently vivid.

In this scene, we are also being introduced to an important character, Nature in the New World, with which all of the other important characters interact in their own way. Malick inserted an exhibition of ravishing nature photography between the scenes of his story. The film got an Oscar nomination for best cinematography. Malick matched the quality of the cinematography with the sound design. In that animated montage during the opening credits, at one point, the music subsides and is strikingly replaced by a panoply of New World nature sounds. I highly recommend you listen with headphones to the beginning of the movie, at the very least, to savor the full richness of the multi-layered sound design.

Meanwhile, Captain Newport chooses the site of their settlement, next to a malarial swamp. Newport then mentions later seeking "… a route to the other sea." It is also called in the film "a passage to the Indies." The other sea was the Pacific and the Indies were Asia, specifically Indonesia, and the route or passage was the fabled Northwest Passage. That was the trade shortcut to Asia that Columbus was looking for when he "discovered" America. It would make all those associated with its discovery very wealthy. Others continued the search more than a century after Columbus, including Henry Hudson, whose crew mutinied in 1611 and set him adrift in a rowboat on the Canadian bay now bearing his name, where he perished.

A crewman asks Newport, "When might we … poke about, sir?" Newport then scolds the would-be pirate, renames what he asked about as "pillage and raid," and reminds him that they are there to establish a colony. Piracy is at the heart of western culture going back to its ancient beginnings. (What was the very first thing Odysseus did after leaving Troy? Raid.) Indeed, much of the European colonization of the Americas can be seen as an extended pirate raid with missionaries.

Next, while Pocahontas plays with her brother in a meadow, we get a full dose of her charm and grace. This sets up the inevitable boy's first meeting with girl. The way this is done is important: Smith is wandering in the same meadow, and the first time he sees Pocahontas, she is hidden in the middle distance, barely visible in the tall grass, barely distinguishable from the natural beauty around them. They move closer and eventually stand staring transfixed at each other until her brother leads her away. From the beginning, Smith's feelings for Pocahontas are blended with his feelings for the New World. At one point as he is making love to her he calls her "My America." She would mean for him a transformed life, as he recognizes in later voice-over musings, "Exchange this false life for a true one. Give up the name Smith."

On first seeing the abundance of the land, one of the Jamestown colonists declares, "We shall live like kings." Not long after that, circumstances reverse and they are, in Newport's words, "Hardly better off than being shipwrecked." The gravity of the situation is conveyed by Newport's order to have a food thief branded and his ears cut off. Newport returns to England for supplies and appoints Smith the head of a diplomatic mission to find Indians with whom to trade for food.

Smith was "the low born son of a farmer" and not a gentleman, as his arch nemesis, the aristocratic Wingfield, points out while arguing against Smith's appointment as captain of the diplomatic mission. (Though not mentioned in the film, Wingfield apparently accused Smith of the mutinous remarks that almost got him hung.)

While Smith wends his way up river on this mission, we get the first of Malick's poetic voice-overs, a stylistic quirk of his. You may want to use the subtitles because these interior monologues are spoken in undertones but they are worth understanding. Smith's first voice-over lays out one of the earliest visions of America as an escape from the oppressive European social structure.

This is a vision that will continue for centuries, to our day, and lure tens of millions of immigrants. "We shall make a new start, a fresh beginning ... Here the blessings of the earth are bestowed upon all ... We shall build a true commonwealth, hard work and self-reliance our virtues... We shall have no landlords to rack us with high rents or extort the fruit of our labor..."

But when this monologue concludes we are startled by behavior that directly contradicts it. While Smith says, "None shall eat up carelessly what his friends got worthily or steal away that which virtue has stored up," his famished men are stripping food from drying racks in an apparently abandoned Indian village. This is Malick reminding us that those high-minded principles are frequently ignored or at best compromised in the application.

The colony is in the territory of the Powhatan Confederacy, composed of thirty Algonquin tribes and ruled by a King Powahatan. That is who Smith is brought to when Indians capture him during that diplomatic mission. Then Powhatan apparently orders his execution and that brings us to the big question: did Pocahontas save his life?

We know about the incident from Smith himself, who could have written honestly about battles but lied about Pocahontas. Indeed, he claims in other writings to have been rescued by a young girl while a captive of the Turks, which could indicate a recurring invention. It used to be the consensus among historians that Pocahontas did *not* rescue John Smith. However, J. A. Leo Lemay, Professor of English at the University of Delaware and author of *Did Pocahontas Save Captain John Smith?* (1992), makes the point that "No one in Smith's day ever expressed doubt in [the story], and many persons who must have known the truth...including John Rolfe [and] Pocahontas...were in London in 1616 when Smith publicized the story in a letter to the queen." Would Smith have lied to the queen while expecting, as he did then, that she would meet Pocahontas? Lemay concludes, "There are eight unmistakable references in Smith's writings to Pocahontas's saving his life... The overall evidence supplied by all eight (and possibly nine) references proves beyond a shadow of a doubt that Pocahontas rescued him."

It has been suggested that the Powhatans were not actually trying to kill Smith when Pocahontas saved him but were putting him through an initiation ceremony that he didn't understand. However, very little is actually known about Powhatan culture, so all we have in the end is speculation about it. Malick uses both Smith's account and the speculation that he was being initiated. When Smith tries to wow the Indians with gunpowder thrown into fire, they answer with a shaman who can induce hallucinations. This is the beginning of what is clearly depicted as some sort of ritual laying-on of the hands by native women on Smith's body. Then a warrior rushes toward Smith with a huge club held aloft and then Pocahontas is suddenly on top of him while the voice-over quotes Smith's written description of the incident.

Before he is captured, when Smith and a small crew are going deep into Virginia forest, the scene is suggestive of Joseph Conrad's later European, Marlow, going into the heart of darkness of an African jungle. Smith even encounters dangling shrunken heads for warning off intruders. But Smith's experience is diametrically opposed to that of Conrad's Kurtz. In the place of "the horror," Smith finds Eden. His vision for a democratic future already exists in native society. "Real, what I thought a dream," he says in voice-over.

While we watch the burgeoning romance between Smith and Pocahontas, handled with consummate delicacy, we also see Smith gradually being seduced by and absorbed into Powhatan society. Eventually he is dancing bare-chested beside a fire at night with other warriors and we know for certain that he has "gone native." Then King Powhatan sends him back to Jamestown, with the understanding that the English are to leave the following spring, once their boats have returned.

This Indian idyll might be considered sentimental over-compensation for past distortions of Native American history except we have the fact that Indian societies were attractive to some whites, drawing them away from the colonies. It became such a problem for the Pilgrims that they outlawed long hair and had hanging as one of the punishments for those who joined the Indians. In other colonies, such people were burned alive. Plus, there are stories of rescued white captives refusing to return to white society.

An early American classic, *Letters from an American Farmer* (1782), says, "Thousands of Europeans are Indians and we have no examples of even one of those Aborigines having from choice become Europeans." Ben Franklin wrote, "No European who has tasted savage life can afterwards bear to live in our societies ... All their government is by Council of the Sages. There is no Force; there are no Prisons, no officers to compel Obedience, or inflict Punishment."

Now enjoy the movie, and after watching it, finish the next section of this chapter.

After

It was fitting that Pocahontas died at the end of this film. By far the most effective European weapon against the indigenous peoples of the Americas was disease. Scholarly estimates for the death toll from disease range as high as ninety per cent. The traumatized survivors of the pandemics were much easier to defeat militarily, and of course, the Europeans considered the diseases a sign that God wanted them to possess these new lands.

Pocahontas died of unknown causes, but in the London of that time, she would have been exposed to things such as smallpox, pneumonia, or tuberculosis for which she, like the rest of the indigenous American population, would have no immunities. This was because they had none of the domestic-cated animals from which the diseases and the immunities to the diseases derived.

If Pocahontas dies young, she dies in the film with a degree of spiritual fulfillment, and an answer to a query at the beginning of the film. She says in voice-over, "Mother, now I know where you live," as the film fades to black over images of nature in the new world. Of course, "The New World" for Pocahontas was England and all things English. She is the bridge between the two peoples, and the film broadly follows her documented life from her youth in the Powhatan village, to the period with the settlers in Jamestown, to her marriage to John Rolfe, and her journey to London and an early death.

Pocahontas' earliest ancestors first migrated into North America from Asia over the Bering Straits that separate Siberia from Alaska (and possibly by other routes) sometime between 15,000 and 40,000 years ago. Scientific advances in the latter half of the twentieth century have led to the conclusion that indigenous American cultures were much more advanced technologically and much more numerous than was previously thought. Estimates range from 50 to 100 million for the population of the Americas at the time of Columbus' arrival.

Once there was a holiday called Columbus Day. It is still formally celebrated in some places but nowhere is it nearly as big as it used to be. Why not? The truth finally got out, as it will, that though he may have been a heroic explorer and navigator of genius, Columbus was also a criminal. The Arawaks were the inhabitants of the Bahamas when Columbus landed there in 1492, and when the natives couldn't supply him with enough gold, he punished them by cutting off their hands. When that didn't produce enough gold, he made up the loss by enslaving the Arawaks and other indigenous peoples and taking them back to Spain. Columbus thus began both the transatlantic slave trade and the destruction of indigenous American cultures for gold that would continue for centuries. All of this is in the first chapter of Howard Zinn's *A People's History of the United States* (which has sold two million copies).

Bartolomé de las Casas, the son of one of Columbus' officers and a Dominican priest who was known as "the Apostle of the Indians," voluminously chronicled for over half a century crimes committed against the Indians. Writing of a period during most of which Columbus was in charge, Las Casas wrote that "from 1494 to 1508, over three million people perished from war, slavery, and the mines. Who in future generations will believe this? I myself writing it as a knowledgeable eyewitness can hardly believe it...." The population of central Mexico alone fell from around twenty-five million in 1519 to little over one million by the end of that century.

Columbus also began what scholars call the "Columbian Exchange:" Europe, Africa, and the Americas exchanging foods, animals, diseases, and human beings. The Indians taught Europeans about tobacco, corn, potatoes, avocadoes, peanuts, tomatoes, and chocolate. Europeans introduced wheat, oats, barley, and rice, plus domesticated animals like horses, pigs, sheep, goats, and cattle. All of what was exchanged of course had far reaching impact on societies and the natural environment.

In *The New World*, infectious diseases haven't had enough time to become a factor in the struggle between English colonists and natives. Armed conflict erupts when Powhatan decides that the English intend to stay. The battle scenes give Malick an opportunity for some box office-fortifying, choreographed violence, which is not to say that there isn't a feeling of authenticity in weapons, formations, and ferocity.

When his arch nemesis, Wingfield, threatens to shoot Smith and instead is shot himself, Malick is able to meet the demands of another box office formula almost as basic as boy-meets-girl: shoot a bad guy. Actually, the real Wingfield wasn't killed, but when Smith was in command of the colony he sent Wingfield back to England "to seeke some place of better emploiment." That "emploiment" turned out to be the writing of several books about Jamestown.

Another departure from history is when Smith is over-thrown by Argall, ostensibly for protecting Pocahontas, and then Smith is bound and whipped. It adds to Smith's cred as a lover, rebel, and persecuted visionary but it didn't happen. Not that he didn't have enemies within the colony, and they even plotted his murder. Historically, Pocahontas was kidnapped by Argal but after Smith had returned to England. Incidentally, Pocahontas did participate in providing life-saving food to Jamestown in the first winter and she did save colonists by warning them ahead of time about an attack, though it wasn't while they were in the fort but while visiting Powahatan.

The biggest departure from history in the film is the romance at its center. While it may or may not be that Pocahontas saved Smith's life, it is extremely unlikely they were lovers, because she was possibly as young as ten years old when they first met. They definitely had a friendship, witness their meeting when she was in London, but the likely subject was the mistreatment of her people since his departure and not their failed romance.

Malick neatly closes his mythical romance with the lines, "Did you find your Indies John?" and "I may have sailed passed them." For all its artistic achievement, and this is the best film by one of the best American filmmakers ever, *The New World* is also an example of the aforementioned scrupulous historical accuracy in everything that doesn't affect the box office formula.

After Smith returns from his period of captivity with the Indians and is made (he was actually elected) leader of the colony, Malick accurately depicts Smith doing what would make him almost as famous as the supposed affair with Pocahontas: taking over the leadership of Jamestown to insure its survival and preserve England's presence in the New World. Malick provides a title card: "The President / Fall 1608."

The desperation of the colony that winter brought to the fore the contradiction of an aristocratic society and forced Smith to adopt stern measures. When he declared in the movie, "He that shall not work, he will not eat," he was quoting the bible. Then Smith added something that is a pretty good formulation of English society in his time, "The labors of honest and industrious men shall not be consumed to maintain the idleness of a few." One of his biggest problems was getting the "gentlemen," who made up about two thirds of the colony, to do manual labor.

Plus Smith also had to deal with true gold-madness. "While they starve, they dig for gold," Smith said in a voice-over while we watched delirious men digging with their hands. Stories about the fabulous wealth stolen from the Aztecs and Incas had enflamed greed throughout Europe. The Disney version of the Pocahontas story includes an extravagant and very effective musical number about the gold-madness that Europeans inflicted on the Americas. In some respects, the rush into the New World was an earlier version of the Gold Rush that opened up California in 1849.

Despite Smith's leadership and his best efforts, by the end of 1608 only 53 of the original 120 Jamestown colonists were still alive. But the next winter, after Smith returned to England, would be called "the starving time." Without Smith and especially his skill at trading with the natives, the colonists descended to cannibalism. One man murdered his pregnant wife, "ripped the child out of her womb, and threw it into the river and afterward chopped the mother in pieces and salted her for his food," according to Smith's successor as President, an ineffectual aristocrat named Percy.

The boiled leather, references to cannibalism, and the ranting madmen in *The New World* would have been more appropriate to "the starving time." Incidentally, the religious rants of several of the characters are important because this was a time of religious fervency in Europe. Known as the Protestant Reformation, it was a religious movement that began as an attempt to reform the Roman Catholic Church and resulted in the creation of Protestant sects and a series of devastating wars that pitted Catholic against Protestant and Protestant against Protestant.

As for what sent Smith back to England, it wasn't the royal summons or the possibility of glory as discoverer of the Northwest Passage that the King through Newport dangled before Smith (which conveniently simplified Smith's dilemma in the movie: love or glory?). Smith was actually forced to return to England because of a serious leg wound, caused by a stray spark that landed in his powder pouch when he was lighting tobacco. He returned to the New World five years later exploring Massachusetts Bay and the coast of Maine and bestowing the name "New England" on the territory. That's where he was when the title card in the movie appeared that said, "Far to the North / Spring 1614."

It is fitting that this most capitalist of countries should be founded for the profit of the Virginia Company, and it is also fitting that tobacco, a popular consumer commodity and addictive drug, helped the country take root and grow. Pocahontas' next love interest, John Rolfe, was the first to develop a sellable tobacco (from stolen Spanish seeds). In the movie, Rolfe mentioned Pocahontas' knowledge of tobacco cultivation as being one of her attractions. The "brown gold" the Rolfes created was Virginia's first cash crop and it would eventually create an entire economy and vast fortunes. It would also lead to the first importation of African slaves.

The scene in the movie in which Rolfe is getting permission from the authorities to marry is muddled and confusing. Some of the dialogue comes from a letter he wrote to the governor requesting permission to marry. He was wracked with guilt about marrying a heathen and he even wondered if his feelings for her were prompted by the Devil. There was a political aspect to their marriage not touched-on in the film: it sealed a temporary peace between the colonists and the Powhatans.

With scrupulous (contemporary) psychological honesty, Malick puts the ache of first love and untenable love at the center of a story about first contact between worlds. And as such films must, most of it is told on the faces of the lovers, and after Smith's departure from Jamestown, it is told mostly on the remarkable face of fourteen year old actress Q'orianka Kilcher, whose father is a Peruvian Quechua Indian. By the time of the making of this film, 2005, there was a long roster of excellent Native American screen actors and this film includes two of the very best, August Schellenberg (Mohawk) who plays King Powhatan and Wes Studi (Cherokee) who plays Opecancanough, younger brother of Powhatan and the counselor who advised killing all the colonists in the scene in which Pocahontas saved Smith.

Opecancanough did not accompany Pocahontas to England as he does in the movie, but you can't blame any director for wanting as much of Wes Studi in front of his camera as he can get. By the way, in that scene in which this "natural" wandered bewildered through a rigidly structured and sculpted English garden, Malick was contrasting the English and Indian views of nature. Opecancanough succeeded Powhatan as king, and in an uprising, slaughtered 347, a third of the colonist population, including Pocahontas' husband John Rolfe who had returned following her death. English reprisals were so ferocious that they nearly wiped out the entire Powahatan tribe.

Something not mentioned in the movie is the fact that Pocahontas was sent to London by the Virginia Company as a living advertisement, proof that the Indians could be civilized, and therefore, it was safe to live in the colony. John Smith became a tireless and insistent champion of British colonization of America, so much so that his literary endeavors for twenty years after he left the colony may have been as important as his actions while in the colony. After 1607, 14,000 people migrated to the colony, but by 1624, only 1132 were living there. Many returned to England but some also starved and some were killed in Indian attacks.

To attract needed craftsmen to the colony, the Virginia Company promised them "the rights of Englishmen" including a representative assembly which would be known as the House of Burgesses and would be the seed of American representative institutions. The company also provided ninety women for wives at a mere one hundred and twenty-five pounds of tobacco each. The same year the House of Burgesses first met, 1619, was also the year when the first cargo of slaves arrived, so that democracy and slavery were, as one historian put it, "born in the same cradle."

The following year, the Pilgrims arrived on the *Mayflower*, founding the second English colony, and that is the setting for our second film, *The Crucible*.

Exploration Timeline 1492–1607

1492 Columbus reaches the Bahamas
1493 Start of permanent settlement (La Isabela on northern Hispaniola)
1497 John Cabot may have reached Newfoundland
1502 Columbus sails along the mainland coast south of Yucatán
1513 Ponce de Leon explores Florida
1521 Hernán Cortés completes the conquest of Mexico
1524 Giovanni da Verrazzano explored the Atlantic coast of North America for the French
1534 Francisco Pizarro conquers the Inca in Peru
1535 Jacques Cartier reaches Quebec
1536 Cabeza de Vaca reaches Mexico City after wandering for years in the North American Southwest
1539 Hernando de Soto explores the interior from Florida to Arkansas
1540 Coronado travels from Mexico to eastern Kansas
1541 French settlement at Quebec City fails
1542 Juan Rodriguez Cabrillo reaches the California coast
     Hernando de Soto claims the Mississippi River for Spain
1565 Pedro Menéndez de Avilés founded St. Augustine
1570 The Iroquois League founded (a Native American confederation of the "Five Nations")
1587 Englishman Sir Walter Raleigh founded Roanoke Colony
1590 The Roanoke Colony was found deserted
1598 Spanish reach Northern New Mexico
1607 The first permanent English colony is founded in Jamestown, Virginia

Recommendations

For the 500th anniversary of his voyage, 1992 saw two films about Columbus. The first and worst, *Christopher Columbus: the Discovery,* was from the producers of *Superman* and featured a muscular comic-book hero Columbus. A Washington Post review dismissed it as "ridiculous." The more promising *1492: Conquest of Paradise* was directed by the Ridley Scott and starred Gérard Depardieu, but the Washington Post dismissed it with "Despite Scott's trademark spectacular imagery, the story's dead in the water." And Variety seconded that calling the film, "a lumbering, one-dimensional historical fresco." Plus, there was Columbus' thick French accent. Of course, neither film had the guts to get close to historical accuracy. Probably the most accurate depiction yet is the film within a film of the excellent Spanish movie *Even the Rain* (2010).

But there are two superb, accurate movies that show colonization customs of other European powers, above and below the U.S. For above, there is *The Black Robe* (1991) which brings together the great Australian director Bruce Beresford and one of the best Irish novelists of the Twentieth Century, Brian Moore. He adapted his own novel of the same name which focuses on a French Jesuit missionary who arrives in Canada in 1634 to convert the Huron Indian tribe to Catholicism, and incidentally, expedite French colonization of Quebec. Relations between the French and Indians were less violent than in Spanish or English colonies. France's Jesuit priests did not require the Indians to immediately abandon their tribal ties or their traditional way of life. Meticulously researched and utterly gripping start to finish, *The Black Robe* won the Genie (Canada's equivalent of the Oscar) for Best Picture.

Robert De Niro, Jeremy Irons, and Liam Neeson star in *The Mission* (1986). It won the Palme d'Or, the top prize at the Cannes Film Festival, and the Academy Award for Best Cinematography. Set in the 1750s, it tells the story of a Spanish Jesuit who enters the South American jungle to build a mission and convert Guaraní Indians. The climax is the Guarani War of 1754–1756, during which the hopelessly out-gunned Guaranis attempted to defend their homes against Spanish-Portuguese forces. It is based on the book *The Lost Cities of Paraguay* (1982) by Father C. J. McNaspy, SJ, who was also a consultant on the film.

For the four hundredth anniversary of Jamestown, there were two new documentaries, National Geographic's *The New World: Nightmare in Jamestown* (2006) and PBS's *Pocahontas Revealed: Science Examines an American Legend* (2007). Both claim to have unearthed new truths with advanced scientific techniques. National Geographic's *America Before Columbus* (2009) covers the same terrain as the book *1491,* discussed with other free book recommendations at www.escalloniapress.com.

Chapter 2 – The Crucible

Before

This film is based on the most popular stage play of one of our greatest playwrights, Arthur Miller, who also wrote the film script. In the 1950s, when it premiered, the play acquired a history of its own, worthy of its own movie, which would blend betrayal and treason and Marilyn Monroe.

This movie version of *The Crucible* could hardly begin more spectacularly. At dawn, deep in the forest, there is a Dionysian celebration full of sexual frenzy with adolescent girls dancing nude and smearing blood on themselves and calling out the names of boys. Their pagan priestess so-to-speak is an African slave who is tending a cauldron boiling with ingredients that could have come from the witches' brew in *Macbeth*. Reverend Parris, the father of one girl, uncle of another, and the local minister, discovers the girls.

These people are Puritans and what the girls were indulging in is the Puritans' greatest evil: witchcraft. This film is about the most famous incident in American Puritan history, the Salem witch trials. The title refers to a container used to heat metals to high temperatures, and a "crucible" is also defined as "a severe test or trial, especially one that causes a lasting change or influence."

Besides the one that settled Jamestown, the Virginia Company had another division, called the Second Colony of Plymouth. Using a map from Captain John Smith's 1614 expedition, the first colonists of the Second Colony of Plymouth landed their ship the *Mayflower* in Plymouth, Massachusetts, in 1620. They did *not* land on Plymouth Rock as legend has it.

The passengers on the *Mayflower* included some ordinary Protestant Englishmen and some "Separatists." For some Englishmen, the protestant Church of England, the official English church, was still too "popish" or tainted with Catholic influence. They wanted to purify it further and were therefore called Puritans. But there were divisions even among the Puritans, and one subgroup wanted to separate themselves completely from the Church of England, and because of that, were driven out of England into the Netherlands. These were the Separatists, known to Americans as "the Pilgrim Fathers." As a wise man said, to know the true nature of anything study its beginnings. To understand the

United States of America, we are going to its beginnings in these religious refugees, Protestants so extreme that other Protestants persecuted them.

As at Jamestown, the Pilgrims arrived in Plymouth too late to plant crops and during the first winter 52 out of 102 perished. They were saved by an English-speaking Indian named Squanto who taught them how to plant corn. The Pilgrims had cordial relations with the Indians at first and invited them to a traditional October harvest feast, which we celebrate today as Thanksgiving.

Before the *Mayflower* landed, a short document was composed in which the signers, forty-one males, agreed to abide by laws made by leaders of their own choosing. That was called the Mayflower Compact and it was the first written constitution in North America.

Less than a decade later, another Puritan colony was founded north of Plymouth by Massachusetts Bay Company, and within the decade after that, the Great Puritan Migration occurred in which around 21,000 Puritan immigrants flooded the area. They would eventually have 16 million descendants, but our story takes place among their grandchildren and great-grandchildren.

The director of the *The Crucible*, Nicholas Hytner, had been an opera director, and his previous film was the highly successful *The Madness of King George* (1994), also adapted from the stage. As with *The New World*, the filmmakers behind *The Crucible* strove "to make the most authentic film possible," according to one of its producers. They shot the outdoor scenes on pristine Hog Island off the coast of Cape Ann, almost within shouting distance of Salem, the site of the historical events, and the indoor scenes were shot on a sound stage constructed in nearby Beverly. Authenticity extended to buildings "authentically stained and aged," to farm animals of the period, to crops of the period growing in the fields, to costumes made by hand (no sewing machines) from antique linens, even to giving the actors an appropriately unbathed appearance, fingernails daily dirtied.

It is significant that the film opens in the forest (though the scene is an invention, and in the play, takes place offstage). The Puritans' towns perched on the coastal edge of a continent the extent of which and the contents of which were unknown. Nature here is not Pocahontas' Great Mother but a monster sleeping just outside the settled area. Poet William Carlos Williams wrote of their situation, "The emptiness about them was sufficient terror for them not to look further."

They didn't need to find any evil spirits in the American forests though, they brought their own supply from Europe, chief among them Satan. These people believed as much in Satan, hell, and eternal damnation as they did in God. When two of the girls, traumatized by being discovered in the forest, are in a coma the next day, the town's people naturally assume the influence of Satan and witchcraft. All Europe believed in witches at this time. In Salem, they believed that all misfortunes were attributable to the work of the Devil. When things occurred like infant death, crop failures, or friction within the congregation, the supernatural was blamed. Evil was something external but palpable. Satan was everywhere, except in their own deficiencies.

The ringleader of the girls who met in the forest is Abigail Williams, Parris' niece, and she is played by the stunning Winona Ryder. Abigail is in love with our hero, John Proctor, played by Daniel Day-Lewis, who is Arthur Miller's son-in-law and the son of British Poet Laureate, C. Day Lewis.

Abigail was a servant in John Proctor's house. He had sex with her and she fell in love with him. During the ritual in the woods, she asks the slave, Tituba, to use witchcraft to arrange the death of Proctor's wife Elizabeth. Notice the first time John and Abigail see each other on screen, while he is engaged in conversation and she is descending stairs. He can barely look her in the face and she is rigid with fright. There is, shortly after, a scene where they are alone and we get the state of their relationship. Abigail's passion for John Proctor will be the spark that ignites the witchcraft hysteria in the movie.

"There are wheels within wheels here," John Proctor says to Mr. Hale the witchcraft expert from outside Salem. What Proctor means is: there are what we would call "hidden agendas." Immediately afterwards, during a shouting match, Reverend Parris complains, "I can never offer one proposition but I face a howling riot of argument." "Welcome to Salem," Proctor says to Hale after both witness this argument. Miller's point here, and this is firmly established by historians, is that the town was ripe for what was to follow due to long-standing disputes over land, village boundaries, and the maintenance of the ministry.

A middle-aged couple named Putnam will be prime movers of the hysteria. In an early scene, they will declare that they only have one child alive out of eight while another townswoman, Goody Nurse, hasn't lost one, and even has had twenty-six grandchildren. (The infant mortality rate was very high then.) The Putnams' remaining child is one of those girls in a coma, and as the hysteria develops, notice in scene after scene, Goody Putnam shouting from the sidelines. Incidentally, "Goody" is short for "Goodwife."

This grief-addled mother will start the madness rolling when she mentions to Tituba the first named suspects, Goody Osborn and Goody Good. Tituba, who has just been whipped and is undergoing a grueling interrogation, in her terror of course accuses whoever she is bid to. After she does, Goody Putnam declares in an ecstasy, "I knew it ... They were midwives to me three times and my babies shriveled in their hands." Then Abigail in a trembling fit seconds Tituba's accusation and then a chorus of demented girls breaks out in a frenzy of accusations shrieking random names of those they have supposedly seen with the Devil. Goody Putnam weeps with joy.

Of course, notice who is the first scapegoat, the slave, the person it is safest to victimize. Then it is a couple of derelict crones, Goody Osborn and Goody Good. The first victims are all outcasts, but then we get a series of scenes illustrating the atmosphere that has been created in the town: a neighbor whose garden has been invaded by a goat curses another neighbor, a girl is looking at a load of logs while it falls off of a sledge, and a neighbor hails Mr. Putnam while a bonfire suddenly flares up. All are thrown into jail for witchcraft. The madness will continue to devour the social structure upwards.

When it touches his home, John Proctor will rant in his despair, "I'll tell you what is walking in Salem ... Vengence! ... The little crazy children are jangling the keys to the kingdom ..."

There had been plenty of witchcraft trials in New England before 1692 and nearly a score of executions. But accusations had usually been directed against obscure and isolated individuals. Only in Salem did accusations of witchcraft get so out of hand that they came close to destroying the whole community. This happened, moreover, at the very time when in Europe witch trials were becoming increasingly anachronistic.

The language used in the play and film is not an exact replication of Puritan speech, which would have been closer to Shakespeare's, but is a poetic recreation for our times drawing on the rhythms and speech patterns of the King James Bible. Miller was peerless for creating poetry out of ordinary speech.

In modern usage, the word "puritan" is most often used to describe "dour prudery." It is a collection of nasty traits such as extreme sexual repression, censorship, prohibition, fundamentalism, and moral hypocrisy. The most famous line about Puritanism is journalist H.L. Menken's definition of it as "the haunting fear that someone, somewhere, may be happy." One obvious legacy of Puritanism in our time is that section of many police departments known as the vice squad, which specializes in "victimless crimes" (or criminalized morality) such as homosexuality, prostitution, gambling, drugs, etc.

William Carlos Williams wrote of Puritans that they "looked black at the world and damning its perfections praised a zero in themselves." But he also wrote, "They were the perfect sprout for the savage continent God had driven them to ... By their very emptiness they were the fiercest element in the battle to establish a European life on the New World."

Alexis de Tocqueville considered the Puritans to be the Founders of America because of their formative influence on American national character. From them came "a democracy, more perfect than any which antiquity had dreamt of." He wrote admiringly in *Democracy in America* (1835) of the Puritans: "The other colonies had been founded by adventurers without family; the emigrants of New England brought with them the best elements of order and morality - they landed in the desert accompanied by their wives and children. ... Nor did they cross the Atlantic to improve their situation or to increase their wealth; the call which summoned them from the comforts of their homes was purely intellectual; and in facing the inevitable sufferings of exile their object was the triumph of an idea ..."

The major twentieth century scholar of Puritanism, Perry Miller, located "the meaning of America" in the experience of the seventeenth-century Puritans. Miller said, "Without some understanding of Puritanism, it may safely be said, there is no understanding of America." Some historians believe the American sense of mission is inherited from the Puritans. In the most famous description of the Puritan community by one of its own, John Winthrop wrote "as a City upon a Hill, the eyes of all people are upon us." More recently, some historians have maintained that the Puritan influence has been exaggerated. Others are focusing more on Puritans as the first immigrants whose experience is a paradigm for understanding all subsequent immigrations.

After 1700, most immigrants to Colonial America arrived as indentured servants—young unmarried men and women, who worked off the cost of their passage, seeking a new life in a more promising environment. Also, between the late 1610s and the American Revolution, Britain shipped an estimated 50,000 convicts to its American colonies.

Religious persecution was a particularly powerful force motivating English colonization. Some 30,000 English Puritans in total immigrated to New England, while Maryland became a refuge for Roman Catholics, and Pennsylvania, southern New Jersey, and Rhode Island, havens for Quakers. Refugees from religious persecution included Baptists, Congregationalists, and Presbyterians, to say nothing of religious minorities from continental Europe, including Huguenots and members of the Dutch and German Reformed churches.

Having been a persecuted religious minority didn't keep the Puritans from persecuting other religious minorities. Not long before the witch trials, they hanged four Quakers in Boston.

The core Puritan religious beliefs were personal Biblical interpretation, shared with Protestants in general, along with lots of preaching in churches where there was little or no ritual, decoration, vestments, images, musical instruments, etc. On moral grounds, the Puritans banned many secular entertainments, such as games of chance, maypoles, and even drama. Music, dancing, celebration of holidays such as Christmas and Easter, were absolutely forbidden, as they had roots in Paganism.

In the first scene of our movie that is set inside the Salem church, when Reverend Parris explains to the assembled townsfolk the possibility that Satan is in their midst, notice in the shots of Parris on his pulpit the two gold candlesticks, one in the lower left and one in the lower right of the frame. Under interrogation later, John Proctor will give as his reason for not attending Parris' church the fact that the minister replaced perfectly acceptable pewter candles sticks with those gold ones. Proctor is a Puritan's Puritan.

Some scholars point out that the actual Puritans weren't nearly so puritanical as they are portrayed. Maybe, but they were puritanical enough. As we see in the film, their funereal clothing, abhorrence of dancing, and obsession with "evil," hardly project joyous affirmation of life. To the Puritans, a person was by nature wholly sinful, totally depraved, and could achieve good only by severe and unremitting discipline. Hard work was considered a religious duty and emphasis was laid on constant self-examination and self-discipline.

After the 17th century the Puritans as a political entity largely disappeared, but Puritan attitudes and ethics continued to exert an influence on American society. They made a virtue of qualities that made for economic success—self-reliance, frugality, industry—and through them influenced modern social and economic life.

The Puritans advocated mass education so everyone could read the Bible for themselves, prefiguring the free public education that would be so indispensable to the development of the United States. The Puritan idea of congregational democratic church government would carry into the political life of the nation as another source of modern democracy. The Puritans in Massachusetts held annual elections and extended the right to vote and hold office to all "freemen." Although this term was originally restricted to church members, it still meant that a much larger proportion of the adult male population could vote in Massachusetts than in England itself (roughly 55 percent in Massachusetts compared to about 33 percent in England).

Hey, what's all this got to do with Marilyn Monroe?! The period of her greatest fame, the 1950s, was also a period when the country and especially Washington was gripped by anti-communist hysteria, called the Red Scare. Arthur Miller attacked it in *The Crucible*, drawing parallels between the anti-communist "witch hunts" and those that took place in Salem in 1692. Conservative politicians then attacked Miller.

He and Monroe were married (sometimes they were referred to as "The Egghead and The Hourglass"). When Miller refused to betray friends before a congressional committee, he was convicted of contempt of congress. The committee chairman let Miller know that things might go easier for him if Marilyn posed for a photograph with the chairman. When Monroe was urged by movie studio executives to abandon Miller for the sake of her career, she refused, later branding them as "born cowards". Miller's contempt of congress conviction was overturned on appeal.

In the After section, we will see how this type of hysteria erupted in our own time, indeed within a few years of the making of the movie, with causes eerily similar to those of the Salem witch trials.

After

This film was made in 1996, and only a few years before, there was a nationwide rash of child molestation trials in which coached five-year-olds were used to convict innocent day-care workers of unspeakable crimes. Victimized children can trigger a particularly deep hysteria. Remember Goody Putnam?

The trials of the day-care workers included uncorroborated allegations of satanic cults, human and animal sacrifices, and even U.F.O. abductions. If this most recent outbreak of Salem-style mass hysteria didn't kill people, it did give innocent people lengthy prison sentences. Recent polls have shown that a majority of Americans say they believe in the Devil's existence and 10 percent say they have communicated with him.

Paul Scofield's brilliant performance makes Judge Danforth so obviously thoughtful and fair, so unmoved by hysteria, that he obliges us to accept the plausibility of the accusations. It is a measure of Arthur Miller's fairness to the Puritans that even those who do not believe the girls, like John Proctor and Rebecca Nurse, nevertheless, cannot offer a viable alternative explanation for the freakish behavior. Even today, though we know it is not caused by evil spirits, we cannot explain with certainty the psychological mechanisms behind mass-hysteria.

To visually underscore the fact that *The Crucible* is about "mass" hysteria, Nicholas Hytner used the movements of large crowds. He also tripled the number of accusers. A big problem for a film director using a play is "breaking out of the stage," making a talky stage play cinematic. Hytner really broke out of the stage best in that scene where the girls started repeating everything Mary Warren said and then ran out of the church pursued by a bird-like invisible spirit-projection of Mary's. What follows is a beautifully choreographed crowd sequence with the girls cowering on the ground and then the overhead camera, from the point of view of Mary's spirit-projection, swooping down on them like a raptor. They jump up and rush toward the sea and the camera pivots and follows as does the entire village fearing the girls will drown themselves. We now have the spectacle of the whole town running furiously together toward the sea. What better illustration of group madness? This scene climaxes with the arrest of the hero, John Proctor.

A writer at the time of the witch trials gave the body count: "And now Nineteen persons having been hang'd, and one prest to death, and Eight more condemned, in all Twenty and Eight ... about Fifty having confest themselves to be Witches, of which not one Executed; above an Hundred and Fifty in Prison, and Two Hundred more accused..." At least five more of the accused died in prison.

Miller wrote in an afterward to the play, "The legend has it that Abigail turned up years later as a prostitute in Boston. Twenty years after the last execution, the government awarded compensation to the victims still living and to the families of the dead ...Some beneficiaries were not victims at all, but informers ...To all intents and purposes, the power of theocracy in Massachusetts was broken."

Theocracy in this context is civil authority and religious authority either mixed together or invested in the same people. Miller shows this in the scenes where Reverend Parris acts as government official, excommunicating the condemned just before their execution and supervising the crushing of Giles Cory. Eventually a complete "separation of church and state," an impenetrable wall between civil and religious authorities, would become one of the most hallowed of American political principles.

Miller did original research in the archives at Salem. Nevertheless, fitting the story into a stage play required changes, and the principal ones were fusing characters and inventing the affair between John Proctor, who was actually 60 at the time of his execution, and Abigail Williams, who was actually 11, making possible the story's sexual catalyst, particularly apt in a society defined by sexual repression. So this film becomes yet another example of scrupulous historical accuracy in everything that doesn't affect the box office formula.

Miller also changed the race of Tituba the slave. All of the primary sources (documents by the people who actually knew her) refer to Tituba as "Indian." By making her African, in a cast otherwise all white, Miller of course is reminding us of the moral affliction of racism that continues into our own day even after we have had an African American president.

Europeans enslaved anybody they could, and there was a thriving, and still little known, trade in Indian slaves. The Carolina Indian slave trade, which included both trading and direct raids by colonists, was the largest among the British colonies, estimated at 24,000 to 51,000 slaves. Most went to the Caribbean plantations where there wasn't a hospitable forest to escape into but where the tropical diseases proved so lethal that Africans with immunities to those diseases eventually became preferable.

Indians were also part of the threat of that haunted the enveloping forest. Miller shows this when Abigail is threatening the other girls to keep them in line and says, "I saw Indians smash my dear parents' heads on the pillow next to mine and I have seen some reddish work done at night."

There were several major Indian wars in the seventeenth century, before the Salem Witch Trials. One involved the Pequots of Connecticut between 1634-1638. They understood that, as Pocahontas' father, Powhatan, told John Smith, "Your coming is not for trade but to invade my people and possess my country." The events leading up to the Pequot War involved the killing of a slaver who was kidnapping Pequot women and children and the Puritans' subsequent demands for the killers. There was an exchange of raids and battles, and it all culminated in a massacre on the Mystic River of "six or seven hundred" Indians by the Puritan's own count. The victims were mostly Pequot women, children, and old men, since the warriors were away at the time. The slaughter appalled the Puritan's Indian allies. The war destroyed the Pequots as a tribe with the few survivors being sold into slavery. *The New World* gave us vivid recreations of Indian attacks and colonist retaliations.

King Philip's War of 1675-1678 was the single greatest calamity to occur in seventeenth-century Puritan New England. "King Philip" was what the colonists called Metacomet, the chief of the Wampanoags, because of his adoption of European dress and custom. Much more difficult to defeat than the Pequots, the Wampanoags and their allies might have triumphed except, though he had two thirds of the tribes, King Philip wasn't able to form an effective coalition. This will be a continuing problem for the Indians in the following centuries.

When King Philip's War was over more than half of New England's towns had been attacked by Native Americans and twelve of the ninety towns destroyed. Five percent (600) of the Puritan population was killed, a higher proportion than Germany, Britain, or the United States lost during World War II. Indian casualties were far higher, perhaps 40 percent (3,000) were killed or fled the region. Most of the participating tribes were all but exterminated, plus the Puritans had extended the war into the territories they coveted of peaceful Indians. King Philip was captured and killed and his wife and son sold into slavery, which the Puritans considered an act of mercy. The Wampanoags were the tribe that helped the Puritans survive their first years and with whom they shared the first Thanksgiving.

Tituba could have been descended from survivors of either the Pequot War or King Philip's War.

After the latter, most of Massachusetts, Connecticut, and Rhode Island were almost completely open to settlement, free of military resistance from the Native Americans. However, King Philip's War devastated for a time the colonial economy, which was highly dependent on the import of staples from England, and was supported by the investments of a number of wealthy immigrants. In New England, the economy was organized around small family farms and urban communities engaged in fishing, handicrafts, and Atlantic commerce, with most of the population living in small compact towns. In Maryland and Virginia, the economy was structured around larger and much more isolated farms and plantations raising tobacco. In the Carolinas, economic life was organized around larger but less isolated plantations growing rice, indigo, coffee, cotton, and sugar.

In 1676, Bacon's Rebellion occurred, an uprising led by 29-year-old planter, Nathaniel Bacon. Sparked by declining tobacco prices, a cattle epidemic, and a belief that the colony's governor, William Berkeley, had failed to adequately protect Virginia against Indian attacks, Bacon's Rebellion caused about a thousand Virginians to rise up (including former indentured servants, poor whites, and free blacks). Rebels took matters into their own hands, attacking Native Americans, chasing Berkeley from Jamestown, and then torching it.

The alliance between former indentured servants and Africans disturbed the ruling class who responded by hardening the racial caste of slavery. While the farmers did not succeed in their goal of driving Native Americans from Virginia, the rebellion did result in Berkeley being recalled to England. But after Bacon's Rebellion, African slaves rapidly replaced indentured servants as Virginia's main labor force.

The Middle Colonies, consisting of the present-day states of New York, New Jersey, Pennsylvania, and Delaware, were characterized by a large degree of diversity—religious, political, economic, and ethnic. The Dutch colony of New Netherland was taken over by the British and renamed New York but large numbers of Dutch remained in the colony. New Jersey began as a division of New York, and was for a time divided into the proprietary colonies of East and West Jersey. Many German and Irish immigrants settled in these areas, as well as in Connecticut.

Pennsylvania was founded in 1681 as a proprietary colony of the Quaker William Penn. Philadelphia, Pennsylvania eventually became the center of the colonies. By the end of the colonial period 30,000 people lived there, having come from diverse nations and practicing numerous trades.

Nearly all the English colonies in America were settled without any significant English government support, as they were used chiefly as a safety valve to minimize religious and other conflicts in England. King Philip's War was the beginning of the development of a greater American identity, for the colonists' trials gave them a group identity distinct from subjects of the English Crown in England.

That identity will be a catalyst for the War of Independence, which is the subject of the next film, actually sections of an HBO miniseries, *John Adams*.

Colonial Timeline 1607- 1692

1607 John Smith founded the Jamestown Settlement.
1614 The Dutch laid claim to the territories of New Netherland.
1619 Slavery was introduced to the Colony of Virginia.
1620 The Mayflower Compact was signed.
       -The Pilgrim Separatists land at Plymouth, Massachusetts.
1622 Indian attacks kill one-third of the English settlers in Virginia.
1625 New Amsterdam (later New York) was founded.
1628 The Massachusetts Bay Colony founded.
1634 The colony of Maryland was founded allowing Catholics to
       settle in it.
       -Theologian Roger Williams was banished from the
       Massachusetts Bay Colony.
1635 The Connecticut Colony was founded by Thomas Hooker.
1636 Roger Williams founded the Colony of Rhode Island, the first
       English colony to grant complete religious tolerance.
       -Harvard College was founded.
1637 The New Haven Colony was founded.
1637 Anne Hutchinson banished from Massachusetts for preaching
       that salvation was achievable through faith alone.
1638 The Delaware Colony was founded.
       -New Sweden was established.
1643 The New England Confederation was created.
1644 Third Anglo–Powhatan War began.
1646 Third Anglo-Powhatan War ended.
       -The execution of the English King Charles I marked the
       establishment of the Commonwealth of England under

Puritan dictator Oliver Cromwell.

1654 The first Jews arrive in New Amsterdam, fleeing the Spanish Inquisition in Brazil.

1660 The Commonwealth of England came to an end with the restoration of King Charles II of England.

1664 Second Anglo-Dutch War began with the English conquest of New Amsterdam.

1667 New Netherlands was ceded to England under the Treaty of Breda.

1675 King Philip's War began in New England.

1676 Bacon's Rebellion Jamestown, Virginia
   -King Philip's War ended, relative to the size of the population, the deadliest in American history.

1680 Pueblo Indian Revolt in Spanish New Mexico.

1682 The Province of Pennsylvania was founded by William Penn.
   -Frenchman de La Salle travelled down the Mississippi River to its mouth.

1685 Charles died. He was succeeded as King of England by James II of England.

1688 Glorious Revolution in which King James was deposed in favor of William and Mary, ending absolute monarchy in England forever.

1692 Salem witch trials took place in the Province of Massachusetts Bay.

Recommendations

Remember the saintly Rebecca Nurse who was hung with John Proctor? She had two sisters: Mary Eastey was also executed, but Sarah Cloyse, although accused, escaped execution. The PBS produced movie *Three Sovereigns for Sarah* (1985), using actual transcripts of the witch trials as the basis for some dialogue, is about Sarah's efforts to prove her sisters' innocence after their deaths. The film sacrifices some dramatic flair for historical accuracy but Sarah is played by Vanessa Redgrave. Member of the Redgrave acting dynasty and proclaimed by Arthur Miller and Tennessee Williams as "the greatest living actress of our times," she is also the only British actress ever to win the Oscar, Emmy, Tony, Cannes, Golden Globe, and Screen Actors Guild awards. As we would expect from PBS, the costumes, locations, buildings, and props are unusually authentic.

There is a movie from 1952 about the Mayflower called *Plymouth Adventure* that still stands up pretty well. All the characters are there from the historical record, however, Spencer Tracy's cynical ship's captain has an unlikely love affair with Gene Tierney, the wife of colony leader William Bradford. It's in color and the effects won an Oscar and still look pretty good. The other most famous literary work about Puritans, after *The Crucible*, is *The Scarlet*

Letter, a classic novel by Nathaniel Hawthorne. None of the film versions do justice to the book. Demi Moore's 1995 version is a laughable mess but can provide some insight into Puritan society and give some feel for the times.

Disney's *Squanto: A Warrior's Tale* (1994) is loosely based on the actual historical Native American figure Squanto, and his life prior to and including the arrival of the Mayflower in 1620. Included are his adventures in England and his return to the discovery that his tribe had been entirely wiped out by European diseases. The last scenes of the film portray the first Thanksgiving celebration.

Cromwell (1970) does not take place in the U.S. but is nevertheless significant. Even though it is riddled with minor inaccuracies, it is an excellent depiction of the Puritans as a political force in England. There is even a scene in which Puritan leader Oliver Cromwell, like John Proctor, has a violent reaction to gold candlesticks in his church. After winning the English Civil War, Cromwell and the other Puritans cut the head off King Charles I who was supposedly appointed by God but not evidently actually protected by him. This execution for treason was one of the most important events in the evolution of democracy in the world and America, conclusively disproving the principle of the "divine right of kings." The French will later second the motion in their revolution when they similarly dispatch their monarchs.

In the period before the English Civil War erupted, some Puritans saw emigration to the New World as a substitute for revolution against the king. Cromwell himself considered emigrating here. The New England Puritan community was openly sympathetic to the Cromwellian revolution, and indeed sheltered two of the regicides and refused to give them up when the monarchy was restored after Cromwell's death.

There is also a 2008 film *To Kill a King* starring Tim Roth as Cromwell. The movie is about Cromwell's strained friendship with the more moderate Puritan General Thomas Fairfax. Though it looks good, it's muddled and meandering.

There is a 1998 History Channel documentary, *In Search of History: Salem Witch Trials*. The first of the six parts of the PBS series *God in America: How Religious Liberty Shaped America* (2010) deals with the Puritans and the religious context of early New England. The History Channel also has a typically thoughtful docudrama on the Pilgrims in *Desperate Crossing: the Untold Story of the Mayflower* (2006). It uses Royal Shakespeare Company actors with scenes and dialogue from the records of participants and eyewitnesses, and was filmed in many of the historical locations.

At www.escalloniapress.com, there are free recommendations of the best books - histories, biographies, memoirs, and even novels -related to the subjects of this chapter.

Chapter 3 · John Adams

This is the best film ever about the American Revolution. It won four Golden Globes and is the holder of the record for most Emmys by a single program in a single year. And it is based on the Pulitzer Prize-winning biography by historian David McCullough, *John Adams*, declared "by far the best biography of Adams ever written" by the dean of Revolutionary War historians Gordon S. Wood. In a review in the *New York Review of Books*, Wood wrote, "None of the other Founders passed on such a rich and revealing body of personal documents as Adams did. He could not hide his feelings, and he spilled out his innermost passions onto the pages of his diaries and his personal letters."

Adams is a perfect entry point into the major causes and major players of the American Revolution. He was closer to an everyman than any of the other Founders. Washington was distant and stiff, Jefferson enigmatic and contradictory, Madison shy and brilliant, Franklin witty and wise. Adams was contentious, cantankerous, prickly, blunt, even offensive, but also brilliant, decent, fair, and always of sterling integrity. Of the first ten presidents, he and his son were the only ones who never owned slaves.

As much as it is about the founding of the republic, this miniseries is also about a marriage, the first and one of the greatest American political marriages, that of John and Abigail Adams. It is well documented through their twelve hundred letters filled with intellectual discussions on government and politics as well as marital intimacy. He was dependent on her advice and craved her approval. Pulitzer-prize winning historian Joseph Ellis maintains that the letters are more revealing than any other correspondence in American history between a prominent husband and wife. Ellis also thinks she was the better letter-writer (even though he was one of the best of the age), and that she was the more resilient and more emotionally balanced of the two. The miniseries takes the same position and her wisdom and insight shines out of scene after scene.

This HBO miniseries is nine hours long and has seven episodes. We will use just enough episodes to cover all the political highpoints of the Revolution and the founding of the Republic. Because of the importance of this chapter, the density of the information, and the length of the episodes, we will use a somewhat different format. Of the seven episodes, we will only use the first, second, and fifth. In the first and fifth we will combine the normal before and after sections into one. "Recommendations" will be after the end of the last episode.

Episode 1 – "Join or Die"

Before and After

It opens onto a desolate snowy night when Adams, brilliantly played by Paul Giamatti, is returning from a journey on horseback. It's typical of the intelligence and skill of this film that there is something important in almost every shot of the opening sequence, before there is a line of dialogue. You will see on a tree trunk a poster with a drawing of a snake in 13 pieces and below it the slogan, "Join or die." This is propaganda by radicals who want a united front by the colonies against what they see as British oppression. The American colonies had a long history of squabbling with one another, and before 1765, relations among the colonies were much more quarrelsome than their relations with Britain.

Then you will see an effigy hanging from a tree branch (popular form of protest at the time) and a sign on it reading, "Tory." This is a term still used in Britain today for political conservatives. In this context, it would mean an American who supports the British government. We get a parting shot of red cloth on the effigy. That is for the red uniforms of the British army.

Adams then enters the town center and we see him pass a Redcoat, as British soldiers are called. We hear boys' shouting voices and then see a group of kids marching in mock military formation in front of the soldier who is standing on guard duty. One voice is distinctly heard yelling, "Go back to England!" As Adams rides out of the square, we see the kids pelting the soldier with snowballs. These kids' shenanigans are about to have a major impact on American history.

Adams arrives home and he is there only minutes when the fire alarm, a clanging bell, is heard. He rushes into the street where, instead of a house on fire, he happens onto the Boston Massacre, gun smoke still in the air. The title card before the opening shot told us it was "Boston / 1770." Though the Revolution is still five years away, on this night it gets its first martyrs. Actually, when the Boston Massacre occurred, John Adams was visiting friends and not at home.

Adams wanders among the Redcoats, who stand about in shock over what they have just done, shot unarmed civilians. Then he looks at the victims. Notice the last one is African American. His name was Crispus Attucks and he was a runaway slave of Wampanoag and African descent who became a seaman ... and one of the first martyrs of the American Revolution. The other colonist who arrives and starts shouting "Murderers!" at the Redcoats, and has to be restrained by John Adams, is his cousin Samuel Adams. Five Americans were killed that night.

In that brief period between John's arrival at home and the fire alarm, we get a foretaste of the warmth and love within the Adams family. And we meet Abigail, whose first comment is a measure of this extraordinary marriage. He is a lawyer and she embraces him and says, "You lost ... I could tell by the set of your shoulders." She knows him *that* well. She is played by Laura Linney who nails Abigail's strength and intelligence perfectly. For their roles in *John Adams*, both Linney and Giamatti each won an Emmy, Golden Globe, and Screen Actors Guild Award, among others.

At a time when love was not considered necessary for a successful marriage, the Adams were not only passionately in love but intellectual partners as well. They were third cousins and descended from Puritans. When they married, she was seventeen, bookish and brilliant, and he was twenty nine and a struggling country lawyer. Four of their six children reached adulthood and two of those died before John and Abigail. One son became president, John Quincy Adams, more on that in a later chapter.

Though John was dependent on Abigail's advice, he goes against it when he is asked to defend the British soldiers involved in the Boston Massacre, saying "Counsel is the last thing an accused person should lack in a free country." This tells us much about the man. In a later scene he will complain to her that, though the trial ought to be decided on the guilt or innocence of the soldiers, the real issue will be "Does the government of King George have the right to tax the citizens of Boston when they are denied representation in the parliament?" The Sons of Liberty expressed that sentiment best in their motto, "No taxation without representation." In that same scene, we get a good insight into John and Abigail's working relationship as she gives him courtroom strategy. Later she will read and critique his summation.

Just before the trial begins, we see a funeral procession and protest demonstration complete with more effigies of hanged redcoats and banners with "Join or die," and a new one, "The Folly of England is the Ruin of America." The procession includes Crispus Attuck's grieving mother and boys wounded in the Massacre. It is lead by Sam Adams (played by Danny Huston, son of one of the greatest movie directors of all time, John Huston). The John Adams family is watching from their doorstep and Sam loudly criticizes for all to hear John's becoming the defense attorney for the British soldiers. The drawing of the Massacre on the flier Sam gives John was by Paul Revere.

John and Sam Adams were second cousins. John was born in 1735, the son of a respectable farmer and shoemaker in the small village of Braintree, Massachusetts, just south of Boston. But he was awarded a scholarship to go to Harvard at age 15, where he "discovered books and read forever." He became one of the most widely and deeply read Americans of that very bookish Age of Enlightenment. His father wanted his son to become a minister, but Adams realized he was not temperamentally suited for a clerical life, and chose the law instead.

While John went into law, Sam, who also graduated from Harvard, squandered a large amount of his family's money mis-managing a business. He was obsessed with colonial rights from a young age and became a charismatic speaker and held several political offices. Sam was not, as John implies in the funeral procession scene, formally a member of the Sons of Liberty. However, Sam's writings showed that he had no disagreements with them. They were a loose knit underground organization of pre-Revolution activist patriots. Formed In 1765, they used public demonstrations, violence, and threats of violence to ensure that the British tax laws were unenforceable.

The trial scene is riveting but it is not of major historical significance. It presents the British soldiers' side of the Boston Massacre. It is another indicator of the fairness of this series about one of America's greatest achievements that it begins with numerous scenes, like the trial, that are unflattering to the Americans. Incidentally, in the book that the series is based on, David McCullough points out that Sam Adams did not object to his cousin John representing the soldiers because both men wanted to prove Massachusetts capable of a fair trial.

There is a scene after the trial in the Adams' parlor when three friends try unsuccessfully to get John to run for office (which actually happened two years before the Massacre) and one of the friends runs down a list of tax abuses by the British, "They've taxed our paper, our glass, the lead in our paint, even our playing cards and dice." These were taxes imposed by the British government at a time when it had incurred an enormous debt after defeating the French in the Seven Years' War, or as it was known in America, the French and Indian War (1754-1763).

The French and Indian War is the name for the North American theater of the Seven Years War, the first global conflict between super powers: France and Spain against England and Germany. The name French and Indian War refers to the two main enemies of the British colonists: the royal French forces and the various Native American forces allied with them, although Great Britain also had Native allies. The war began near the site of present-day Pittsburgh, Pennsylvania, when Virginia militiamen under the command of the British officer George Washington ambushed a French patrol.

Britain's victory in that war confirmed its position as the dominant colonial power in the eastern half of North America but at the cost of nearly doubling its national debt. Parliament thought it only fair that the colonies share in the cost of their defense plus some of the costs of protecting and administering the empire. But in the absence of a French threat, colonists believed the colonial militias (which were funded by taxes raised by colonial legislatures) were sufficient to deal with any trouble with natives on the frontier.

The Americans, who were taxed far less than citizens in Britain, didn't object to paying taxes (they were already supporting local legislatures and militias). They objected to paying taxes to a parliament in which they had no representatives. Parliament said that they had "virtual representation," meaning the whole of parliament represented the whole of the English people. But most Americans rejected this. They believed that only the colonial assemblies, where the colonists *were* represented, should be able to levy taxes upon the colonies.

The most incendiary of Parliament's taxes was the Stamp Act of 1765, the first direct tax (as opposed to a customs duty) levied on the colonists. It imposed a tax on all newspapers, legal documents, playing cards, dice, almanacs, and pamphlets. It caused a firestorm of opposition through resolutions of local legislatures and public demonstrations and even violence. The Sons of Liberty ransacked the mansion of the governor, Thomas Hutchinson. The Americans organized a boycott of British goods, and affected merchants convinced Parliament to repeal the taxes. The boycott became the weapon of choice against unpopular acts of Parliament.

But the next year Parliament passed the Declaratory Act, asserting that parliament retained full power to make laws for the colonies "in all cases whatsoever." Policy makers thought it was time to rein in colonial subjects who had been allowed near-autonomy.

But in 1767 came the Townsend Acts requiring the colonists to pay an import duty on tea, glass, oil, lead, paper, and paint. Parliament soon repealed all the Townsend duties except the one on tea. On December 16, 1773, about a hundred and fifty Sons of Liberty dressed like Mohawk Indians and led by Sam Adams, boarded ships of the government-favored British East India Company and dumped their tea into Boston harbor. This event became known as the Boston Tea Party and remains a significant part of American patriotic lore. In the film it only gets a passing reference from Jonathon Sewall, the attorney general of Massachusetts and the close friend who arranged for John Adams to get a royal appointment.

There is a scene in the film where John Hancock, after being confronted by a British customs official, orders a crowd to "Teach him a lesson, tar the bastard." Hancock and Samuel Adams then look on while the official is tarred and feathered, to the disapproval of John Adams. This scene is fictional and does not appear in McCullough's book. According to Samuel Adams' biographer Ira Stoll, the scene succeeds in "tarring the reputations of Hancock and Samuel Adams." Historian Jeremy Stern writes that, "Despite popular mythology,

35

tarrings were never common in Revolutionary Boston, and were not promoted by the opposition leadership."

John Hancock *was* accused of smuggling and a customs official by the name of John Malcolm *was* tar-and-feathered but only from his waist up and not on a shipping dock in the middle of day as in the film. Nevertheless, there was a great deal of mob violence in the period just before the war. Frightening for the savagery of the unleashed mob, this fictitious tar-and-feathering scene supports John Adams' often repeated belief in the law before all else. The scene also illustrates his belief stated later to Abigail while they are reading late at night before a fire that "People all need strong governance, Abigail. Restraint! Most men are weak and evil and vicious."

It is also in this scene of the tar-and-feathering that we meet John Hancock, wealthiest man in New England, shipping magnate, and friend of Sam Adams. His was the first and boldest signature on the Declaration of Independence which gave rise to the phrase "Put your John Hancock there" for signing a document. As for whether or not he was a smuggler, historians are still divided. Britain tried to block American trade with the French, Spanish, or Dutch empires using the Navigation Acts, which Americans avoided as often as they could, thus becoming "smugglers." Incidentally, notice in the scene with the tar-and-feathering the quick shot of slaves, brought to a dockside stage for an auction that must wait for the tar-and-feathering to finish.

Then there is a scene in which new laws are proclaimed from a balcony. These were the Coercive Acts of 1774, or the Intolerable Acts, as the colonists called them. They were Parliament's response to the Boston Tea Party as well as other offences. Jonathon Sewall reads the proclamation which says, "No goods or merchandise whatever [shall] be transported to or brought from any other colony or country [to Boston] ... " The British closed the harbor of Boston to importing and exporting. " ... All disturbers of the King's peace are to be transported to England for trial ..." They also replaced the elected local officials with those appointed by the crown; families had to let soldiers live with them; and four thousand soldiers were now in Boston to enforce the new laws. King George III had told his prime minister, "The die is cast. The colonies must either submit or triumph."

In late 1772, Samuel Adams created the Committees of Correspondence, which linked Patriots in all 13 colonies and eventually provided the framework for a rebel government. Between 7000 and 8000 served on the Committees of Correspondence and they became the leaders of the American resistance to British actions, and largely determined the war effort at the state and local level. During the boycotts of British products, the colonial and local Committees examined merchant records and published the names of merchants who attempted to defy the boycott. They promoted patriotism and home manufacturing, advising Americans to avoid luxuries and lead simpler lives.

From late 1774 into early 1775, they supervised the elections of provincial conventions, which took over the operation of colonial governments.

The Coercive Acts were intended to make an example of Massachusetts and the other colonies got the message. Their Committees of Correspondence created the First Continental Congress to deal with the threat and John Adams was chosen as a delegate from Boston. This first episode ends with Sam and John going off together to the First Continental Congress in 1774 in Philadelphia. With fifty-six delegates from twelve of the thirteen colonies, it was convened as a vehicle for deliberation and collective action and would eventually become the governing body of the United States during the American Revolution.

In the film, John makes a rousing first political speech the night he is introduced to the citizens of Boston as a delegate. That meeting ends with the singing of a religious hymn reminding us how intensely religious these people were. In the 1730s and 1740s, the most important event in American religion during the eighteenth century occurred, the Great Awakening, a series of emotional religious revivals that spread across the colonies. The Great Awakening was ignited by Jonathan Edwards, whose sermons emphasized human depravity and divine omnipotence.

Pulitzer Prize winning historian Bernard Bailyn argues that the evangelism of the era challenged traditional notions of natural hierarchy by teaching that the Bible taught that all men are equal, so that the true value of a man lies in his moral behavior, not his class. The Great Awakening was the first single experience shared by large numbers of people throughout all the American colonies, and therefore contributed to the growth of a common American identity. It also sent a powerful spiritual message: that God works directly through the people, rather than through churches or other public institutions.

After the death of Oliver Cromwell, the English monarchy was reinstated, but forced onto the new monarchs was the 1689 English Bill of Rights which listed certain rights that were "true, ancient, and indubitable rights and liberties of the people" of England. It limited the powers of the king in such matters as taxation and keeping a standing army. In the colonies, as in England itself, Americans would celebrate these English liberties as their birthright.

Between 1680 and 1776, a distinctly American society emerged, with features that set it apart from Britain. These included the absence of a titled, hereditary aristocracy; a widespread distribution of land; an unprecedented degree of ethnic and religious diversity; and broad eligibility to vote. In contrast to the way Britons conceived of Parliament, the colonists thought of the members of the colonial assemblies as representatives of the people, accountable to their constituents, and obligated to follow public instructions. Popular participation in decision making was much more pronounced in general in the colonies, where militia officers were often selected by their companies and ministers were often hired by their congregations.

Another key difference between the mother country and the colonies was the presence in the latter of slavery. Between 1500 and 1700, over 60% of the 6 million people who traveled to the New World were slaves. By the beginning of the Revolution in 1776, one-fifth of the inhabitants of the American colonies, north and south, lived in bondage. The widespread presence of slavery made adult white males acutely aware of the difference between independence and dependence. Colonial Americans knew what it was like to be subjected to the will, authority, and domination of another person. When Parliament began to tax Americans, regulate their trade, station troops in their midst, deny colonists the right to expand westward, many Americans perceived these efforts as part of a design to deprive them of their property and reduce them to slavery.

This episode ends with John leaving with Sam for Philadelphia while we learn that Abigail is pregnant. This separation at such a critical time is the first of many sacrifices that we will witness this family making for America.

Pre-Revolution Timeline 1702-1774

1702 William died and was succeeded by Queen Anne of Great Britain.

1727 George I of Great Britain died and was succeeded by George II.

1732 First Great Awakening

1754 French and Indian War began.
  -At the Albany Congress, a "Union of Colonies" was proposed.

1760 King George II of Great Britain died and was succeeded by his grandson George III.

1763 The Treaty of Paris, under which France ceded much of its North American territory to Great Britain but surrendered Louisiana to Spain, formally ended the French and Indian War.
  -Beginning of Pontiac's War in which Indians alarmed by British policies attacked British forts destroying eight forts and killing or capturing hundreds of colonists.

1764 The Sugar Act, intended to raise revenues, was passed by the British Parliament.

1765 To help defray the cost of keeping troops in America, the British Parliament enacted the Stamp Act 1765, imposing a tax on many types of printed materials used in the colonies.
  -The British Parliament also enacted the Quartering Act, requiring citizens in the Thirteen Colonies to provide housing, food, and other provisions to British troops.
  -Virginia's House of Burgesses adopted the Virginia Resolves, which claimed that under British law Virginians could be taxed only by an assembly to which they had elected representatives.
  -In the Stamp Act Congress delegates from nine colonies adopted the Declaration of Rights and Grievances, which petitioned Parliament and the King to repeal the Stamp Act.

1766 Pontiac's War ended.
  -The British Parliament repealed the Stamp Act and issued the Declaratory Act, asserting Parliament's "full power and authority to make

laws and statutes... to bind the colonies and people of America... in all cases whatsoever."

1767 The Townshend Acts impose duties on many items imported into America.

1770 Boston Massacre

1772 Sam Adams organized the Committees of Correspondence, patriot shadow governments.

1773 The British Parliament passed the Tea Act, to which the Sons of Liberty responded with the "Boston Tea Party," in which, disguised as Indians, they destroyed an entire shipment of tea.

Episode 2 – "Independence"

Before

In the opening scene, before the credits, we watch the Adams cousins, John and Sam, endure the First Continental Congress in Philadelphia, convened on September 5, 1774, in response to the Coercive Acts. Their impatience is indicative of their role as prime agitators for, first, a military response by the colonies, and later, for independence. This is contrasted to the caution of their colleagues, most especially, John Dickinson.

This episode opens with Dickinson's droning recitation of the "Declarations and Resolves," the accomplishments, of the congress. He says they will publish a statement of grievances, boycott British goods, and send a petition, the "Olive Branch Petition," to the king seeking reconciliation. Not mentioned in the film: a call for another Continental Congress in the event that their efforts were unsuccessful in halting enforcement of the Intolerable Acts.

Dickinson will be John Adam's chief political sparring partner throughout this episode. He was a wealthy, cultivated Philadelphia lawyer who wrote the most popular pamphlet of the 1760s, in which he held that Parliament had no right of taxation and calling for a boycott of British goods. Nevertheless, he will be a leader of those colonists most reluctant to break with the mother country.

Dickinson ends the pre-credits sequence with a dinner toast in which he says "May Boston's troubles soon be at an end and her peoples' natural rights as Englishman be fully restored..." The war will start and be fought for well over a year for no other purpose that to restore the colonists' rights as Englishmen. As Benjamin Franklin would later put it, "No one drunk or sober was talking about independence" at this time. Note how John Adams will throw that phrase "natural rights as Englishmen" back in Dickinson's face in their first clash in the Second Continental Congress.

At one point Adams will attack Dickinson's Quakerism illustrating Adams' primary flaw: his bluntness and lack of tact toward his political opponents, a flaw that would make him many enemies and that would plague his political career. It would also, eventually, contribute to historians' disregard for his many achievements. "I am obnoxious, suspected, and unpopular ..." Adams says to Thomas Jefferson in the movie.

This episode is a remarkable dramatization of the political side of the Revolution. In our next movie, *The Crossing*, which is about George Washington, we will cover most of the military side. But not all of the military side, because, after the credits and after we have watched two future presidents knead manure, this episode opens with a scene of the aftermath of the opening battle of the Revolution, the Battle of Lexington and Concord.

This is an invention of the filmmakers. Adams didn't actually visit the battle scene until days afterward. But in the film he does so minutes afterward, affording images of carnage: dead animals, wounded and dead Redcoats, and, as he will later describe the Americans to Abigail, "plain country boys with no experience of professional soldiering, but their faces shining like the sun through a church window..." Some of those plain country boys also lay wounded and dead down the road from their own farms and with their mothers and wives wailing over them.

On April 19, 1775, to cut off the rebellion before it got started, British General Thomas Gage sent seven hundred redcoats to the Massachusetts village of Concord to capture the main cache of rebel arms. They were stopped at Lexington Green by seventy-seven "Minutemen," local farmers who had to be ready to go into battle in a minute. The two sides stood looking at each other and exchanging epithets and then a shot was fired. It would later be called "the Shot Heard 'Round the World" because of the effect on global democracy of the revolution it started. It was the unordered, anonymous, maybe accidental first shot of the military action of the Revolution. At the end of a brief battle, eight Minutemen were dead and ten wounded. No British, yet.

The British moved on to Concord, where a detachment of three British companies was engaged and routed at the North Bridge by a force of 500 Minutemen. The British did not find the rebel arms and as they retreated back to Boston, thousands of militiamen attacked them along the roads. The Minutemen chased "the bastards back to Boston" to quote General Warren in our movie when John encounters him during his surveying of the aftermath of the Battle of Lexington and Concord. 73 British troops were killed and 200 were wounded or missing in action. The patriot losses were 49 dead and 46 wounded or missing.

The night before the Battle of Lexington and Concord was the subject of "Paul Revere's Ride," by Henry Wadsworth Longfellow, the most famous of American patriotic poems and a recommended fun read. Much of the poem is accurate: he did ride through the countryside rousing the Minutemen (though the poem doesn't mention he was detained by the British). But there are inaccuracies too, for instance, he didn't receive the signal of a lantern in the Old North Church but sent the signal. Not mentioned in the poem, General Gage that night was also out to arrest Sam Adams and John Hancock who were hiding in Concord, and it was Revere who warned them.

The Battle of Lexington and Concord roused the 13 colonies to call out their militias and send troops to besiege British-held Boston. The first formal battle of the Revolution, the Battle of Bunker Hill, followed on June 17, 1775. The British had to charge uphill in blistering heat, and though it was formally be a British victory, it was at a cost of about 1,000 British casualties compared to 500 American casualties from a much larger force. The Americans only gave ground because they ran out of ammunition.

The night before the Battle of Bunker Hill, British ships in Boston harbor bombarded rebel positions, which gave our filmmakers an opportunity to create one of the most remarkable scenes in this or any other film. Abigail and the children watch the bombardment from a ridge near the farm. Because the beauty of the visual imagery is equaled by the sound design, I urge you to listen to this scene with headphones, which is the only way to get the full percussive resonance of the cannons and to *hear* the trajectory of the cannon balls. Notice too the distancing device of having the sound of the cannon fire arrive sometime after the flash.

The next day, while Abigail and the children are in the road giving water to the Minutemen retreating from Bunker Hill, the war is brought into the Adams home even more when Abigail recognizes the corpse of Joseph Warren in a wagon heaped with dead. This too is an invention because the retreating Americans would not have passed the Adams farm.

Throughout this episode we will be going back and forth between the impact of the war on the Adams family (which could be any middle class family of the time) and the intellectual war inside congress. Right after the Battle of Lexington-Concord, we are in the middle of the Second Continental Congress, where the Adams cousins clash with Dickinson. Then, after the Battle of Bunker Hill, we see John describe to congress the killing and desecration of the same General Warren he met after the Battle of Lexington-Concord, who was also the Adams' family physician. John then brilliantly maneuvers the congress into creating a Continental Army, an army representing the colonies collectively, by turning the issue into a vote on the popularity of George Washington.

Note later the value Abigail puts on her letters to John when she gives them to Washington for him to deliver to John. Note also that Washington understands their value to the cause. Those letters are now some of the greatest documents in U.S. history and they make this film possible.

Before the twentieth century most soldiers died of disease and starvation not battlefield wounds. When John visits General Washington and gets a tour of the Continental Army (notice the African American and Native Americans among the soldiers), we get our first view of the small pox that was decimating that army. As war-time plagues usually did, this one will spread to the civilian population and, most dramatically, right into the Adams family. The film features a scene where Abigail courageously trusts science and allows her children to be inoculated against the disease, a new and daring treatment.

This episode introduces some of the indispensable Founders, such as Benjamin Franklin. He was a leading author, printer, political theorist, politician, postmaster, scientist, musician, inventor, satirist, civic activist, statesman, and diplomat. As a scientist, he was a major figure in the Enlightenment and in the history of physics for his discoveries and theories regarding electricity. He invented the lightning rod, bifocals, the Franklin stove, a carriage odometer, and the glass 'armonica' (a musical instrument). He formed both the first public lending library in America and the first fire department in Pennsylvania. Proudly from a working class background, he is considered the first "self-made man." He is also the wittiest, wisest, and most charming character in our film. He is played to perfection by the great British actor Tom Wilkinson, most of whose lines are taken from Franklin's writings.

Note the relationship between Franklin and Thomas Jefferson, who shared many traits. Another important Founder we will meet in this episode, Jefferson was the principal author of the   Declaration of Independence and the third President of the United States. He represented Virginia in the Continental Congress, which is where we first meet him in the movie. He then served as wartime Governor of Virginia (1779–1781). Just after the war ended, Jefferson served as a diplomat in Paris with John Adams. He was the first United States Secretary of State (1790–1793), during the administration of President George Washington. Upon resigning that office, he organized the Democratic-Republican Party with his close friend James Madison. Jefferson was elected Vice-President in 1796, under his opponent John Adams.

Elected president in 1800, he purchased the vast Louisiana Territory from France (1803), and he sent the Lewis and Clark Expedition (1804–1806) to explore the new west. His second term was beset with troubles at home, such as the failed treason trial of his former Vice President Aaron Burr and troubles abroad such as escalating friction with Britain.

A leader in the Enlightenment, Jefferson was a polymath who spoke five languages and was deeply interested in science, invention, architecture, religion, and philosophy. He designed his own large mansion on a 5,000 acre plantation near Charlottesville, Virginia, which he named Monticello. As part of the Virginia planter elite and, as a tobacco planter, Jefferson owned hundreds of slaves throughout his lifetime. After Martha Jefferson, his wife of eleven years, died in 1782, Thomas remained a widower for the rest of his life; his marriage produced six children, with only two surviving to adulthood. He also fathered children by a slave, Sally Hemings, with whom he had a thirty-eight year relationship, from the time she was fourteen.

There is a Founding Father vital to the theme of this episode who is nevertheless missing and that is Thomas Paine. He has been called "a corset maker by trade, a journalist by profession, and a propagandist by inclination." He immigrated to the American colonies in 1774 just in time to participate in the Revolution. His principal contributions were the powerful, widely read pamphlet

Common Sense (1776), the all-time American best-seller that advocated colonial America's independence from Great Britain. His *The American Crisis* (1776–1783) was a pro-revolutionary pamphlet series. *Common Sense* was so influential that John Adams said, "Without the pen of the author of 'Common Sense,' the sword of Washington would have been raised in vain."

Paine lived in France for most of the 1790s, becoming deeply involved in the French Revolution. In December of 1793, he was arrested and imprisoned in Paris, then released in 1794. In 1802 he returned to America where he died in 1809. Only six people attended his funeral as he had been ostracized for his ridicule of Christianity.

Adams and Paine had an intense dislike for each other. Adams at first praised *Common Sense* but then attacked it. Paine was the most radical of the Founders, concerned with economic equality as well as political; for instance, he advocated that people without property be allowed to vote, which was just too far out for Adams.

After

The Olive Branch Petition that the Second Continental Congress sent to the crown attempting reconciliation was refused, and King George III issued instead the Proclamation of Rebellion which called for hanging the revolutionary leadership, and which is read aloud in one of this episode's most dramatic scenes. From that point on, their lives were at stake.

"We must all hang together or most assuredly we will all hang separately," Franklin famously summed up their dilemma.

Not only would they be hanged if they lost the war but, what is not mentioned in the film, their estates would go to the Crown and their families would be destitute. That is the meaning of the word "Fortune" in the famous ending of the Declaration of Independence: "And for the support of this Declaration... we mutually pledge to each other our Lives, our Fortunes and our sacred Honor."

John Adams says after the Proclamation of Rebellion is read to Congress, "The question is no longer whether or not there shall be independence but when." Thomas Jefferson later called Adams, for his leadership on the issue, "the colossus of independence."

From that point on, this episode is about the hard political slog to declaring independence, intercut with Abigail's and the kids' ordeal at home. The illness of the daughter Nabby following the inoculation was portrayed inaccurately in the film in that it was their son, Charles Francis, who developed small pox and was unconscious and delirious for 48 hours. This is an odd change to make considering the ultimate fates of Charles and Nabby (covered in the next section).

Nor did Henry Knox go by the Adams house in the rain with artillery stolen from the British as he does in the movie, but he did use the artillery as depicted to help Washington drive the British out of Boston.

The scene with Franklin, Adams, and Jefferson revising the Declaration of Independence is one of the gems of the entire miniseries. Jefferson wrote of the Declaration of Independence: "Neither aiming at originality of principle or sentiment, nor yet copied from any particular and previous writing, it was intended to be an expression of the American mind, and to give to that expression the proper tone and spirit called for by the occasion."

Jefferson's most immediate sources were his own draft of the preamble of the Constitution of Virginia and George Mason's draft of the Virginia Declaration of Rights. They were, in turn, directly influenced by the 1689 English Declaration of Rights, which formally ended the reign of King James II and was seen as a model of how to end the reign of an unjust king. The English political theorist John Locke, whom Jefferson called one of "the three greatest men that have ever lived," was also a primary influence.

The Declaration of Independence is a philosophical tract about "natural rights," the rights all human beings are born with, but it is also a legal document, an indictment against King George for violating the rights of the colonists. As much space is dedicated to an itemized list of "repeated injuries and usurpations" by the King as is dedicated to the poetry about rights.

The second paragraph, with its talk of self-evident truths and unalienable rights (both of which phrases are emphasized in the movie), was applicable long after the war ended of course. Because the Constitution and the Bill of Rights lacked sweeping statements about rights and equality, advocates of marginalized groups have turned to the Declaration for support. Starting in the 1820s, variations of the Declaration were issued to proclaim the rights of workers, farmers, women, and others. In 1848, for example, the Seneca Falls Convention, a meeting of women's rights advocates, declared that "all men and women are created equal". The Declaration would have its most prominent influence in the debate over slavery.

Remember when Washington visits Abigail in this episode and she muses out loud, ""Could it [this war] be punishment for the sin of slavery?" She once single-handedly forced her reluctant Quincy neighbors to accept the presence of a free black boy in the local school.

The contradiction between the claim that "all men are created equal" and the existence of American slavery attracted comment when the Declaration was first published. English abolitionist Thomas Day wrote in a 1776 letter, "If there be an object truly ridiculous in nature, it is an American patriot, signing resolutions of independency with the one hand, and with the other brandishing a whip over his affrighted slaves." In the 19th century, the Declaration took on special significance for the abolitionist movement.

"I have never had a feeling politically that did not spring from the sentiments embodied in the Declaration of Independence," Abraham Lincoln said. He argued that the Declaration of Independence was a founding document of the United States, and that this had important implications for interpreting the Constitution, which had been ratified more than a decade after the Declaration. Lincoln believed that "all men are created equal" was part of the nation's founding principles and he expressed this belief in the opening sentence of the Gettysburg Address: "Four score and seven years ago our fathers brought forth on this continent, a new nation, conceived in Liberty, and dedicated to the proposition that all men are created equal."

Note that when the Declaration is read to the people in the closing scene of this episode, the last hold out against the Declaration, John Dickinson, listens while mounted and in a military uniform. All of the patriots are now united behind independence.

During the debate over independence in the movie, the anti-independence delegate from South Carolina asks John Adams, "Who will join us in this folly?"

"France," Adams immediately shoots back.

And he will go there in the third episode to help gain indispensable financial and especially military support from England's traditional enemy, which is ready to seek revenge for the loss of its North American colonies in the Seven Years' War (French and Indian War). We will be skipping the third and fourth episodes because though they are extremely well done and fascinating history they are outside the scope of an overview like this.

In the third episode, "Don't tread on Me," after a wrenching break with Abigail and the family, Adams and son John Quincy go to France to join Benjamin Franklin in the diplomatic delegation. Father and son experience an exciting and beautifully detailed naval battle during the crossing. Then we are in the decadent French royal court where this descendent of puritans is comically out of place and eventually insults the very people he most needs to seduce. Franklin summed up his view of Adams: "He means well for his country, is always an honest man, often a wise one, but sometimes and in some things, absolutely out of his senses." Franklin has him transferred to Holland where he struggles to get a war loan.

In episode four, "Reunion," with the war over, Adams is posted to Paris again, this time with Jefferson. Abigail joins them, alone (though in reality the children accompanied her). A rich friendship develops between the three but with glimpses of an ideological rift between John and Jefferson that will later develop into a bitter political rivalry. Adams becomes the first American ambassador to England and afterwards returns to a tumultuous welcome in America and reunion with his now grown children. He and Abigail are gray and middle aged.

Adams is elected the first Vice President and the fourth episode ends with the stirring and magnificent scene of Washington being sworn-in as the first

President of the United States with Adams standing beside him. I urge you to see episodes 3 and 4 but the next section of this chapter will be about episode 5. To prepare you for that episode it is necessary to describe the biggest domestic event in the Adams' years abroad, the event second in importance only to the Revolution itself: the Constitutional Convention.

Adams was a diplomat abroad during the convention and that is why it is not featured in the film. Just as Tom Paine was the indispensable man missing from the movie during the independence struggle, James Madison is the indispensable man in the Constitutional Convention. Indeed, Madison has been called the Father of the Constitution.

James Madison, Jr. (1751-1836) was a statesman and political theorist, and the fourth President of the United States (1809–1817). Besides fathering the Constitution, he was the key champion and author of the Bill of Rights. Slight, frail, and reserve, he served as a politician most of his adult life. Like other Virginia statesmen, he was a slaveholder and part of the élite. He inherited his plantation, known as Montpelier, and owned hundreds of slaves during his lifetime to cultivate tobacco and other crops. Madison's wife Dolly, one of the great beauties of the day, virtually invented the role of First Lady. Madison's presidency will be covered in the next section of this chapter.

Prior to the Constitution, the thirteen states were bound together by the Articles of Confederation, essentially a military alliance among sovereign nations to fight the Revolutionary War. Under it, Congress had no power to tax, and as a result was not paying the debts left from the Revolution. Break-up of the union and national bankruptcy were feared. Shays' Rebellion, an armed debtors' uprising, is often cited as the event that forced the rewriting of the national charter.

As Madison wrote, "a crisis had arrived which was to decide whether the American experiment was to be a blessing to the world, or to blast forever the hopes which the republican cause had inspired." What was needed was a redefinition of the relationship among the states, the national government, and the people.

Partly at Madison's instigation, a national convention was called in 1787. The Convention was intended to only revise the Articles of Confederation, but from the outset, many, chief among them James Madison and Alexander Hamilton (who is described in detail in the next section), were determined to create a new government rather than fix the existing one. The delegates elected George Washington to preside over the convention.

During the Convention, Madison spoke over two hundred times, and his fellow delegates rated him highly. For example, William Pierce wrote that "...every Person seems to acknowledge his greatness. In the management of every great question he evidently took the lead in the Convention... he always comes forward as the best informed Man of any point in debate."

One of Madison's goals in devising the U.S. Constitution was to create a republic that would endure despite its large size and that would not have to depend entirely on the virtue of the country's leaders. He believed that in a large republic, diverse and conflicting interests would balance and neutralize each other. This was a unique and original insight contrary to conventional wisdom that held that conflicting interests were the bane of democracies.

In our next episode there will be a cabinet luncheon where Adams tells Jefferson that the federal and state governments must "check and balance" each other? This was one of the most famous phrases concerning the Constitution. To prevent concentrations of power, the framers established a system of checks and balances which meant that, as a blueprint for the American government, the Constitution called for a government in which authority was divided between the federal and state governments and was further divided among the three branches of the federal government.

This idea came from a French aristocrat and political philosopher by the name of Montesquieu. He proposed that, to prevent any one branch from becoming too powerful, each of the other two would have a check on it. The Congress (legislative branch) can remove the President (executive branch) and Congress must approve justices of the Supreme Court (judicial branch). The President can veto Congress's bills and he nominates justices for the Supreme Court, which has the ultimate and final word on the Constitutionality of laws. This is the common meaning of the phrase "checks and balances."

According to the dean of Revolutionary War scholars, Gordon Wood, the ultimate question before the Constitutional Convention was not how to design a government but whether the states should remain sovereign, whether sovereignty should be transferred to the national government, or whether the constitution should settle somewhere in between. Madison believed that the problem was restraining the excesses of the states. Most disagreements were ultimately disputes over the balance of sovereignty between the states and national government.

Other contentious disputes included the composition and election of the senate, how "proportional representation" was to be defined (whether to include slaves or other property), whether to divide the executive power between three persons or divest the power into a single president, how to elect the president, how long his term was to be and whether he could stand for reelection, what offenses should be impeachable, the nature of a fugitive slave clause, whether to allow the abolition of the slave trade (not ownership), and whether judges should be chosen by the legislature or executive.

Most of the time during the convention was spent on deciding these issues, while the powers of the legislative, executive, and judiciary branches were not heavily disputed. Once the convention began, the delegates first agreed on the principles of the convention, then they agreed on Madison's Virginia Plan and began to modify it. Then it was sent to the states for "ratification," approval by state conventions held for that purpose only. They approved it and it became the "supreme law of the land" and the blueprint for a new kind of government. This was the first time in history that anyone sat down and deliberately and calculatedly created a nation.

During the period of national debate over the Constitution prior to ratification, Madison, along with Hamilton and John Jay, authored *The Federalist Papers*. These were a series of eighty-five essays promoting and explaining the Constitution and, to this day, the single most important source for Constitutional interpretation. Hamilton wrote the most but Madison wrote the most important one, Number 10.

Madison has also been called the "Father of the Bill of Rights" which is the name for the first ten amendments to the Constitution. They were introduced by Madison to the First United States Congress in 1789. The Bill of Rights is a series of limitations on the power of the federal government, protecting the natural rights of liberty and property including freedom of speech, a free press, free assembly, and free association. It guarantees a speedy, public trial with an impartial jury, and prohibits double jeopardy (being tried more than once for the same crime). In addition, the Bill of Rights reserves for the people any rights not specifically mentioned in the Constitution.

In episode five, we will watch in action the government the Constitution created.

Political History of the Revolution Timeline

1774 -In reaction to the Boston Tea Party, the British Parliament passes "Intolerable Acts," which close the Boston harbor, forbid unauthorized public meetings in Massachusetts, and require Massachusetts citizens to house and feed British troops in their homes.
-The First Continental Congress meets in Philadelphia and calls for opposition to the Intolerable Acts.
1775 The Second Continental Congress convenes in Philadelphia and selects George Washington to be commander in chief of the Continental Army.
1776 Thomas Paine's pamphlet *Common Sense* is published.
-The Olive Branch Petition attempting a reconciliation is sent to King George III.
-Second Continental Congress enacts the Lee Resolution declaring independence from the British Empire.
July 4 Second Continental Congress approved Declaration of Independence.
-Second Continental Congress adopted the Articles of Confederation.
1778 France signs a treaty with the United States.
1779 Spain declares war on England.
1783 The Treaty of Paris ended the American Revolutionary War.

Episode 5 – "Unite or Die"

Before and After

There is an old political joke that goes: "Once there were two brothers. One explored the Amazon and got lost, and the other became Vice President. Neither man was ever heard from again."

The fifth episode begins with Vice President John Adams fulfilling one of the few responsibilities of the office, presiding over the Senate, and on this day, presiding over the debate over what to call the new President. We see that Adams has become an old fuddy duddy who is openly mocked by the senators. His nickname among them was "His Rotundity."

After the credits, we drop right into an argument between John and Abigail. Throughout this episode, we will see strains in the marriage and the family, the latter concerning an over ambitious son-in-law, the resentful spurned middle son Charles, and the loss of the oldest and youngest sons to overseas diplomatic postings. The story of the family is intercut with scenes of the infant republic finding its legs, beginning with a scene of the cabinet having lunch.

Many of the topics of conversation at this luncheon will be major themes of this episode and major issues of contention among the Founders. The first conflict erupts, however genteelly, between Thomas Jefferson and Alexander Hamilton, secretaries of State and Treasury respectively. This is appropriate, because they will become the most significant political and ideological opponents of the era. Late in this episode President Washington will complain bitterly about their constant bickering in cabinet meetings.

"The future prosperity of this nation rests chiefly in trade," Hamilton expounds in the movie. "Trade depends, among other things, on the willingness of other nations to lend us money ... Our first step would be to incur a national debt ... I have recommended to the president that congress adopt all the debts incurred by the individual states during the war through a national bank ..."

"If the states are indebted to a central authority, it increases the power of the central government," Jefferson complains. "The moneyed interest in this country is all in the North, so the wealth and power would inevitably be concentrated there in a federal government to the expense of the South."

There we have two key issues from the Constitutional Convention, issues which will also be worked out in the republic's earliest years, and indeed they are still issues in today's politics: fear of a central (federal) government and regional conflict; in this case, South versus North.

Then Adams joins the conversation on the side of Hamilton, supporting "powerful central government," though with concessions to Jefferson's concerns. Adams and Hamilton will create one of the first two American political parties. In the very next scene, in conversation with his friend and fellow Founder, Doctor

Benjamin Rush, Adams will name himself a "Federalist," and that was the name of his and Hamilton's party, the Federalist Party.

The Federalists promoted Hamilton's financial system which emphasized federal assumption of state debts, a tariff to pay off those debts, and a national bank to facilitate financing. Their opposition was the Democratic-Republicans, the party created by Jefferson and James Madison, based in the plantation South. They opposed a strong executive power, were hostile to a standing army and navy, demanded a limited reading of the Constitutional powers of the federal government, and strongly opposed the Hamilton financial program. Perhaps even more important was the conflict over foreign policy. That is the area emphasized by this episode.

In the opening dialogue of that cabinet luncheon, Jefferson says, "I have been in Revolutionary France where the streets are filled with songs of liberty and brotherhood and the overthrow of the ancient tyrannies of Europe ..." A little later, in a scene with Abigail, John, and Jefferson together again, we hear some of Jefferson's most famous lines on the French Revolution and its excesses, including, "You cannot expect a people so long oppressed to be transported from despotism to liberty on a feather bed ... The tree of liberty must be refreshed from time to time with the blood of patriots and tyrants ..."

In 1793, revolutionary France and conservative Britain went to war, opening a period of intense European conflict that lasted until 1815. American policy was neutrality, with the Federalists hostile to France, and the Democratic Republicans hostile to Britain. Federalists favored Britain because of its political stability and its importance as a trading partner. Jefferson was especially fearful that British aristocratic influences would undermine democracy.

The most dramatic scenes of this episode are concerned with the Jay Treaty of 1794, a peace treaty with Britain which provoked purple-faced shouting matches in Congress and violent mobs in the streets, as we see in the movie. The Jeffersonians mobilized their supporters nationwide to defeat the treaty, and the Federalists followed suit in an intense, nasty battle. The treaty passed in 1795 when Washington threw his prestige behind it. Incidentally, George Washington, while officially nonpartisan, generally supported the Federalists and they made him their iconic hero.

In the same scene in which Hamilton is lurking behind a door and Washington tells John that John Quincy is being given an overseas diplomatic posting, Washington also tells Adams about the diplomatic mission of John Jay that will result in the eponymous treaty. The mission involved crucial claims of trade, freedom of the seas, and the integrity of America's borders. It was the failure of the treaty to resolve most of these issues while nonetheless granting Britain special trade status that principally sparked widespread public anger. This is a particularly important point since the unresolved issues of naval impressments (kidnapping American sailors for the British navy) and maritime freedom would ultimately culminate in the War of 1812.

The climax to the Jay Treaty in the movie includes two of the most inaccurate scenes of the series. One scene is inaccurate because it violates common sense that a president and vice president would stand next to a large window with a mob yelling against the Jay Treaty just a few feet outside that window. Another scene violates historical accuracy. The final vote on the Jay Treaty in the senate did not entail a tie that was broken by John Adams. It was passed, as the Constitution says it must be, by a two-thirds vote of the senate.

"Creating a fictional crisis and a constitutional absurdity for the sake of Adams-centered 'drama,' is simply unjustifiable," wrote historian Jeremy Stern about the miniseries. "The vice president could not (and cannot now) introduce business to the Senate. The Federalist/Republican schism, Adams's virtual exclusion from the government by Washington, and his own growing split with Jefferson over the French Revolution are handled well, especially given the complexity of the issues involved."

The film does an excellent job with Alexander Hamilton though. Brit actor Rufus Sewell captures the arrogance and brilliance of the man in that cabinet luncheon and later when he visits Adams and enlists him to run for president. Hamilton (1755-1804) was a soldier, economist, political philosopher, one of the country's first constitutional lawyers, and the first Secretary of the Treasury. He played a major role at the Constitutional Convention and during the ratification process, writing over half of the *Federalist Papers*.

Of illegitimate birth and raised in the West Indies, Hamilton was effectively orphaned at about the age of 11. Recognized for his abilities and talent, he came to North America for his education, sponsored by people from his community. He attended King's College (now Columbia University) and became Washington's aide-de-camp in the Continental Army during the Revolutionary War. As his most recent and probably best biographer, Ron Chernow, wrote of him: "In all probability, Alexander Hamilton is the foremost figure in American history who never attained the presidency, yet he probably had a much deeper and more lasting impact than many who did." Hamilton's status is recognized by having his face on the ten dollar bill.

In that same scene in which Adams arrives for a meeting with Washington, and Hamilton suddenly appears from behind a door, working at a desk, there is an implied intimacy between Washington and Hamilton in the staging. Throughout this episode notice how Hamilton is always around when Washington is in the scene. He was the senior aide-de-camp and confidant to Washington throughout the war.

In that scene, when Hamilton visits the Adams' farm, we learn that Hamilton has a mean streak when he says of Jefferson, "The Secretary of State suffers from a womanish attachment to France. There are those who say he is more Frenchman than American." Adams is forced to defend his old friend. At the end of this episode, we learn that Hamilton is also capable of treachery, when Benjamin Rush reveals to Adams that Hamilton, his fellow Federalist, had intrigued against him in the first presidential election and is still intriguing against him in the election of 1796, when Adams is running for the presidency after Washington's retirement.

Embarrassed when an extra-marital affair with Maria Reynolds became public, Hamilton resigned from the Washington administration in 1795 and returned to the practice of law in New York. However, he kept his hand in politics and was a powerful influence on the cabinet of President John Adams (1797–1801). As the sixth episode, about the Adams' presidency, makes clear, the first loyalty of much of Adams' cabinet was to Hamilton.

The election of 1800, says McCullough, was "a contest of personal vilification surpassing any presidential election in American history." Adams was running for reelection in 1800 and Hamilton helped defeat him. Opposing the candidate of his own party cost Hamilton prominence within the Federalist Party. When Thomas Jefferson and Aaron Burr tied in the Electoral College president-ial election, Hamilton helped to defeat Burr, whom he found unprincipled, and to elect Jefferson, despite their profound political differences. When Burr ran for governor in New York State, Hamilton's influence in his home state was strong enough to prevent a Burr victory there also. Taking offense at some of Hamilton's comments, Burr challenged him to a duel in which he wounded Hamilton, who died after a couple days of intense suffering. Hamilton's son had died in a duel held in the same location three years before.

Hamilton's economic program was one of the major accomplishments of the Washington administration and it deserves the attention given it in this episode. The program included new tariffs and taxes, one of which provoked the Whiskey Rebellion in 1794, when western settlers protested against a federal tax on liquor. The Whiskey Rebellion was the first serious test of the federal government. Washington called out the state militia and personally led an army. The insurgents melted away and the power of the national government was firmly established.

Washington remains the only president to have received 100 percent of the electoral votes. Aware that everything he did set a precedent, Washington attended carefully to the pomp and ceremony of office, making sure that the titles and trappings were suitably republican and never emulated European royal courts. He preferred "Mr. President" to the more majestic names suggested by John Adams in the movie.

Washington reluctantly served a second term. But he refused to run for a third, establishing the tradition of a maximum of two terms for a president. As we see at the end of this episode, he was greatly relieved to retire. Besides laying the foundation of the presidency and suppressing the Whiskey Rebellion, he defeated an Indian confederacy in the Ohio country and negotiated Britain out of its western forts.

His Farewell Address in 1796 was very influential. Drafted primarily by Washington himself, with help from Hamilton, it gives advice on the necessity and importance of national union, and the value of the Constitution and the rule of law. It calls for men to move beyond partisanship and serve the common good. It warns against bitter partisanship in domestic politics and the evils of political parties. It warns against involvement in European wars and entering into "foreign entanglements". It says the United States must concentrate primarily on American interests. The address quickly set American values regarding foreign affairs.

This episode, the fifth, ends with John Adams' inauguration as the second president. The sixth episode, "Unnecessary War," and the seventh, "Peacefield," (the name of the Adams' farm) are beautifully done and well worth watching for their drama, history, and the virtuosic acting of the three principles, John, Abigail, and Jefferson. But these two episodes deal with subjects outside the purview of this book. John Adams' was not a major presidency.

To summarize the Adams' presidency and the sixth episode, "Unnecessary War": during his one term, Adams encountered ferocious attacks by the Jeffersonian Republicans, as well as the dominant faction in his own Federalist Party led by his bitter enemy Alexander Hamilton. Adams signed the controversial Alien and Sedition Acts (a disastrous curtailment of rights that made it a crime to publish "false, scandalous, and malicious writing" against the government or certain officials). He built up the army and navy in the face of an undeclared naval war with France. The major accomplishment of his presidency was his peaceful resolution of the conflict in the face of Hamilton's opposition. He went into retirement in 1800 content with that accomplishment.

Not in the film, but important enough, in his final hours in office Adams appointed John Marshall to the office of Chief Justice of the Supreme Court. Marshall has a minor role in the film as a presidential assistant but he had a short stint as Adams' Secretary of State before the Supreme Court. Serving until his death in 1835, Marshall dramatically expanded the powers of the Supreme Court and provided a Federalist interpretation of the Constitution that made for a strong national government. He established the principle of judicial review, which enables the courts to review the constitutionality of federal laws and invalidate acts of Congress when they conflict with the Constitution.

In 1962, President John F. Kennedy hosted a White House dinner for America's Nobel Laureates. He told those assembled that that night was "probably the greatest concentration of talent and genius in this house except for those times when Thomas Jefferson dined alone."

Jefferson (1743 - 1826) succeeded Adams, becoming the third President of the United States (1801–1809). At the beginning of the American Revolution, Jefferson served in the Continental Congress, representing Virginia and then served as a wartime Governor of Virginia (1779–1781). Just after the war ended, from mid-1784 Jefferson served as a diplomat, stationed in Paris, to help negotiate commercial treaties. In May 1785, he became the United States Minister to France. Jefferson was the first United States Secretary of State

(1790–1793). Upon resigning his office, with his close friend James Madison he organized the Democratic-Republican Party. Elected Vice-President in 1796, under his opponent John Adams, Jefferson with Madison secretly wrote the Kentucky and Virginia Resolutions, which attempted to nullify the Alien and Sedition Acts.

Elected president in what Jefferson called the Revolution of 1800, he oversaw a peaceful transition in power, purchased the vast Louisiana Territory from France (probably his most important act, it nearly doubled the size of the nation), and commissioned the Lewis and Clark Expedition. This was the first transcontinental expedition to the Pacific coast undertaken by the United States. It was led by two Virginia-born veterans of Indian wars in the Ohio Valley, Meriwether Lewis and William Clark. Their objectives were both scientific and commercial – to study the area's plants, animal life, and geography, and to learn how the region could be exploited economically.

Jefferson's second term was beset with troubles at home, such as the failed treason trial of his former Vice-President Aaron Burr, and escalating trouble with Britain. With Britain at war with Napoleon, he tried aggressive economic warfare against them; however, his embargo laws did more damage to American trade and the economy. Jefferson has often been rated in scholarly surveys as one of the greatest U.S. presidents, though since the mid-twentieth century, some historians have increasingly criticized him for his failure to act against domestic slavery.

A leader in the Enlightenment, Jefferson was a polymath who spoke five languages and was deeply interested in science, invention, architecture, religion and philosophy, interests that led him to the founding of the University of Virginia after his presidency. He designed his own large mansion on a 5,000 acre plantation near Charlottesville, Virginia, which he named Monticello. While not an orator, he was an indefatigable letter writer and corresponded with many influential people in America and Europe.

Although Jefferson owned slaves, he was a consistent opponent of slavery throughout his life and considered it as something that was contrary to the laws of nature and a blight on civilization and expressed his willingness to support any feasible plan to eradicate the institution. Jefferson privately struggled with the compatibility of owning slaves and the ideals of the American Revolution. Yet, he owned 200 when he wrote the Declaration of Independence and freed only five slaves at the time of his death.

After Martha Jefferson, his wife of eleven years, died in 1782, Jefferson remained a widower for the rest of his life; his marriage produced six children, with only two surviving to adulthood. In 1802, allegations surfaced that he was also the father of his slave Sally Hemings' children. In 1787, Sally Hemings at the age of 14 was chosen to accompany Polly, the youngest daughter of Jefferson, to Paris to rejoin her father; the widower was serving as the US Minister to France. Hemings and Jefferson are believed to have begun a sexual relationship then or after their return to Monticello. She had a total of six children of record born into slavery; four survived to adulthood and were noted for their resemblance to Jefferson. Sally Hemings served in Jefferson's household as a domestic servant until his death. The Thomas Jefferson Foundation, which runs Monticello, conducted an independent historic review in 2000, as did the National Genealogical Society in 2001. In both, scholars concluded Jefferson was likely the father of all Hemings' children. There are a couple of good movies on this subject in the recommendations section.

The seventh and final episode, "Peacefield," covers Adams's retirement years. There is a terrible scene in which his daughter, Nabby, has a mastectomy before the invention of anesthesia. She dies of breast cancer anyway and then Abigail succumbs to typhoid fever. Though he is ninety at the time, Adams does live to see his son, John Quincy, become the sixth president. Paul Giamatti's ninety year old Adams is a comic masterpiece that puts all of Adams' squinty-eyed orneriness on the surface. Even though Adams discovers that Jefferson was secretly behind the most offensive newpaper attacks against him, Adams and Jefferson are reconciled through correspondence in their last years. Both die mere hours apart on July 4th on the 50th anniversary of the Declaration of Independence. Jefferson was 83, Adams was 90.

After serving eight years as Jefferson's Secretary of State, James Madison won the U.S. presidential election of 1808, largely on the strength of his abilities in foreign affairs. At the time Britain and France were both on the brink of war with the United States. In response to continued British interference with American shipping, including impressment (kidnapping) of thousands of American sailors, and to British aid to Indians in Ohio and the western territories, Congress declared war on Britain. The subsequent War of 1812 was certainly the biggest event of Madison's two terms.

Westerners and Southerners were the most ardent supporters of the war, given their concerns about defending national honor and expanding western settlements, and having access to world markets for their agricultural exports. The war featured the burning of the U.S. capitol, Washington D.C., in August 1814 by the British, and the crushing defeat of the British by American general Andrew Jackson in the Battle of New Orleans in January 1815.

The War of 1812 allowed the United States to solidify its control over the lower Mississippi River and the Gulf of Mexico. It encouraged New England merchants to invest in textile factories. Though the Americans gained no territory, they gained a sense of victory in what they called a "second war of independence". The war was a major loss for Native American tribes in the Northwest and Southeast who had allied themselves with Britain and were defeated on the battlefield. It effectively destroyed Indians' ability to resist American expansion.

The war opened opportunities in national politics to generals like Andrew Jackson and William Henry Harrison (both of whom were president) as well as to civilian leaders like James Monroe and John Quincy Adams (both of whom were also president). New England was making a fine profit trading with England and its Federalists opposed the war, almost to the point of secession. The Federalist reputation collapsed in the triumphalism of Jackson's victory and the party ceased to have a national role.

The United States' only Federalist president was John Adams. After 1800, the party dominated Congress and most state governments outside New England. It selected presidential candidates through its caucus in Congress, but in the late 1820s, that system broke down and the party split between Andrew Jackson and the incumbent President John Quincy Adams. Jackson's faction founded the Democratic Party. The other faction, led by John Quincy Adams and Henry Clay, formed a new party known as the National Republicans which evolved into the Whig Party, the northern wing of which eventually became the Civil War-era Republican Party.

Episode seven, and the series, ends with John Adams saying in voice-over, "Oh posterity, you will never know how much it cost us to preserve your freedom. I hope that you will make a good use of it. If you do not, I shall repent in heaven that I ever took half the pains to preserve it."

Early Republic Timeline

1783 The British withdraw from ports in New York and the Carolinas.
-The Treaty of Paris officially ends the war.
1786 Shays' Rebellion (debtors' armed uprising)
1787 The Northwest Ordinance of 1787 was passed establishing
the precedent for westward expansion across North America.
-Constitutional Convention convened in Philadelphia with
George Washington presiding.
1789 The first presidential election
-The United States Constitution came into effect.
-George Washington was inaugurated as President in New
York City. John Adams was chosen as Vice President.
-First United States Congress passed the Judiciary Act of 1789
and the Hamilton tariff.
1791 The United States Bill of Rights was ratified.
-The First Bank of the United States was chartered.
1792 Washington was reelected President.
1793 Eli Whitney invented the cotton gin, which revives the dying
institution of slavery.
1794 Whiskey Rebellion, a tax revolt by farmers in western Pennsylvania who
object to a tax on whiskey, suppressed by Washington.
1795 The Jay Treaty was signed.
1796 Adams was elected President. Thomas Jefferson was elected Vice
President.
1798 The Alien and Sedition Acts were passed.

1799 Washington died.
1800 The Library of Congress was founded.
   -In the presidential election, Jefferson and Aaron Burr tied
   in the Electoral College.
1801 Jefferson was elected President by the House of Representatives. Burr
   became Vice President.
   -Adams appointed John Marshall Chief Justice.
1803 The Supreme Court establishes the principle of judicial review in Marbury
   v. Madison, and for the first time, rules a federal law unconstitutional.
   -Louisiana Purchase in which Jefferson bought 800,000 square miles for
   $15 million from Napoleon.
1804 Alexander Hamilton killed in a duel with Aaron Burr.
   -The Lewis and Clark Expedition sets out from St. Louis exploring to the
   Pacific Ocean.
   -Jefferson reelected President.
1806 Lewis and Clark return.
1807 Robert Fulton invented the steamboat.
1808 Congress ended the slave trade.
   -James Madison was elected president.
1812 War of 1812 began over British interference with American shipping and
   kidnapping of American seamen.
   -Madison was reelected President.
1814 British troops burned Washington, D.C. but were forced back at Baltimore.
   -Francis Scott Key writes "The Star-Spangled Banner."
   -The Treaty of Ghent ended the War of 1812.
1815 Unaware of the Treaty of Ghent, Andrew Jackson scored stunning defeat
   of British at Battle of New Orleans.
1816 James Monroe was elected President.

Recommendations

Whereas there are dozens of fine films on World War II and at least a half
dozen good ones on the Civil War, as mentioned before, there is a comparative
paucity of good films about the Revolution.

The Last of the Mohicans is a 1992 historical epic film set in 1757 during
the French and Indian War. Directed by Michael Mann, it's loosely based on
James Fenimore Cooper's classic American novel of the same name. It's
exciting, intense, and visually stunning and includes actual battles and some of
the politics of that war. It also focuses on the simmering tensions and
resentments between the Americans and their English colonial masters that will
lead to the Revolutionary War eighteen years later.

Jefferson in Paris is a 1995 film about the early relationship between slave
girl Sally Hemings (played by Thandie Newton) and Thomas Jefferson (Nick
Nolte). By the legendary team Merchant-Ivory, this film is set in pre-Revolution
France while Jefferson was ambassador there. *Sally Hemings: An American*

Scandal is a 2000 television miniseries. As PBS noted about it in a Frontline program, "Though many quarreled with the portrayal of Hemings as unrealistically modern and heroic, no major historian challenged the series' premise that Hemings and Jefferson had a 38-year relationship that produced children."

There are numerous documentary series covering the revolution but the best by far is PBS's *Liberty! The American Revolution* (1997). It is a model of the form cramming all the relevant information into an entertaining mere six hours. It includes top actors in costume speaking into the camera the actual words of participants. Also from PBS is the excellent 2006 doc *The War That Made America: the Story of the French and Indian War.* Master documentarian Ken Burns created the three hour *Thomas Jefferson* (2004). PBS' American Experience presented an excellent docudrama in 2006, *John and Abigail Adams.* PBS also has a 2002 documentary, *Benjamin Franklin,* and a 2007 one, *Alexander Hamilton.* Plus American Experience has one titled *The Duel* (2011) about that fatal confrontation between Hamilton and arch enemy Aaron Burr. PBS has a 2 *The War of 1812* (2005) *The War of 1812* (2011) doc and the History Channel a 2005 one, both titled *The War of 1812* (2005) Ken Burns also made the superb doc *Lewis & Clark - The Journey of the Corps of Discovery* (1997). Incidentally, it is shameful that there is no documentary about James Madison.

At www.escalloniapress.com, there are free recommendations of the best books - histories, biographies, memoirs, and even novels - related to the subjects of this chapter.

Chapter 4 - The Crossing

Before

It is ironic that the nation most famous for its movies didn't until recently make any memorable movies about its founders. This one is the best so far on George Washington, "the father of his country," and it is going to help explain why he is "first in the hearts of his countrymen" and why they named the federal capitol and a state after him and put his face on the most common currency.

The Crossing was a made-for-TV production of A&E which garnered a Peabody Award, an American Society of Cinematographers' Award, and an Emmy nomination. It was based on a novel of the same title by Howard Fast, who also wrote the script and who was one of the best and most prolific American historical novelists. *The Crossing* focuses on the darkest moment of the American Revolution, Christmas 1776.

You'll remember the beginning of the war from *John Adams*, when Adams rode into woods amid the wounded and dying colonials after the opening battle of the Revolution at Lexington-Concord on April 19, 1775. A friend there told Adams that the colonials had confronted the British and stopped them from taking their objective: a cache of colonial arms at Concord. The colonial militia then surrounded Boston, limiting resupply of the British army inside the city. Meanwhile, at the Second Continental Congress, John Adams nominated and the Congress approved George Washington for command of the Continental Army. Washington joined the army's Siege of Boston in the field in July 1775.

He reorganized the army during the long standoff and in November sent a bookseller-turned-soldier named Henry Knox to bring to Boston heavy artillery that had been captured from the British at Fort Ticonderoga. Knox is a major character in *The Crossing* and you met him in *John Adams* when Abigail came out of her house in the rain and spoke with a jovial portly man on horseback as he and a contingent of soldiers were bringing artillery to Boston. By putting that artillery on hills overlooking the city and its harbor, Washington eventually forced the British to withdraw.

He then moved his army to New York City where British General William Howe had launched a massive naval and land campaign to seize the city. The Continental Army under Washington, for the first time as the army of the newly independent United States, met the enemy at the Battle of Long Island in August 1776. It was the largest battle of the entire war. The Americans were badly outnumbered, many deserted, and Washington was badly beaten. He made a daring nighttime retreat across the East River without loss of materiel or a single life in what has been seen as one of his greatest military feats.

At White Plains, north of New York City, Washington again was defeated and again had to retreat this time to the hills of New Jersey. Meanwhile two major American forts, Lee and Washington, were surrounded and captured with 2,800 prisoners and the loss of sorely needed artillery and supplies. Disorganization, shortages of supplies, fatigue, sickness, and above all, lack of confidence in the leadership caused mass desertion in the American ranks.

As the narrator at the beginning of *The Crossing* puts it, the American Army has been "decimated" by defeat after defeat and is on the run from the British who are taking their time finishing-off the "cold, tired, and sick" continentals. What he doesn't mention is that there is also open talk in Congress about replacing Washington. It's at this moment that Washington will come up with a daring and brilliant plan that turns everything around.

Remember the scene in *John Adams*, earlier in 1776, when Washington escorted Adams on a tour of the Continentals' camp in Boston? That scene was more detailed than the similar scene in the beginning of this film and the scene in *John Adams* included images of something not mentioned in this film, small pox. Before the twentieth century, most soldiers died of disease and starvation, not battlefield wounds. The wretchedness of the army's conditions is portrayed identically in both films.

The opening scenes of *The Crossing* illustrate the narrator's theme that the American Army is on the verge of collapse. You will first see the wounded bedraggled Americans fleeing through falling snow on a road in New Jersey. The first time you see Washington he is ordering the abandonment of a cannon stuck in the mud. When a soldier puts a hole in the barrel, he is making the cannon unusable for the British. Then, as the Americans scramble to escape across the Delaware River into Pennsylvania, you will see an army routed, fleeing their enemy, and being shot by him.

The condition of the colonial army is most graphically conveyed in the tracking shot (moving camera) through the American camp the next day. Part of that shot follows Washington riding through the camp and his expression tells us his assessment of his army. The shot ends on the black frostbitten feet of a soldier being tended by a woman, who could be the soldier's wife. It was common at this time for wives even families to accompany their men into war.

In the scene immediately after the tracking shot, Washington articulates their situation for his staff and us. In six months, their army has gone from twenty thousand men and three hundred pieces of artillery to less than two thousand men and eighteen pieces.

"And we presume to fight against the most powerful nation on the face of the earth," Washington says.

In a few days, the Delaware River will freeze over and twenty thousand British troops can cross it and destroy them.

Later that day Washington has his great idea, which almost no one else believes in besides him. Watch the movie to find out what it is. Suffice it to say that it entails fighting the Hessians, German mercenaries, who are described in the film by Hugh Mercer, Washington's best friend and top doctor, as "the best soldiers on earth," and who Washington's soldiers "fear like a Salem pastor at the sight of a witch." At the staff dinner at which Washington announces his plan, it provokes such a fiery argument with General Horatio Gates that Washington has to have Gates removed from the camp at gunpoint.

This is the culmination of a sub theme you will notice about Washington's other battlefronts: against jealous colleagues and an unsupportive congress. After that first staff meeting, an officer forces Washington to hear the officer's suspicions about fellow American Generals Charles Lee and Gates. He tells Washington that they envy and hate him and hope for and work for his downfall. The officer's suspicions will prove accurate and both generals will eventually come to bad ends.

In the above-mentioned scene in *John Adams*, when Adams toured the Continentals' camp, Washington said of Congress, "Nothing has yet come from all their promises of powder, muskets, supplies…" A couple scenes later, Adams appealed to Congress for Washington and was ignored completely. *The Crossing* echoes this in an early scene in which Washington dictates a letter to his secretary, Alexander Hamilton, pleading for funds for his troops, some literally barefoot in winter.

You're also going to learn of the critical role of "a pretty little wench named Mrs. Loring" who is nightly sharing a bed with British General Howe, and why, as Hugh Mercer suggests to Washington in the movie, the fetching adulteress detaining Howe may be credited with the "continuing existence" of the American army.

Also at that same staff dinner where he announces his new scheme to save the Revolution, Washington reads a letter from Congress that says they have fled Philadelphia and he is "in full command with the power to make all decisions concerning the future of our struggle." At this historical moment, Washington *is* the Revolution.

When they enact his plan, the password for that night shows how desperate they are: "Victory or death." Incidentally, the subject of this movie was also the subject of one of the most iconic of American paintings, *Washington*

Crossing the Delaware, by German immigrant Emmanuel Leutze. That's the one with Washington posed heroically at the prow of a boat in a winter landscape. Prints of the painting hung on the wall in many one-room schoolhouses in the nineteenth century. Soldiers in various wars were even recruited under prints of it.

The movie will show you how Washington actually crossed the Delaware River. However, the painting got one thing right that the movie didn't. The river was more dangerous than it is portrayed in the movie and more like it is in the painting, full of huge free-floating blocks of ice.

After

British historian Sir George Otto Trevelyan wrote about the victory at Trenton that: "It may be doubted whether so small a number of men ever employed so short a space of time with greater and more lasting effects upon the history of the world."

Inspite of its historical significance, the Battle of Trenton, as the battle in the movie is known, was small even by the standards of the Revolutionary War, with fewer than three thousand men participating, and, as you saw, many Americans armed with what were essentially spears.

What's wonderful about this movie is its grubbiness, its complete lack of cinemascopic grandeur. To say it's grubby is not to suggest there isn't beauty here, it did win an American Society of Cinematographers' Award. Washington's last meeting with his officers by a blazing hearth just before the crossing, in which he wishes them a Merry Christmas, has a stylized lighting reminiscent of the illustrations by N.C. Wyeth in Thirties adventure books.

Inspite of some shots of canned Hollywood violence, the look and feel of the climactic clash on a plowed field seems accurate. As they attacked, notice no one had uniforms except the officers and that Washington shouted, "Stay with your officers men, for God's sake, stay with your officers!" The American Army is in its raw infancy. Notice too that even at this early date we are a nation of immigrants. A unit of German immigrants who speak no English plays a critical role especially in the aftermath of the battle.

The young sharpshooter who shot Hessian Colonel Rall and who we first met in a tent in the rain smoking cow dung because tobacco wasn't available, was obviously an invention of Howard Fast. The sharpshooter was illustrating the common accusation that Americans violated 18th Century war etiquette by deliberately shooting enemy officers, democrat-ically refusing to recognize the officers' special status.

This is from Washington's own letter describing the Battle of Trenton. "I crossed over to Jersey the Evening of the 25th about 9 miles above Trenton with upwards of 2000 Men and attacked three Regiments of Hessians consisting of fifteen hundred Men about 8 o'clock next Morning. Our Men pushed on with such Rapidity that they soon carried four pieces of Cannon out of Six, Surrounded the Enemy and obliged 30 Officers and 886 privates to lay down their Arms without firing a Shot. Our Loss was only two Officers and two or three privates wounded. The Enemy had between 20 and 30 killed." This contradicts what Washington is told in the movie, that no Continentals were wounded or killed in the battle. It is correct that there were no deaths in the battle itself but two soldiers froze to death on the march to Trenton, which says much about the extremity of the conditions.

After the battle, Washington forced his men to immediately recross the Delaware River because he feared a possible massive British counterattack, but he had another reason for the quick retreat not mentioned in the movie. Some of the men may have been so exhausted they were sleeping by the road, as an officer in the movie complains, but some had gotten into the Hessians' hogsheads and gotten drunk. Washington was afraid of losing control of them.

A few days after his victory at Trenton, Washington had another victory at Princeton and together these victories established his reputation as a leader of resourcefulness and decision. They also significantly boosted the Continental Army's flagging morale and inspired re-enlistments.

John Adams said one third of the colonial population was indifferent to the Revolution, one third supported it, and one third was Loyalist. In The Crossing, you saw examples of each. An example of the first would be the shepherd who with his son encountered the American Army just before the battle and was more dazzled by Washington's celebrity than charged with patriotic fervor. Examples of supporters were the gentleman who courteously offered his house as Washington's headquarters and whose family later that night at the staff dinner expressed support for the Revolution. Another example of a supporter was the charming Irish publican who offered his inn for headquarters during the crossing. An amusing example of a Loyalist was the businessman who came out of his privy one morning and discovered himself surrounded by the Continental Army, and who, after the Continentals confiscated his boats, said of Washington "God damn him for the bandit he is" and who furiously predicted failure for the Revolution.

That staff dinner at which the attack on Trenton was announced is the turning point of the film, everything after that is the execution of Washington's plan. At that dinner, during the same conversation in which the host's family expressed support for the Revolution, the contentious officer John Glover scolded his compatriots and insulted his host over such fripperies as their powdered wigs. What was that all about?

Remember in the chapter on The Crucible that you learned that this country's earliest founders, the Puritans, were Protestants so radical other Protestants persecuted them. This friction between Protestant sects was still alive in Washington's time and it erupted at that staff dinner. Glover mentioned his compatriots and hosts being "high church" which was a conservative faction of Anglicanism or the Church of England, the officially approved form of Protestantism. He then described himself as "a Marblehead fisherman of the Congregational persuasion." Congregationalism is a factional descendant of the Puritan Separatists, the sect of the Pilgrim Fathers.

The next pivotal victory for the Americans, after those at Trenton and Princeton, was the Battle of Saratoga (it was actually a series of battles stretched out over days). It came the next year, 1777. The presiding general was Horatio Gates, the same one escorted out of Washington's camp at gunpoint. Gates may have spent the Battle of Saratoga in his tent. He was essentially a paper pusher and really didn't know what to do on a battlefield. The big hero of Saratoga was General Benedict Arnold. He and Gates had argued and Gates had stripped him of his command. Arnold was disobeying orders by even being on the battlefield where he was seriously wounded but kept on fighting, rallying the troops.

Saratoga was a stunning and savory victory over the arrogant British general "Gentleman" Johnny Burgoyne. The Americans lost 500 killed or wounded to 1000 for the British and the remaining nearly 6000 British soldiers became prisoners of the Americans.

As we saw in *John Adams*, the Americans always knew they needed a superpower ally to defeat a superpower and that was why they sent Benjamin Franklin and John Adams to Paris. The French, though hungry for revenge after their defeat in the French and Indian War, were reluctant to commit until Saratoga convinced them that the Americans could win. The French then provided their army and navy plus financial support. Some of the latter also was provided by the Netherlands (John Adams' effort to get a loan there is featured in his HBO series). The war then became a global conflict, forcing the British to divert resources to the West Indies and Europe, and to rely on what turned out to be the illusion of Loyalist military support in North America.

"Saratoga was the turning point," Gordon Wood, the dean of Revolutionary War historians, has written. "It suggested that reconquest of America might be beyond British strength. It brought France openly into the struggle. And it led to a change in British command and a fundamental alteration in strategy."

During the negotiation for the French-American alliance, the Continental Army, still ill-fed, disease-ridden, clothed in tatters with boots ruined by long marches, survived another horrible winter this time in Valley Forge. But during that winter, it was trained and drilled to a polish by one of those democracy-loving European aristocrats, Baron Friedrich Wilhelm von Steuben.

That "alteration in strategy" by the British after Saratoga was a shift of the war to the South. Horatio Gates received the command of the main American army in the South where he suffered a disastrous defeat in 1780 at the Battle of Camden. He lost nearly a thousand men and was at the forefront of a panicked retreat. (Compare that with Washington's retreat from Long Island to Manhattan when he was the last man in the last boat.) Gates was relieved of his command in disgrace and faced a court martial inquiry.

Incidentally, Washington's other nemesis among his own generals, Charles Lee, who was mentioned but not shown in *The Crossing*, also met a disastrous end. You'll remember in the movie when Washington encountered part of his army on a road and was told that its commander, Lee, had been captured by the British. That was just the beginning. While a British prisoner, Lee (a former British officer) drafted a plan for British military operations against the Americans. He was eventually traded back to the Americans for a captured British general, and at the Battle of Monmouth in 1778, Washington ordered him to attack the retreating enemy, but instead, Lee himself retreated directly into Washington's advancing troops. Lee was arrested and court-martialed.

Unquestionably, the American general who hurt Washington the most was Benedict Arnold, the most aggressive of his generals and a popular battlefield hero and eventually the most famous traitor in American history. When Arnold switched sides, it was the biggest disappointment of Washington's life.

After Gates' disgraceful exit from the scene, command of the American Army in the South was given to Nathaniel Greene. In *The Crossing*, it was he who briefed the officers on the eve of the attack and had the memorable line, "We're attacking at dawn gentlemen with cold steel." After the battle, it was he who convinced Washington to see the dying Colonel Rall. When Washington said "Do you want me to weep for those bastards, men who kill for profit?" Greene replied: "Our own cause at its heart is a fight against taxation is it not? In the end, we all kill for profit, the British and the Hessians and us." (More on that exchange later.) By the way, the actor looks surprisingly like the real Greene according to his portraits.

Greene was the most prominent absence in the thumbnail biographies at the end of the movie. Raised a Quaker, he is generally considered the best American field commander of the war. Washington felt that if anything happened to him, Greene should take command of the American forces. Greene's brilliant performance in the South set up the climactic victory at Yorktown, Virginia. After the war, he twice refused the post of Secretary of War and retired to a Georgia estate awarded him for his service.

One of Greene's aides at the time of the Battle of Trenton was Tom Paine the passionate pamphleteer whose simple but stirring rhetoric was such an important rebel weapon and who was mentioned in *John Adams*. Though he is featured in the novel, for some reason Howard Fast left him out of the movie. This is odd, and it may have been due to budget constraints, because Paine wrote one his most famous essays just before the Battle of Trenton, "The American Crisis," supposedly on a drumhead. It begins, "These are the times that try men's souls: The summer soldier and the sunshine patriot will, in this crisis, shrink from the service of their country... Tyranny, like hell, is not easily conquered... and it would be strange indeed if so celestial an article as freedom should not be highly rated." Washington ordered it read to his troops just before the crossing.

Someone who is included in the thumbnail biographies at the end of the movie but who was not actually at the Battle of Trenton is Alexander Hamilton. We covered him already in *John Adams* where he had the same role as in *The Crossing* of omnipresent assistant to Washington. Howard Fast inserted Hamilton into the movie in order to show the close relationship between Hamilton and Washington. Washington never had a son and Hamilton, along with the young French supporter of the Revolution, the Marquis de Lafayette, both of whom were about the age a Washington son would have been, served as surrogate sons. Among those who were at Trenton but not featured in the movie were the future killer of Alexander Hamilton in a duel of honor, Aaron Burr, and James Monroe, the fifth president and the last who was a Revolutionary War combat veteran.

In achieving that "climatic victory at Yorktown" that Greene set up for him, Washington went up against General Charles Cornwallis. In our movie, Washington told his friend Hugh Mercer that Cornwallis was the only British general "who's not an idiot." In 1781, Cornwallis and an army of 8,000 were at Yorktown on Chesapeake Bay in Virginia. In early September, a French fleet arrived and defeated a British fleet thus blocking any escape by sea for Cornwallis. In late September, Washington's army and a French army arrived and the combined land and naval forces completely surrounded Cornwallis. Washington began several weeks of heavy bombardment of the British positions and after successful American and French infantry attacks, the British surrendered and peace negotiations between the United States and Great Britain began, resulting in the Treaty of Paris in 1783.

In *John Adams* we already covered what follows, the Constitutional Convention, which Washington presided over, and the Washington presidency. This brings us back to that original question in this chapter about Washington: why do the Americans love this guy so much?

The great American poet William Carlos Williams, who also authored a classic on early American history, probably expressed the consensus opinion when he wrote of Washington: "No doubt at all, he personally, was ninety percent of the force which made of the American Revolution such a successful issue." Historian David McCullough wrote, "Above all, Washington never forgot what was at stake and he never gave up." This is exemplified in the movie, when Washington says at the first staff meeting, "So long as I command a corporal's guard, I'll make some endeavor" to endure.

If he is loved for his perseverance (a favorite word in Washington's writings) and determination in the face of daunting odds during the Revolution, he may be loved even more for what he did after the Revolution, something that no victorious general had ever done before, something that shocked the entire world, he relinquished power.

As historian Richard Norton Smith said in PBS's *Liberty!* "He could have been king. Congress in effect offered him a crown. He spurned it, and in the process, he gave us a whole new definition of greatness, which was renunciation of power, not the embrace of it. And it's no accident that on his death bed, Napoleon said, 'They wanted me to be another Washington.' " Jefferson declared, "The moderation and virtue of a single character... probably prevented this revolution from being closed, as most others have been, by a subversion of that liberty it was intended to establish."

So what kind of flesh-and-blood man was this living icon? The most recent and, at more than 900 pages, perhaps most monumental biography, *Washington: A Life* (2011) by National Book Award winner Ron Chernow, was reviewed by the Harvard historian of the American Revolution, Jill Lepore. She wrote in the *The New Yorker*, "Washington isn't like Adams, effusively cantankerous; he's not like Jefferson, a cabinet of contradictions. He's not funny like Franklin or capacious like Madison... He was a staged man, shrewd, purposeful, and effective. Not surprisingly for an eighteenth-century military man, he held himself at a considerable remove from his men. But he also held himself at this remove from just about everyone else... Washington's theatrical reserve can look, now, like mysteriousness. But what he was going for was an imperturbability that had to do with eighteenth-century notions of honor, gentility, and manliness; its closest surviving kin, today, is what's called military bearing... Washington came to embody the new nation's vision of itself: virtuous, undaunted, and incorruptible."

We have two actors' portrayals of him. Both offer much of Lapore's "considerable remove" and "theatrical reserve" and "imperturbability." In *John Adams*, David Morse, as a vital but secondary character, is stiff, aloof, and monumental. The star of *The Crossing*, Jeff Daniels, is the same height and at the time of filming was the same age that Washington was during the Battle of Trenton. He gets a chance to present a more rounded Washington, not that the remove and reserve aren't there. They are brought to the fore in the central scene of the staff dinner when Gates accuses Washington of "looking down that long nose" at him.

Lapore wrote, "Chernow's aim is to make of Washington something other than a 'lifeless waxwork,' an 'impossibly stiff and wooden figure...' That has been the aim of every Washington biographer, and none of them have achieved it." Howard Fast inserted several scenes that tried to counter the same problem. Always a meticulous researcher, he discovered and used an anecdote of humanizing barracks humor in which Washington says, loud enough for the troops to hear, to the portly artillery officer Henry Knox as they enter a boat during the crossing, "Move your fat ass Henry and don't swing your balls or you'll swamp the boat."

But the most humanizing scene has to be the one after the battle, when an exhausted Washington confesses to his best friend Hugh Mercer (who will be killed in the next battle) that he has been worried sick and sleepless about sending "these beautiful lads" to their deaths (the sixteen and seventeen year olds that make up what is left of his army). This was a man who never had children of his own.

What the movie couldn't include are the life facts. He was born in Westmoreland County, Virginia, in 1732. His father died when he was eleven. When he was sixteen, he went on a surveying trip in the Shenandoah Valley and, three years later, travelled to the West Indies. His military experience began in the French and Indian War.

In 1754, before that war began, Major Washington of the Virginia militia led an expedition to assist in the construction of a fort at present-day Pittsburgh, Pennsylvania. Along the way he, his men, and their Indian allies ambushed a French scouting party. Its leader was killed. The exact circumstances of his death were disputed, but this peacetime act of aggression is seen as one of the main causes of the global Seven Years War between France and England, or as it is known in the U.S., the French and Indian War.

In 1755, Washington was the senior aide to General Edward Braddock on the largest British expedition ever in the colonies. The French and their Indian allies ambushed it, Braddock was killed, and the British were catastrophically defeated. But Washington performed well and he was made "Colonel of the Virginia Regiment." This gave him command of a thousand soldiers in brutal campaigns against the Indians in the west with 20 battles in 10 months in which he lost a third of his men.

In 1758, he left the military and the next year married the wealthy widow Martha Dandridge Custis while, according to surviving letters, he may have been in love with the wife of a friend. Nevertheless, it was a solid marriage and, though they never had children of their own, he helped raise her two children from a previous marriage. For the sixteen years before the Revolution, he lived the aristocratic life of a successful Virginia planter: dances and parties and the theater, fox hunting, races, and even cock fights.

It has been claimed that Washington was the richest man in America. He was at least one of the richest men in Virginia and much of that wealth was in slaves. He owned over three hundred. Gordon Wood has written, "Of all the well-known founders who were major slaveholders, including Jefferson, Madison, and Patrick Henry, Washington was the only one who actually ended up freeing his slaves." Plus he created a trust fund to help them adjust to freedom. Wood goes on, "He arrived at his conclusion that slavery was immoral and inconsistent with the ideals of the Revolution gradually, privately, and with difficulty." He wanted slavery to be abolished "by slow, sure, imperceptible degrees." Washington told the abolitionists privately how much he hated slavery and promised to support emancipation in Virginia if it ever came to a vote. He made no secret of his disdain for the institution, but neither did he have the courage to broadcast his views or act on them publicly.

Americans like to believe that the country's rise to dominance was inevitable because of the truth of its founding principles. Maybe. But it is certain that America has been lucky enough to have great leadership during each supremely critical crisis, when its very existence was at stake, starting with Washington and continuing through Lincoln and up to Franklin Roosevelt.

Military Timeline of the Revolution

1775

Apr 19 Battles of Lexington and Concord begin the war

May 10 Fort Ticonderoga was captured by revolutionaries Ethan Allen, Benedict Arnold and the Green Mountain Boys.

Jun 17 In the Battle of Bunker Hill, the British force the Patriots to retreat, but there are over 1,000 British casualties.

Jul 3 Washington arrives in Massachusetts and becomes Commander-in-Chief of an army of untrained undisciplined farmers and workers.

1776

Jan 24 Henry Knox arrives in Boston with fifty-nine captured British cannons.

Aug 29 In New York, British forces under General Howe route the Americans, forcing Washington make a nighttime retreat across the east River to Harlem Heights.

Sept 22 Nathan Hale is executed by the British. His famous last words were, "I only regret that I have but one life to lose for my country."

Nov 16 At the Battle of Fort Washington in Manhattan, Howe again defeats the Americans, forcing Washington to retreat toward the Delaware River pursued by British General Cornwallis.

Dec 26 American victory in Battle of Trenton

1777

Jan 3 American victory in Battle of Princeton

Sept 11 At Brandywine Creek, Pennsylvania, Washington and Howe meet again. Both sides suffer heavy losses and Washington retreats toward Philadelphia.

Oct 17 The British plan to separate New England from the rest of the colonies fails when General John Burgoyne and his army of 7,700 surrender at Saratoga, New York.
-France recognizes America's independence.

Dec 17 Washington sets up winter camp at Valley Forge, Pennsylvania. Morale is low, disease and frigid temperatures decimate the soldiers. German General Baron Von Stueben trains them.

1778

Jun 28 Clinton and Washington's armies meet at Monmouth, New Jersey. The battle was inconclusive, but American General Charles Lee ordered a disastrous retreat.

1780

May 12 Charleston, South Carolina, surrendered to the British.

1781

Jan 17 American forces under Daniel Morgan defeat British

forces at Cowpens, S.C.

Mar 15 British General Charles Cornwallis defeated Nathanael Greene at Guilford Courthouse, North Carolina; however, British casualties were such that it was the intended strategic victory for the Americans.

Aug 1 Cornwallis chooses Yorktown, Virginia as resting place.

Sept 28 The siege at Yorktown begins. Washington's army encircled the British while French naval forces continuously bombard them.

Oct 19 Cornwallis formally surrenders at Yorktown ending all formal combat.

1783

Sept 3 The Treaty of Paris ends American Revolutionary War.

Recommendations

From 1985, there is *Revolution*, as it was originally titled. It has since been reissued and recut and is now *Revolution Revisited* (2009). Directed by Academy Award nominee Hugh Hudson and starring Academy Award winner Al Pacino, the film was scandalously panned by critics and audiences alike. It's chief weakness is a miscast and mumbling Pacino with a hippie hair style. It is not a great film but it is a good one, and ideal for our purposes. It is a compelling fictional story with excellent period detail about fur trapper Pacino and his son who are part of the one third indifferent to the Revolution but who are swept up into it anyway. It ends with the Revolution itself at the Battle of Yorktown. What adds to the fun is that Brits made it in the U.K.

There is an excellent movie *Benedict Arnold: A Question of Honor* (2003) with a miscast Kelsey Grammer as Washington but a superb Aiden Quinn as Arnold. *Not* recommended is Mel Gibson's *The Patriot,* a total mess, lacking in historical veracity throughout, plus having a plot riddled with logical inconsistencies.

PBS's American Experience has a documentary titled *George Washington: Man Who Wouldn't Be King* (2011). It's only sixty minutes and stops at the end of the Revolutionary War when he resigns his commission. The History Channel's *Washington the Warrior* (2006) covers the same ground more or less. A&E's Biography series produced *George Washington: American Revolutionary* (2009) which covers the whole life in 50 minutes.

It would almost be possible to teach a history course just using the novels of Howard Fast, some of which were made into great movies, such as *Spartacus* (1960), and some were made into watchable movies, such as *April Morning* (1988). That is a 1988 Hallmark Hall of Fame made-for-TV movie starring Tommy Lee Jones. It is about the Battle of Lexington-Concord and it gets the period detail and history right for the most part (and adds some teenage romance). A major exception is when they have an invented character surreptitiously fire "the shot heard 'round the world," as the opening shot of that battle by persons and for reasons unknown is called.

When *The Crossing* first aired in 2000 on A&E, there was an explosion of outrage among conservatives over the lines quoted above from Nathaniel Greene, "Our own cause at its heart is a fight against taxation is it not? In the end, we all kill for profit, the British and the Hessians and us." None of the articles seriously criticized anything about the film except those lines and none failed to mention that Howard Fast had been a member of the Communist Party in the Thirties. Fast had an intense if critical love of this country which he evinced in dozens of historical novels close to eighty million copies of which have been sold.

At www.escalloniapress.com, there are free recommendations of the best books - histories, biographies, memoirs, and even novels - related to the subjects of this chapter.

Ch. 5 – Amistad

Before

This movie has one of the most powerful beginnings in film history: in the dead of night, during a lightning storm, a black man by the name of Cinque digs a nail out of wood with bleeding fingernails. He uses the nail to unlock his shackles and then unlocks other black men in the hold of a sailing ship. Thus begins the slave uprising of the Spanish ship "La Amistad" (which means friendship in Spanish). The terror, rage, and despair of those recently enslaved explodes onto the crew just two of whom the slaves leave alive to pilot the ship back to Africa.

This 1997 Steven Spielberg film, based on an actual incident of 1839, is actually two films in one: the shorter is about the unspeakable nightmare that was the life of a slave and the longer is about the politics of slavery in the 1840s. The former is a technical tour-de-force from one of our greatest filmmakers; there is nothing like it on film; it is stunning first shot to last. Some of the political drama surrounding it is sluggish and has unwarranted distortions of the history, but there is quite a bit of the politics of that period between the Revolution and the Civil War, so this is our film for slavery.

The ordeal of the slaves on the ship after the uprising, as they head back (they think) to Africa, occupies the first twenty minutes of the film. (The most gruesome scenes set on the slave ship, appear in flashback, later in the film.) After the slave ship is captured by the U.S. Coast Guard, we enter the political realm where most of the conflict is in the arena of the courtroom. As in his *Lincoln* (2012), which is the subject of chapter eight, Spielberg has constructed an historical drama here based on legal technicalities. The legality and morality of slavery itself is not the issue in the Amistad trials. The various courts must decide whether the defendants were born of slaves (in which case they are guilty of murder) or were illegally brought from Africa (and therefore had a right to defend themselves against kidnapping). Though slavery is flourishing in the South at this time, since 1808 the importation of slaves into the U.S. has been illegal, and it is also illegal internationally by treaty by the time of the Amistad uprising.

In this film, we will meet both historical and fictional characters from the era. At the center is the historical character, Cinque, played by Djimon Hounsou, who brings a fierce mesmerizing integrity to the role. From the African country of Benin, Hounsou is a former model who appeared in the music videos of Paula Abdul, Janet Jackson, and Madonna among others. *Amistad* was his first starring role. Today he is well established with a long filmography that includes two Oscar nominations for Best Supporting Actor.

The African captives in this film are not meek mute damp-eyed victims. They can be ferocious, as we see in the opening sequence, and fascinating to watch, as they react to this alien world in which they are stranded. Spielberg keeps their perspective in the foreground of the story and even takes us deep into the psyche of Cinque, in an acting tour-de-force by Hounsou, as he describes the killing of a lion that made him a chief. Real West Africans speaking their own dialect play the black captives. Normally slaves would not necessarily have known each other's language, which was a deliberate calculation by the slavers to prevent rebellions, but it so happened that the 53 captives on the Amistad were all from the Mende tribe in Sierra Leone.

A fictional character near the center of the film is Theodore Joadson, supposedly a former-slave and abolitionist activist, played by Morgan Freeman. There were numerous African American abolitionists, and some were involved in the Amistad trials, but by far the most famous African American abolitionist was Frederick Douglass (1818 - 1895). It might have made more sense to use Douglass as a character and simply fictionalize his involvement in the Amistad incident (he was still a slave at that time). Morgan Freeman read from Douglass' writings in a voice-over for the classic documentary *Ken Burns' Civil War* (1990).

Douglass was one of the all time great Americans and the author of a world classic, *Narrative of the Life of Frederick Douglass, an American Slave, Written By Himself* (1845). There is nothing else like it for understanding the life of someone born into slavery in America. It is less than a hundred and fifty pages and written in a remarkably clear and direct prose, a prose fashioned into a weapon by the urgency of his need to tell the truth about slavery.

After escaping slavery, he became a leader of the abolitionist movement and a living counter-example to slaveholders' arguments that slaves did not have the intellectual capacity to function as independent American citizens. During the Civil War, he met Abraham Lincoln and they became friends. After the war, Douglass spent the rest of his life working for the rights and equality of all people: black, female, Native American, and recent immigrant.

An important historical figure we meet in this film is John Quincy Adams (1767 – 1848), superbly played by Oscar and Emmy winner Anthony Hopkins, who bears a striking resemblance to Adams. While still a slave, Frederick Douglass read to other slaves a speech by Adams attacking slavery, and the knowledge that this fight was going on gave the slaves hope. Some historians consider John Quincy Adams the most distinguished public figure of the entire era between the Founders and Lincoln. In his Pulitzer Prize–winning history book *Profiles in Courage*, which describes acts of courage and integrity by eight U.S. Senators, John F. Kennedy starts with John Quincy Adams.

Of course, we first met Quincy Adams in the miniseries *John Adams* where he went from childhood to manhood during the Revolution. His life is a good link between that era and the one in this movie. As we saw in *John Adams*, he witnessed the Battle of Bunker Hill at age eight. He also fought under Washington, negotiated an end to the War of 1812, engineered the annexation of Florida, and served in congress when Lincoln did, in front of whom, Adams suffered a stroke at his desk in the House chamber, dying at the age of eighty. He was also the sixth President of the United States (1825–1829) and one of the most brilliant and well-qualified men ever to occupy the White House. He read Biblical passages at least three times a day--once in English, once in German, and once in French. He was fluent in seven languages including Greek and Latin.

He had a difficult fifty-year marriage to a strong brilliant woman producing three sons, a daughter who died in infancy, and nine miscarriages. His son Charles Francis Adams, as Lincoln's ambassador to Great Britain, made the vital contribution to victory in the Civil War of keeping the British from recognizing the Confederacy. The son of Charles Francis, Henry Adams, was one of the greatest American historians.

Besides being President, John Quincy Adams was senator, ambassador to six countries, and one of the greatest secretaries of state. He authored the Monroe Doctrine, the 1823 proclamation by the United States that the Western Hemisphere was closed to further European colonization and that the U.S. would use force to stop it. It was a defining moment in U.S. foreign policy.

John Quincy Adams is the only president to be elected to congress after he left the presidency (and that is when he served with Lincoln). With greater success than he had in the presidency, Adams was a U.S. Representative from Massachusetts from 1830 until 1848. As a congressman, he was known to sympathizers as "Old Man Eloquent," and to Southerners, as "the Madman from Massachusetts." It is in that role of congressman that he is featured in our film.

Of course, recently the U.S. had a president who was the son of a president. Indeed, George Herbert Walker Bush's nickname for his son George Walker Bush was "Quincy." The latter also shared with Quincy Adams the fact they both lost the popular vote but still gained the presidency.

Another historical character you're going to meet in *Amistad* is President Martin Van Buren, a nonentity, which makes him perfect for us. He can stand in for the rogues' gallery of nonentities who occupied the White House between Andrew Jackson and Abraham Lincoln, and who somehow got through a term or two without confronting the dominant political issue of the era, slavery. Because of an economic depression brought on by the policies of his predecessor and mentor Andrew Jackson, Van Buren faced an uphill struggle for reelection in

1840. So, in the movie, we will see him desperately trying to appease a key constituency of his reigning Democratic party, the increasingly volatile slave-holding South.

Speaking of which, John C. Calhoun is quoted by John Quincy Adams at the Amistad trial in our film: "There has never existed a civilized society in which one segment did not thrive upon the labor of another ... In Eden, where only two were created, even there, one was pronounced subordinate to the other ..." That is probably what Calhoun is best known for: his intense and original defense of slavery as something normal and even positive. Known as the "Cast-Iron Man" for his ideological rigidity, Calhoun was an inspiration to the secessionists who started the Civil War. He was also a "war hawk" who for the sake of American honor helped push the U.S. into the War of 1812. Besides being John Quincy Adams' Vice President, as mentioned by Adams in our film, he was also congressman and senator from South Carolina, and secretary of war and state. He is accurately portrayed in our film. That's him at the Presidential banquet, cutting his meat while defending slavery and threatening Van Buren with civil war.

Those unforgettable scenes on the slave ship depict what was called the Middle Passage, the journey slaves took west from Africa across the Atlantic. The First Passage was their capture and transport to a port in Africa, and the Final Passage was their transport inside the Americas to their final destination.

The Middle Passage usually took more than seven weeks and was one segment of a triangular trade route in which ships departed Europe for Africa with manufactured goods, which were traded for kidnapped Africans, who were transported across the Atlantic and then traded for agricultural products, which would be transported back to Europe to complete the voyage. For two hundred years, 1440–1640, Portuguese slavers had a near monopoly, but later other European powers also became slavers such as Britain, Spain, France, the Netherlands, Denmark, and Sweden.

Between ten and sixteen million Africans were forcibly transported across the Atlantic between 1500 and 1880. Forty percent died during the First or Middle Passage. Before 1800, more people came to the U.S. from Africa than anywhere else and they came in chains. The first census in the U. S. after independence found blacks, slaves and free, to be about twenty percent of the country's population. The U.S. had slavery longer than it has been independent.

The biggest difference between American and ancient slavery is the racial distinction between slave and master. In the ancient world slavery was not necessarily a permanent condition nor even necessarily the lowest status. Some slaves were even imperial administrators. In the New World, slavery provided the labor force for a profit-making capitalist system of plantation agriculture producing cotton, sugar, coffee, and cocoa for distant markets. In a typical plantation in the American South, the slave-men might be required to pick 80 pounds-per-day of cotton, while women were required to pick 70 pounds. If any slave failed in his or her quota, they were given lashes of the whip for each pound they were short. The whipping post stood next to the cotton scales.

Apologists for slavery have maintained that it could not have been so bad since slaves were property and no one abuses their own property (except of course when that property tries to escape or threatens rebellion or does anything whatsoever that offends its owner). The historical record is conclusive that, illogical as it may well be, treatment of slaves was very brutal, including punishment by whipping, shackling, beating, branding, imprisonment, and hanging. After slaves were whipped, overseers were known to order the wounds rubbed with turpentine and red pepper. Mutilation such as castration or the cutting off of ears was relatively common during the colonial era. Punishment was most often meted out for disobedience or perceived infractions, but sometimes just to assert dominance.

In addition to the dehumanizing brutality was the psychological impact of such common occurrences as family members sold at auction or daughters raped. Slaves were at a continual risk of losing family members, the average slave being sold once or twice in a lifetime. Narratives by escaped slaves often included accounts of families broken up and women sexually abused. One of those narratives is the basis for the movie *12 Years a Slave*, which provides as powerful a glimpse into the life of the average American slave as *Amistad* does into the Middle Passage. *12 Years a Slave* is thoroughly discussed in the Recommendations section.

Of course, white Southern society abhorred sexual relations between white women and black men as damaging to racial purity, but sexual relations between white men and black women were good for business, with the children of slave mothers always classified as slaves. During the early nineteenth century, popular Southern literature characterized female slaves as lustful promiscuous "Jezebels" who shamelessly tempted white owners, a stereotype obviously used to rationalize rape. By 1860, there were four hundred eleven thousand slaves classified as mulatto (biracial) out of a total slave population of nearly four million.

One of the arguments of the abolitionists against slavery was that it encouraged incest; for instance, between a master and his slave daughter. This is a theme in some of the work of the South's greatest novelist, Nobel Prize winner William Faulkner. Though a political conservative, Faulkner hated racism, and in one of his masterpieces, *Absalom, Absalom* (1936), he made the case that Southern racism is a bigger perversion than incest.

When George Washington married Martha Custis, he became the owner of her slaves and faced the ethical conundrum of owning two of his wife's half-sisters. Despite the fact that Thomas Jefferson was a lifelong slaveholder, he included strong anti-slavery language in the original draft of the Declaration of Independence, but other delegates took it out. Benjamin Franklin, also a slaveholder for most of his life, was a leading member of the Pennsylvania

Society for the Abolition of Slavery, the first recognized organization for abolitionists in the U. S.

Ken Burns' epic documentary *The Civil War* uses in its narration a memorable quote from a former slave: "No day ever dawns for the slave. Nor is it looked for. For the slave it is all night. All night forever." Only four slaves out of a hundred lived to be sixty. And the whites knew how bad it was. A white Mississippian, also quoted by Ken Burns, said, "I'd rather be dead than be a nigger on one of these plantations."

After

The box office calculation is obvious when the filmmakers have a hunk like Matthew McConaughey playing the scrappy young lawyer, Roger Baldwin. The real Baldwin (1793 –1863), who could hardly have been less like his screen counterpart, was a middle-aged, successful, and respected New Haven, Connecticut attorney. Grandnephew of a signer of the Declaration of Independence, Baldwin would eventually be governor of Connecticut and then one of its U. S. senators. His antislavery credentials were impeccable. He took the Amistad case as a matter of conscience and accepted no more than a token fee.

There was no box office calculation in the mind-boggling distortion the filmmakers inflicted on Lewis Tappan (1788–1873). Played by Stellan Skarsgård, Tappan is the white abolitionist working beside Joadson, and for most of the film, Tappan is accurately portrayed. He was a very successful businessman who started The Mercantile Agency in 1841 in New York City, which was the precursor to Dun & Bradstreet (still in existence today) and other modern credit-reporting services. Tappan was also an early and radical abolitionist.

Lewis was the brother of Senator Benjamin Tappan and abolitionist Arthur Tappan. In 1835, the Tappans helped establish Oberlin College in Ohio, which admitted students of both genders and all races. The Tappan brothers were Congregationalists (sectarian descendants of the Puritans) and uncompromising moralists; even within the abolitionist movement, other members found their views extreme. Lewis Tappan advocated intermarriage as the long-range solution to racial issues. He dreamed of a "copper-skinned" America where no one would be defined by race. Although Tappan was popular among many, his homes and churches he built were targets of pro-slavery arson and vandalism.

Lewis Tappan characterized the arrival of the *Amistad* and its Africans on American shores as a "providential occurrence" that might allow "the heart of the nation" to be "touched by the power of sympathy." That was when the abolitionists still believed that "moral suasion" was enough to end slavery. Tappan attended each day of the *Amistad* trials and wrote daily accounts of the proceedings for the New England abolitionist paper *The Emancipator*, which we observe him do in the movie.

Then at one point, the filmmakers have their Tappan utter the preposterous suggestion that it might be better for the cause if the Amistad captives died. They make him sound like a Bolshevik, something that could not possibly be less characteristic of the actual man.

There are other equally bewildering distortions in this film: John Quincy Adams did not have to be talked into representing the Amistad captives, he was involved in the case from the beginning. At the time of the Amistad trials, Adams was the most prominent national leader opposing slavery, the leading abolitionist in congress, and the leading opponent of the "Slave Power," the enormous political power concentrated in a small group of Southern slave owners.

When he was president, Lincoln pursued the policies of John Quincy Adams, who shared Lincoln's loathing for slavery and who supported much the same program of federal aid to transportation, education, and industrialization that Lincoln enacted. Though he died before they occurred, Adams foresaw not only the Civil War and Emancipation, but he even predicted the mechanism by which emancipation would occur— through use of the presidential war powers (which was how Lincoln did it). Virtually none of Adams' famous eight hour, two day summation before the Supreme Court in the Amistad trial made it into his on-screen speech which is vague and rambling. In a couple shots where Adams refers to the Founders, there is first a painting and then a bust of his father in the frame behind Quincy Adams.

Another unwarranted change in the film concerns the judge for one of the Amistad trials, Andrew Judson, who was proslavery but still found in favor of the captives. The filmmakers however have him replaced by a fictitious crypto Catholic, Coglin, in a failed attempt to rig the trial. Whaaaa...?! What conceivable point were they making...if any? Some of these distortions seem arbitrary if not even frivolous.

Remember the Catholic priest who was blessing the slaves as they were put on the ship? He's representing those who believe that Africans should be grateful for slavery because it enabled them to become Christians and Americans. Slaveholders defended their "peculiar institution," as they called it, with the Bible, pseudo-scientific theories of racial superiority, and reminders that, as John C. Calhoun put it at the presidential banquet in our film, slavery was "the life blood" of the economy. Even when conceding that slavery was inefficient, slavery apologists still saw advantages in its uniting Southern whites and avoiding the class antagonism and labor unrest that plagued the North and Europe. Most in the North held to the "free labor" argument against slavery: that it was backward, inefficient, and degrading, and that it should not be allowed to spread. To abolitionists, slavery was a grievous sin.

Lewis Tappan along with other activists founded the American Anti-Slavery Society in Philadelphia in 1833. From the 1830s on, the abolitionist movement grew, especially among religious women in the Northeast, who were affected by the Second Great Awakening, a religious movement during the early nineteenth century by which believers could be saved through revivals. *Amistad* is rife with religious imagery and sentiment that reflects the Second Great Awakening: from the abolitionists who sing hymns kneeling outside the prison after the Africans first arrive to the women holding up crucifixes through the opening in a fence at the manacled slaves passing on the street.

The pioneers of religious opposition to slavery were the Quakers, a radical Protestant sect based in Pennsylvania, from where in the mid-to-late-eighteenth-century they set in motion the American antislavery movement. Although devout pacifists, Quakers were willing to disobey unjust laws, such as the Fugitive Slave Acts. Because of the Quaker presence and its proximity to slaveholding Maryland, Pennsylvania became a principal way station for runaway slaves on the way to Canada, the famous Underground Railroad.

Never centrally organized, the Underground Railroad was a network of secret routes and safe houses for escaping slaves, involving abolitionists, white and black. Most famous among the latter was the legendary Harriet Tubman (1822 – 1913). Born into slavery, Tubman escaped and made about thirteen missions to rescue approximately seventy enslaved family and friends. She later helped John Brown recruit men for his raid on Harpers Ferry, and in the post-war era, she struggled for women's suffrage.

Other famous abolitionists were: William Lloyd Garrison, publisher of the abolitionist newspaper *The Liberator*, and mentor to the young Frederick Douglass; the popular Quaker poet John Greenleaf Whittier; and Harriet Beecher Stowe who, to give meaning to the devastating loss of a young son, wrote the abolitionist *Uncle Tom's Cabin* (1852), which reached millions around the world as both a novel and a stage play. Set apart from the other abolitionists by his commitment to violence was John Brown, who was also active in the Underground Railroad for several years.

The Amistad slave uprising and Cinque's leadership held special significance for John Brown. In 1850, he said, "Nothing so charms the American people as personal bravery. Witness the case of Cinque, of everlasting memory, on board the Amistad." In 1859, Brown raided the federal arsenal at Harper's Ferry, Virginia, seeking arms for a slave uprising. The raid failed miserably but electrified the nation, and it became a major catalyst of the Civil War. In the raid, Brown killed 4 and wounded 9 but 10 of his 21 men were killed (including two of his sons), and he himself was captured, tried, and hanged, along with 4 followers.

Two other famous outspoken abolitionists, America's two greatest philosophers, who were also close friends, Henry David Thoreau and Ralph Waldo Emerson, were also friends, supporters, and passionate defenders in speeches and print of John Brown. They were alone among public figures in doing so. Emerson famously and scandalously said of Brown that he would "make the gallows as glorious as the cross." Thoreau called Brown "the most American of us all." By the time of the Civil War, only a year and half or so after Harper's Ferry, Thoreau and Emerson had elevated public opinion of Brown such that the Union's most popular marching song became "John Brown's Body," which though it "lies a-mouldering in the grave, / His soul keeps marching on." Brown's historical significance was captured by Herman Melville, author of *Moby Dick*, in his poem "The Portend," where he called John Brown the "meteor of war," a divine forewarning.

Though his court appointed attorney and the South proclaimed John Brown insane, for obvious reasons, there were some among his fellow abolitionists who agreed, and so "Mad John Brown" has been the accepted image of him since. But his calm demeanor, acceptance of responsibility for his actions, and eloquent pronouncements during and after his trial belied the notion of insanity. Virginia's proslavery Governor Henry A. Wise, who met several times with Brown, pronounced him "remarkably sane." The majority of scholars today believe that John Brown, whatever else he may have been, was not insane. The hottest issue among the experts is whether or not Brown would qualify as a terrorist.

For 50 of the 72 years between the elections of George Washington and Abraham Lincoln, a slaveholder served as president. John Quincy Adams became president by defeating one of those slaveholders, Andrew Jackson, in the controversial 1824 election. That election introduced the first campaign buttons, first public opinion polls, and the first campaign biographies. Jackson won the popular vote by quite a lot but neither he nor Adams received the majority of electoral votes. As stipulated in the Constitution for a case like that, the election was thrown into the House of Representatives, where Adams cut deals to win.

Andrew Jackson (1767–1845) is an important historical character of the era that we *don't* meet in this film. He defeated Adams in their rematch of 1828 in one of the bitterest campaigns in American history. In that election, the Jackson campaign was the first to use a professional political organization. Skilled organizers created an extensive network of campaign committees and subcommittees to organize rallies, parades, and barbecues, and to erect hickory poles, Jackson's symbol. His nickname was "Old Hickory" because of his tough aggressive personality; he fought in duels, some fatal to opponents.

During this period, voter participation soared; twice as many votes were cast in the election of 1828 as in 1824, four times as many as in 1820. The 1828 election signaled the beginning of a new democratic age, when the patrician republic of the Founders gave way to a mass democracy in which nearly all white males, not just landowners, could vote. The 1830-1850 period later became known as the era of Jacksonian Democracy. An illustration of Jackson's status today is his face on high-use currency. That's him on the twenty-dollar bill.

At the age of 13, Jackson volunteered to fight in the American Revolution during which he was captured and severely beaten. By the end of that war all but one of his immediate family had died. Later, Jackson was a victorious general whose defeat of the British at the Battle of New Orleans in 1815 is the most lopsided victory in American military history: British casualties, 2042; American, 71. Jackson was the first such described "self-made man," rising from poverty to wealth as an attorney, land speculator, and cotton planter. He also owned more than 100 slaves and was a passionate opponent of abolitionism.

So, he was a wealthy slaveholder who became the champion of the common man against the wealthy elite. He strengthened the presidency, which he saw as spokesman for the entire population, as opposed to Congressmen from specific small districts. He was supportive of states' rights, but during the Nullification Crisis, he declared that states do not have the right to nullify federal laws. When he left office, he made sure Martin Van Buren had been elected as his successor. As we see in our movie, Van Buren failed to win reelection.

Jackson is usually praised for his expansion of democracy and defense of the Union, but criticized for his support of slavery and especially his aggressive enforcement of the Indian Removal Act of 1830 (against a ruling by the Supreme Court). Jackson said that Indians had "neither the intelligence, the industry, the moral habits, nor the desire of improvements." This early example of ethnic cleansing was known as the "Trail of Tears." It resulted in the forced relocation of tens of thousands of Native Americans 800 miles from the southeast to Indian Territory (now Oklahoma) in the center of the country. Many died of exposure, disease, and starvation along the way; for example, almost 17,000 Cherokee were relocated, and an estimated 4,000 died.

In 1831, the Cherokee, Chickasaw, Choctaw, Muscogee Creek, and Seminole (known as the Five Civilized Tribes) were living as autonomous nations and successfully assimilating. By 1837, 46,000 of them had been forcibly removed from what would be called today the Deep South, thereby opening 25 million acres for white settlement. Much of that land would be made profitable with slaves.

Like Spielberg's *Saving Private Ryan*, *Amistad* is a B movie based on historical material with an A set piece of around a half hour (the slave uprising here, the Normandy landing in *Private Ryan*). There is an element of feel-good Spielbergian fantasy here: the Amistad is one of the very few slave uprisings to succeed. Righteous revenge is of course the raw material of the Hollywood product, so we can expect a Hollywood film to reflexively strike back for American slavery, one of history's most monstrous crimes. That's certainly what that scene at the end is about when the righteous naval artillery of Britain destroys the Lomboko Slave Fortress on the African coast. The historical reality is that most slaves did not rebel because the Southern terror state was so effective, and instead, for centuries for millions it was "all night forever."

Eric Foner had some strong criticisms of this film that are worth noting because he is a leading Civil War historian and winner of every history prize in sight including the 2011 Pulitzer Prize, the Bancroft Prize, and the Lincoln Prize for *The Fiery Trial: Abraham Lincoln and American Slavery*. Foner points out anachronisms such as Van Buren campaigning for reelection on a train at a time when candidates didn't campaign and people referring to a imminent Civil War when it was actually twenty years in the future. He accuses the filmmakers of an "orgy of self-congratulation" when in fact the main characters are white and the black characters are "foils for white self-discovery and moral growth."

"Rather than being receptive to abolitionist sentiment [as in the film], the courts were among the main defenders of slavery. A majority of the Amistad justices, after all, were still on the Supreme Court in 1857 when, in the Dred Scott decision, it prohibited Congress from barring slavery from the Western territories and proclaimed that blacks in the United States had 'no rights which a white man is bound to respect.' " Seven of the nine Supreme Court justices in the Amistad case were slave-owning Southerners.

Certainly there are many historical errors in *Amistad*, nevertheless the broad outline of the film's plot is accurate. There was a revolt; the slaves were led by Cinque; the case was a factor in the 1840 presidential contest; various bewhiskered abolitionist lawyers appealed it through US courts up to the Supreme Court where John Quincy Adams successfully represented the slaves' case. Those who survived the ordeal returned to Africa accompanied by missionaries. The Amistad incident contributed to the growth of abolitionism.

There is a small tidbit of Hollywood history in the making of this film: Spielberg got the liberal Supreme Court Justice Harry Blackmun to play Supreme Court Justice Joseph Story, the one who read the Supreme Court's decision in the Amistad case. Blackmun is most famous for writing the decision Roe v. Wade, which legalized abortion.

In 1829, Andrew Jackson arrived in Washington for his first inauguration in a carriage, and eight years later, he left on a train. That illustrates the rapid pace of change in this era of revolutionary innovations in transportation and communications. In an economy previously based on small-scale farming and local commerce, a national market was gradually emerging with canals, steamboats, and railroads connecting the inland regions with the Atlantic ports. The telegraph, the steam-operated printing press, and cheaper paper encouraged the proliferation of newspapers and magazines. The press in turn facilitated the development of nationwide mass political parties. Many newspapers were put out by political parties (or factions within parties) and existed more to give voice to a viewpoint than make a profit.

At one point slavery was actually dying out on its own, but then Eli Whitney got a patent in 1794 for the cotton "gin" (short for engine) that separated the cotton fiber from its seeds and that revolutionized the Southern cotton industry and made slavery profitable again. The mechanization of agriculture continued in the period of our film with Cyrus McCormick's invention of the reaper in 1831 and John Deere's steel plow in 1837. Agriculture was central to the economy: tobacco and cotton in the South, grains and livestock in the North and West.

Eli Whitney also established the first factory to assemble muskets with interchangeable parts, marking the advent of modern mass production, and eventually providing the guns for the Union to defeat the Confederacy. In the North, factories were also manufacturing textiles (using Southern cotton), shoes, clocks, guns, railroad cars, etc. Techniques of mass production were starting to transform manufacturing's age-old artisan traditions and laying the groundwork for the industrial revolution later in the century. By mid century, American inventions – clocks and locks, Colt revolvers and sewing machines, reapers and railroads – were the talk of Europe.

During the era in our film, unsettling social changes led to utopian experimentation, religious revivals, and various reform movements. Among the latter were efforts to suppress the drinking of hard liquor; to rehabilitate criminals; to establish public schools; to care for the mentally ill, the disabled, the deaf, and the blind; to abolish slavery; and to extend women's rights.

All the while, Americans continued their relentless westward expansion, spilling over the Appalachian Mountains and spanning the Mississippi River. By the 1840s, settlers had reached the Pacific Ocean.

Our next film, *One Man's Hero*, will deal with the obscure but immensely important U.S.–Mexico War of 1846. The main political issue that caused the Civil War was whether or not to allow slavery in the "new territories" taken in the U.S.–Mexico War.

Early 19th Century Timeline

1816 James Monroe was elected President.

1817 Harvard Law School was founded.

1819 Panic of 1819: first major peacetime financial crisis followed by a general collapse of the economy persisting through 1821.

1820 The Missouri Compromise between the pro-slavery and anti-slavery factions in Congress, involving the regulation of slavery in the western territories.

-Monroe was reelected President.

1823 The Monroe Doctrine proclaimed that the Americas were off limits to further European colonization and the U.S. would use force to stop it.

1825 John Quincy Adams was elected President by the House of Representatives.

-The Erie Canal was completed linking the Hudson River with Lake Erie.

1826

July 4 Founders and former Presidents Thomas Jefferson and John Adams died within hours of each other, fifty years to the day after the signing of the Declaration of Independence.

1828 Andrew Jackson was elected President. Calhoun continued as Vice President.

1830 Second Great Awakening began, religious revival movement
-The Oregon Trail came into use by settlers migrating to the Pacific Northwest.
-The Indian Removal Act passed allowing forcible relocation.

1831 Slave revolt led by Nat Turner foiled, resulting in 55 white deaths and at least 100 black deaths.
-Publication of abolitionist *The Liberator* began.
-Cyrus McCormick invented the mechanical reaper which reduced human labor on farms while increasing productivity.

1832 Jackson was reelected President; Martin Van Buren was elected Vice President.

1833 American Anti-Slavery Society was founded in Philadelphia.

1835 Texas Revolution (covered in next chapter)
Alexis De Tocqueville's *Democracy in America* published.

1837 Rev. Elijah P. Lovejoy is murdered by a proslavery mob in Alton, Illinois, and becomes the first abolitionist martyr.

Recommendations

12 Years a Slave did not have to be as good as it is. Even a mediocre film on this subject would have been powerful, but *12 Years a Slave* is a great film and historically important. It won the 2013 Academy Award for Best Picture, Best Supporting Actress, and Best Adapted Screenplay. It was awarded the Golden Globe Award for Best Motion Picture – Drama, and the British Academy of Film and Television Arts recognized it with Best Film and Best Actor awards.

Some critics were fooled by screenwriter John Ridley's dialogue finding it "stilted and formal." Actually, this film has some of the most authentic 19th century conversation in cinema, which of course sounds "stilted and formal" to us. Ridley refused to fall back on the "contemporary casual" that would have been so familiar and comfortable for his audience; instead, he took language from the book of the same name that is the basis of the film. Ridley streamlined the narrative, compressing it into a few events on mainly two plantations.

12 Years director Steve McQueen is a Brit and in 1999 he received the highest Brit award in the visual arts, The Turner Award, and in 2011 he received the Commander of the Order of the British Empire, for his service to the visual arts. As a film director, he distinguishes himself in this age of wall-to-wall, ever-finely cut montage with his long, unflinching, defiant, excruciating close shots of physical torture. Incidentally, the star of *12 Years*, Chiwetel Ejiofor, has a role in *Amistad*. That's him as the interpreter for the captives, the historical character James Covey.

Since slaves could no longer be legally imported, there was a steady trade in kidnapping free black men and women from the North and then selling them into slavery in the South, so the experience of Solomon Northrup in *12 Years a Slave* was common. As does Frederick Douglass in his writings, this film also shows the moral and psychological damage slavery did to Southern whites. *12 Years a Slave* has an elegant and devastating ending in which all the torture and injustice of American slavery is concentrated into a single girl, an American Ann Frank.

Several critics mentioned the obvious Kafkaesque aspect to this story: an everyman wakes up one day in an alien world where he is brutalized and utterly powerless. It is a brilliant framing device independent of its authenticity as a true story. This story also attracted the multi-talented Gordon Parks who made a TV movie of the book for PBS in 1984 titled *Solomon Northup's Odyssey*. The 2013 version is much better, nevertheless Parks did well within the confines of a made-for-TV budget and his version is quite powerful at times.

The star as well as the director of *12 Years a Slave* are Brits, so in the category of best film about slavery exclusively by Americans, we have *Nightjohn* (1996). With the riveting Carl Lumbly in the title role of the man who escaped slavery only to voluntarily return to it in order to teach literacy to slaves. Based on a classic young adult novel of the same name, bad acting sinks parts of the film but most of it works well, and it has a powerful ending. It was made for TV, never had theatrical release, and had no stars, other than its director, Charles Burnett, the dean of African American filmmakers.

The Journey of August King (1995), though a minor classic, is essentially a two person play and has little on screen about actual slave life, though it is rich in period details of North Carolina in 1810. It shows that abolitionist sentiments were openly expressed and acted-upon even that early, and it brings up the important issue of slavery and incest.

Django Unchained (2012) was just revenge porn with a blood bag ballet and especially disappointing coming around the same time as Spielberg's magisterial *Lincoln*. There was a slew of films about slavery made in the '60s and '70s. *Slaves* (1969) was very low-budget and very crude. *Goodbye Uncle Tom* (1971) was chaotic, crude, and as much as possible, nude, but this pseudo-documentary by two Italians in which a camera crew time-travels back to the antebellum South has some stunning cinematic imagery. *Mandingo* (1975) and its sequel were crass and lurid. The TV miniseries sensation *Roots* (1977), the final episode of which is still the third-highest-rated US television program ever, and *A Woman Called Moses* (1978), starring the amazing multi-award-winning Cecily Tyson as Harriet Tubman, brought the subject into public discourse, but both had the production values of the industrial-strength TV of their day.

The excellent Canadian film *Race to Freedom: The Story of the Underground Railroad* (1994) focused mainly on the flight from slavery. *Alex Haley's Queen* (1993), starring a young unknown Halle Berry, and *Oprah Winfrey's Beloved* (1998), based on the powerful novel of the same name by

Nobel Prize winner Toni Morrison, focused primarily on the aftereffects of slavery. *Beloved* is based on the true story of a former slave who murdered her own daughter rather than allow her to be a slave. *The Middle Passage* (2000), by a French African director, is a documentary with reenactments that expands the set piece in *Amistad.*

12 Years a Slave is historically important because it is the first film devoted exclusively to the experience of being a slave with production values and talent equal to the gravity of the subject. There has yet to be a feature-length film devoted to the slave experience on the scale of the Confederate white-suffering epics, which have a long Hollywood tradition that continues into our own time and on which we will focus in a later chapter.

PBS' *The Abolitionists* (2013) is an extraordinary three hour docudrama focused on five leaders of the movement: Frederick Douglass, William Lloyd Garrison, Harriet Beecher Stowe, John Brown, and Angelina Grimké, a white Southern woman who courageously turned on her family and community. This film also pushes the documentary form in a new direction with much longer and more fully dramatized reenactments such that it comes close to being a standard narrative movie.

PBS has done well presenting the truth about slavery, with three extraordinary documentary series. PBS described *Africans in America: America's Journey through Slavery* (2000): "Nearly ten years in the making, this landmark six-hour set exposes the truth through surprising revelations, dramatic recreations, rare archival photography, and riveting first-person accounts." *Slavery and the Making of America* (2004) PBS described as "a landmark, four-part series that examines the history of slavery in the United States and the integral role it played in shaping the new country's development ... (It uses) dramatic re-enactments to take viewers back in time and deep into the slave experience. Much of the story is presented from a unique vantage point - through the eyes of the enslaved." Morgan Freeman narrates.

The African Americans: Many Rivers to Cross (2014) "explores in six episodes the history of African Americans from Jamestown to today, as well as their cultural institutions, political strategies, and religious and social perspectives." This one is hosted and produced by Harvard history professor, scholar, and TV personality Henry Louis Gates Jr. It is much more personal, compressing the time given to the overview and focusing more on heroic, obscure individuals in the struggle against slavery and the semi-slavery that followed the Civil War. It's also more personal in that Gates engages in conversation the experts that would normally be just talking heads. Also, Gates serves as the viewers' personal guide through the history.

At www.escalloniapress.com, there are free recommendations of the best books - histories, biographies, memoirs, and even novels - related to the subjects of this chapter.

Chapter 6 – One Man's Hero

Before

"Poor Mexico, so far from God, so close to the U.S." This film illustrates that old saying. This film is also the most direct answer to the question: where did this particular country get the land and the people?

The movie opens with a snare drum roll that cues us that the subject is military. After the written prologue fades, notice the white map of the U.S. and Mexico that was the background for the prologue. On the left, Mexico juts up into what are now the western states of the U.S. (you can see San Francisco in the upper left corner). That territory is what Mexico will lose in the U.S.-Mexican War of 1846-48, the subject of this film.

Remember the beginning of *The New World,* our first movie? It used prints and drawings of the period to provide a general outline of the story. *One Man's Hero* does the same but even more effectively. The credits begin with the mournful keening of Irish folk music while the first drawings and prints appear, depicting the mass death of the "Irish Potato Famine" of 1845–52. Notice a drawing of a troubled man surrounded by other men, creditors, shoving paper debts at him. Then there is a drawing of homelessness as a man pulls a cart loaded with all of his family's belongings out of a village. Then there are actual photos from the period, the second of which shows an emaciated young family slumped on the dirt floor of their hovel. That is followed by a photo of policemen outside the door of a small cottage in the process of evicting the poor tenants.

In addition to famine, the Irish suffered from failed rent payments hence the hounded debtors and the evictions and the homelessness. Their landlords were the English who had been an occupying invader for nearly three centuries at this point. It became cheaper for their English overlords to ship the impoverished, starving Irish to America. There is a print in this sequence with a sailing ship listing in a storm followed by one showing the dejected passengers in a hold considerably more spacious and cleaner than these pestilential holes actually were. Those ships killed so many of their passengers that they would be known to history as the "coffin ships." They finally arrive in America and we see the bustling New York waterfront in prints the last of which is a segue into the first scene of the movie which is on that waterfront.

In the opening scene, we watch a young Irish man join the army to gain citizenship for his family and much needed money. The Irish are important because they are the first refugee population of immigrants (other than the original Pilgrims of course). Remember, everyone in America is an immigrant or a descendent of an immigrant, even the indigenous people, who are Asians that came fifteen to forty thousand years before anyone else. We'll deal with immigration again in chapter 10, but here we'll deal with Irish immigration. Today Americans of Irish descent comprise 12% of the U.S. population.

The Irish faced the same prejudice and discrimination many immigrants are still facing today. Though it didn't entail darker skin, there was even a ethnic aspect, as the Irish are Celtic and their overlords in England and America were Anglo-Saxon. Some factories and businesses famously put up signs saying, "Irish need not apply." The Irish competed for the lowest jobs and were seen as disposable labor. Sound familiar? Sadly, some of the children and grandchildren of this first generation of Irish Americans will attack Chinese immigrants in San Francisco later in the nineteenth century.

"One Man's Hero" tells the little-known story of John Riley and the "St. Patrick's Battalion," or "San Patricios," a group of mostly Irish and other Catholic immigrants who deserted from the mostly Protestant U.S. Army to the Catholic Mexican side during the U.S.- Mexican War. Just before the war starts, a couple of Sergeant John Riley's men in the U.S. Battalion are whipped for "desertion" when they travel to the Mexican side of the border to attend Mass. Riley and the men eventually escape to Mexico hoping to find a ship back to Ireland, instead they find out that the war has just begun and if they are captured they will be hanged.

This movie was a U.S.–Mexico co-production and was filmed in Mexico and makes excellent use of the Mexican countryside. The cinematography and the battle sequences are generally excellent though some of the dramatic sequences are stilted. There is an unconvincing, fumbling but box-office fortifying romance in the foreground, featuring the gorgeous Daniela Romo as Marta. There is also some feel-good cultural intermixing between the Mexicans and the Irish. Our hero, John Riley, based on an historical character of the same name, is adequately acted by over-the-title star Tom Berenger, who has to wrestle the brogue on occasion. By the way, you won't see these U.S. Army uniforms in any other movie. They are just another of the fleeting versions of military uniforms between the Revolution and the Civil War.

If the vicious anti-Catholic bigotry of the junior officers and the merciless whippings of the Irish soldiers seem over the top, they aren't. In this country founded by Protestants so radical they were persecuted by other Protestants, that attitude was abroad throughout the US at that time. By the early 1850s, numerous anti-Catholic secret orders grew up, reaching out especially to those who were lower middle class or skilled workmen. One semi-secret organization was known as the "Know-Nothings". When a member was asked about its activities, he was supposed to reply, "I know nothing." Not mentioned in the film, the Know-Nothings were characterized by political xenophobia, anti-Catholicism, and occasional bouts of violence against targeted Catholic immigrants, who were often regarded as hostile to republican values and controlled by the Pope. Mainly active from 1854 to 1856, the Know-Nothings eventually fragmented over the issue of slavery.

We will return to immigration, nativism, and anti-Catholicism in later chapters. In this film, they are actually sub themes to the war itself. This is the only movie on this vitally important but little-known war. As mentioned before, the issue of whether or not to permit slavery in the "New Territories," as the land taken from Mexico will be called, will be a precipitating factor of the Civil War. That land will also be the states of California, Arizona, New Mexico, Nevada, Utah, and Colorado.

Many of the military leaders on both sides of the American Civil War fought as junior officers in the U.S.-Mexican War: Ulysses S. Grant, Robert E. Lee, George McClellan, Stonewall Jackson, James Longstreet, George Meade, and the future Confederate President Jefferson Davis. This war's colorful and victorious U.S. Major General Zachary Taylor became the 12th president of the U.S. The crotchety character actor James Gammon, who bore a striking resemblance to Taylor, plays him in the film.

Of all U.S. wars, this one is the most blatant land grab. The first cause of the war was the annexation of the Republic of Texas in 1845. When Mexico won its independence from Spain in 1821, Mexican Texas was part of the new nation. To encourage settlement, Mexican authorities allowed organized immigration from the United States, and by 1834, over 30,000 Anglos lived in Texas, compared to only 7,800 Mexicans. That same year, General Antonio López de Santa Anna, then dictator of Mexico, decided to quash the semi-independence of Texas, and Stephen F. Austin called Texans to arms. They declared independence from Mexico in 1836, and after Santa Anna defeated the Texans at the Alamo, a Texan Army under Sam Houston, defeated and captured Santa Ana at the Battle of San Jacinto and a treaty recognizing Texas' independence was signed.

Another contributing factor to the U.S.-Mexico War was the American ambition, publicly stated by President Polk, of acquiring California. (Incidentally, that is a portrait of President Polk in an early scene on the wall behind the desk of the officer who berates Riley for requesting permission to attend mass.) In 1842, the American minister in Mexico, Waddy Thompson, Jr., wrote about California that it was, "the richest, the most beautiful and the healthiest country in the world ... with the acquisition of Upper California we should have the same ascendency on the Pacific ... France and England both have had their eyes upon it." Indeed, the British minister to Mexico Richard Pakenham wrote at about the same time to his government urging it "to establish an English population in the magnificent Territory of Upper California." He contended that there was "no part of the World offering greater natural advantages ... California ... should not fall into the hands of any power but England ... daring and adventurous speculators in the United States have already turned their thoughts in this direction."

Meanwhile the Republic of Texas claimed the Rio Grande River as its southern boundary, but Mexico said it was the Nueces River, farther north. After U.S. annexation of Texas, Polk claimed the Rio Grande boundary. In July 1845, Polk sent General Zachary Taylor with an army of 3,500 (half the U.S. Army at the time) to the Nueces River, prepared to defend Texas from a "Mexican invasion."

On November 10, 1845, Polk secretly sent John Slidell to Mexico City with an offer of $30 million for the Rio Grande border in Texas and Mexico's provinces of Alta California and Santa Fe de Nuevo México. Mexico was not inclined nor able to negotiate. In 1846 alone, the presidency changed hands four times, the war ministry six times, and the finance ministry sixteen times. However, Mexican public opinion and all political factions agreed that selling the territories to the United States would tarnish the national honor.

On April 25, 1846, a 2,000-strong Mexican cavalry detachment attacked a 70-man U.S. patrol that had been sent into the contested territory, killing 16 American soldiers. With this incident and the Mexican government's rejection of Slidell, Polk believed he had enough cause to ask Congress for a declaration of war. "Mexico has passed the boundary of the United States, has invaded our territory and shed American blood upon American soil," Polk said. So Congress approved a declaration of war on May 13, 1846.

Meanwhile hostilities had already begun with the Siege of Fort Texas on May 3 when Mexican artillery at Matamoros opened fire on Fort Texas, which replied with its own guns. This is discussed in an early scene of the film after the date of "May 6, 1846" appears on the screen. In California, U.S. Army Major and famed explorer John C. Fremont (who arrived in late 1845 claiming to be on a mission to find a route to the Pacific) was encouraging rebellion among the Anglo-American settlers. As a result, thirty-three of them in Sonoma declared a revolt on June 14, 1846 and raised a homemade flag with a bear and star. Their actions were later called the "Bear Flag Revolt." It lasted 26 days then the U.S. Army took control of the area.

Also, in June of that year, Stephen Kearny led the "Army of the West" into New Mexico and took Santa Fe without firing a shot and then he moved west eventually into southern California where he joined forces with Fremont and Stockton for a few small battles against Californios (Mexican Californians).

Throughout these years, Americans had been asserting a right to colonize North America beyond the borders of the Louisiana Purchase. The U.S. and Great Britain had jointly administered the Oregon Territory since 1819, but the two nations fell into disputes over the territory. Polk negotiated a compromise that gave half the area to the U.S. (present day states of Oregon and Washington) along the line of the current border with Canada.

By the mid-1840s, U.S. expansionism was articulated in the ideology of "Manifest Destiny". ("Manifest" in this context is an adjective that means "revealed and obvious.") The phrase was coined by journalist John L. O'Sullivan, an influential advocate for Jacksonian democracy, who proclaimed that "Our manifest destiny [is] to overspread and to possess the whole of the continent which Providence has given us for the development of the great experiment of liberty and federated self-government entrusted to us."

In other words, God wants white people to own North America. Indeed this war was another chapter in the juggernaut of European imperialism, white people taking what they wanted from weaker darker people and pretending it was about spreading Christianity or civilization or democracy. European imperialists would eventually even convince themselves this was a philanthropic moral obligation that they called "the white man's burden."

The United States was experiencing a periodic high birth rate and increases in population due to immigration, growing from more than five millon in 1800 to more than 23 million by mid-century. It's estimated that nearly 4,000,000 Americans moved into the various versions of the western territories between 1820 and 1850. Also, there were two economic depressions, one in 1818 and a second in 1839, that drove people to seek new opportunities in frontier areas. Also, merchants saw opportunity in building West Coast ports for trade with China and other countries of the Pacific.

There is another player in the U.S.–Mexican War and that of course is Mexico. It is an adjacent neighbor and source of many of our place names, customs, and citizens, and therefore it is worth some space here. As the gorgeous Marta tells our hero in their first romantic scene together, "I see my home, a village where my blood goes back a thousand thousand years ... I am mestiza. My mother was Azteca and ... my father from Spain. Those two cultures are what Mexico is made of ..." Mexico is 80% mestizo (mixed race) and the indigenous part of Mexico is proudly displayed at the center of their flag in the Aztec symbols of an eagle on a cactus with a serpent in its beak. At the time of the U.S.-Mexico War, Mexico had been an independent nation for barely two decades.

On September 16, 1810, independence from Spain was declared by priest Miguel Hidalgo y Costilla, in the small town of Dolores, Guanajuato. After he was captured and executed in 1811, leadership of the rebel armies was assumed by another priest, José María Morelos, who was captured and executed on 1815. In subsequent years, the insurgency was near collapse, until 1820, when General Agustín de Iturbide was sent against the insurgent troops of Vicente Guerrero, but instead of attacking, Iturbide joined forces with Guerrero. On August 24, 1821, representatives of the Spanish Crown and

Iturbide signed the Treaty of Córdoba and the Declaration of Independence of the Mexican Empire with Iturbide as "emperor."

The first decades of the post-independence period were marked by economic instability and constant strife between liberals, supporters of a federal democratic form of government, and conservatives, proponents of a traditional hierarchical form of government. Military rebellion became the normal means for resolving any political disagreement and social upheaval was always latent. In the war with the United States, it was proposed to arm the peasants, in order to beat the North American army in a guerrilla war. But such proposals were rejected by conservatives for fear that, after eliminating the foreign enemy, the majority lower class masses could threaten the established social order. Therefore, the choice for conservatives was to suffer and sacrifice whatever was necessary, even a huge territorial loss, rather than risk democracy and endanger the hierarchical social order.

In the scene in the movie when Cortina, the Mexican rebel leader, is agreeing to rejoin the Mexican Army, it is mentioned that he fought at the San Jacinto Bridge, the decisive battle of the Texas Revolution. That shows Cortina's value, as veteran officer, to the government army. Cortina, as a patriot and a rebel has divided loyalties of his own paralleling those of the San Patricios. This character is based on Juan Cortina (1824–1894), a Mexican rancher, politician, military leader, outlaw, and folk hero. According to Robert Elman, author of *Badmen of the West*, Cortina was the first "socially motivated border bandit."

Cortina did fight at Matamoros against Zachary Taylor but there is no evidence Cortina fought with the Patricios. After the Mexican-American War, with the self-appointed purpose of defending the rights of Tejanos (Texan Mexicans), Cortina gathered, trained, and armed a private army, and on many occasions used it to resist the eviction of Tejanos from their lands. "The Robin Hood of the Rio Grande" to some and "the Red Robber of the Rio Grande" to others, his followers were known as the "Cortinistas," and during the "Cortina Wars," he led them against the United States Army, the Texas Rangers, and the local militia of Brownsville, Texas. Eventually Texas Rangers attacked Cortina's family villa killing his wife and children.

In the movie, Cortina is also supposed to symbolize the tradition of Mexican rebels, many just regional, fighting against oppression and often trying to recover stolen land. This tradition will culminate with Pancho Villa and Emiliano Zapata, who will become world-famous in the 1910-1920 Mexican Revolution. Incidentally, that snarling shaggy villain Dominguez, who leaves Cortina's band and eventually tries to rape Marta when his, Dominguez's, own men are sacking a village, is supposed to be the criminal element that attaches itself to all revolutions (including that of the U.S.).

The film gives due dramatic weight to the awesome decision to fight against one's own country. The title of our film comes from an old saying that Riley gives voice to in an early scene, "One man's hero is another man's traitor."

Incidentally, after the Mexican government offers them amnesty and land in exchange for fighting the Americans, there is a pithy exchange between two Patricios that captures their dilemma:

"We've heard that tune before ... Join the army and become an American citizen..."

"And get stung by the lash instead."

The first major battle for the Patricios against the U.S., the Battle of Monterrey, is handled accurately. After Zachary Taylor entered Mexico he drove south defeating larger Mexican armies at Palo Alto, Resaca de la Palma, Monterrey, and finally and most dramatically in early 1847, at Buena Vista. That is a pass where after two bloody days Santa Anna's army, three times the size of Taylor's, withdrew. The immediate aftermath of this battle is shown in the film and the rivalry and disdain Taylor felt for fellow American General Winfield Scott is accurate. Taylor, a Whig, became so popular back in the U.S. after his string of victories that Polk, a Democrat, was put under political pressure to replace him. So, Polk handed the baton to General Winfield Scott. He was a hero of the 1812 War and also a Whig who could and did challenge Taylor for his party's nomination in the next presidential election. Scott would also advise Lincoln during the Civil War.

That reasonable attitude Taylor shows in the film toward the Mexicans rankled Polk who wanted someone more aggressive, like Scott. So Scott was put in charge of the final campaign of the war. That began with an eighteen day siege of the fortress port city of Vera Cruz that included a long bombardment that killed many civilians. Scott took the city and drove inland with 12,000 men, winning hard-fought battles at Cerro Gordo, Puebla, Contreras, and Churubusco, where the fate of our heroes, the San Patricios, is decided and to learn that you now must go to the film.

And yes that horrific and macabre ending really did happen that way; indeed, what really happened was even worse.

After

On July 24, 1846, America's two greatest philosophers stared at each other through jail cell bars. Ralph Waldo Emerson asked his close friend Henry David Thoreau, "Henry, what are you doing in jail?" To which Henry replied, "Waldo, what are you doing *out* of jail?" Since they both equally opposed the U.S.-Mexican War, Henry thought Waldo should have refused to pay his taxes in protest, as Henry had, and Waldo should have been sharing the cell with Henry. The next day Thoreau was freed when someone, likely his aunt, paid the tax against his wishes.

Thoreau wrote about the experience and the reasoning behind his act in the classic American essay, *Civil Disobedience,* which was, as already mentioned, an inspiration to Gandhi and Martin Luther King. Thoreau was not the only famous opponent of the war. Former President John Quincy Adams also expressed the opinion of many before the House of Representatives on May 25, 1846, that the war was primarily an effort to expand slavery (which is also mentioned by Zachary Taylor in the film). And then there was a little known Whig Congressman from Illinois, Abraham Lincoln.

Lincoln spoke out against the U.S.-Mexico War, which he attributed to President Polk's desire for "military glory—that attractive rainbow, that rises in showers of blood". Polk insisted that Mexican soldiers had, as Lincoln said, "invaded our territory and shed the blood of our fellow-citizens on our own soil". Lincoln drafted and introduced his "Spot Resolutions" that demanded that Polk show Congress the exact spot on which blood had been shed and prove that the spot was on American soil. Congress never enacted the resolution or even debated it, the national papers ignored it, and it resulted in a loss of political support for Lincoln in his district. The *Illinois State Register* newspaper declared him "a second Benedict Arnold." His anti-war position would dog Lincoln's political career up to and including the presidency.

Another president, Ulysses S. Grant, who as a young army lieutenant had served in Mexico under General Taylor, recalled in his *Memoirs* that: "I was bitterly opposed to [it] and to this day regard the war as one of the most unjust ever waged by a stronger against a weaker nation. It was an instance of a republic following the bad example of European monarchies, in not considering justice in their desire to acquire additional territory." Grant also expressed the view that the war against Mexico had brought punishment on the United States in the form of its Civil War: "The Southern rebellion was largely the outgrowth of the Mexican war. Nations, like individuals, are punished for their transgressions. We got our punishment in the most sanguinary and expensive war of modern times."

Zachary Taylor in the film neatly sums up the attitude of those swept up in morally questionable wars, "It doesn't pay to ponder the right or wrong of it. Yesterday's a coulda-been, tomorrow we're gonna have us a thunderous gonna-be."

The "gonna-be" was the Battle of Monterrey and after the American victory, a Mexican general asks Taylor, "Why do you invade my country?"

"Orders, man. You understand that." He then sums up the national ambivalence toward the war.

Generally, the war was popular in the south and west and unpopular in the north and east. At the time of the U.S.-Mexico War, the U.S. was becoming increasingly divided by sectional rivalry, so the war became a partisan issue. Southern Democrats, animated by a popular belief in Manifest Destiny, supported the U.S.-Mexico War in hopes of adding slave-owning territory to the South and avoiding being outnumbered by the faster-growing North. Northern abolitionists attacked the war as an attempt by slave-owners to strengthen the grip of slavery and thus ensure the Slave Power's continued disproportionate and nefarious influence in the federal government.

Of course, whatever penalties Lincoln and Thoreau may have paid for opposing the war, they were nothing compared to those of Riley and the Patricios after they were captured at the Battle of Churubusco (which means "Place of the War Gods" as we are told in the film). The execution did take place exactly as in the movie except 30 were hung that day, even more than in the film, and 20 the day before. And Riley was actually branded. Incidentally, in the film, one of the Patricios is praying on the scaffold and is told by an acculturated Irish-American officer "Enough of that old language." The Patricio is praying in Gaelic, the first language for most of the Irish of the time, and one that the officer would have been embarrassed by.

The next battle, the Battle of Chapultepec, is memorialized by the opening lines of the Marines' Hymn, "From the Halls of Montezuma to..." What wasn't mentioned in the song or the film was that the Battle of Chapultepec, the one watched by the Patricios from the scaffold and the last major battle of the war, and the one that opened Mexico City to conquest, it was a battle fought in part against students. Six Mexican military cadets refused to fall back when ordered to retreat and instead fought to the death. According to legend, the last of the six grabbed the Mexican flag, wrapped it around himself and to prevent the flag from falling into enemy hands, leapt to his death from the high battlements. There is hardly a city in Mexico without a broad thoroughfare named after "Los Niños Héroes" ("The Children Heroes").

As for our hero, John Riley was not a sergeant at the start of the war, as in the film, but a private. He did form the battalion but lead it as a brevet major, not a captain, as in the film. Not shown for some reason in the movie is the fact that the battalion included some African Americans who had escaped from slavery. Also not mentioned are the atrocities committed by the U.S. soldiers against Mexican civilians. Here is then Lieutenant Ulysses S Grant writing to his then fiancée Julia Dent from Monterrey:

> Some of the volunteers and about all of the Texans seem to think it perfectly right...to murder them [Mexican civilians] where the act can be covered by the dark.... I would not pretend to guess the number of murders that have been committed upon the persons of poor Mexicans and the soldiers, since we have been here, but the number would startle you.

According to their own commander, General Winfield Scott, American soldiers "committed atrocities—horrors—in Mexico.... Murder, robbery, & rape on mothers & daughters, in the presence of the tied up males of the families, have been common all along the Rio Grande."

Remember how after their fistfight over her, Riley tells Cortina that Marta represents Mexico for him? In a scene at the end, with the branded Riley kneeling at her feet, seeking refuge from the gringos, Marta is draped in the

Patricios' flag. The image created would remind every Mexican of the most popular image of the Virgen of Guadelupe, Mexico's patron saint.

Unfortunately, Riley did not ride off into the good life with his gorgeous Mexicana as stated in the closing voice over. Updated research has established that he died in Vera Cruz in 1850 at age forty-five, "as a result of drunkenness, without sacraments," according to church records. However, that pompous ass General Winfield Scott did lose his bid for the presidency and Zachary Taylor, who saw the war for what it was, won the presidency, even if he did die before he could finish his first term.

The total of American deaths, 13,283 (seven eighths of them from disease), represented 17 percent of all American soldiers, the highest rate for any war except the Civil War. There was some talk after the war about annexing all of Mexico but American racism spared the Mexicans losing their independence altogether. As the *Cincinnati Herald* asked, what would the U.S. do with eight million Mexicans "with their idol worship, heathen superstition, and degraded mongrel races?"

The Treaty of Guadalupe Hidalgo ending the war was signed on February 2, 1848. It increased the size of the U.S. by a third, decreased the size of Mexico by half, and ceded over half a million square miles to the U.S. The U.S. paid Mexico $15,000,000 for the territory. The Gadsden Purchase, in 1853, added southern Arizona, which was needed for an anticipated railroad route.

What made the loss even more galling for the Mexicans was the fact that, a week before the Treaty of Guadalupe Hidalgo was signed, gold was discovered by James Marshall at Sutter's Mill on one of the great ranches that dotted California's Sacramento Valley. This kicked off the California Gold Rush, considered by most historians the second most important event, after the Civil War, in nineteenth century America. Actually, a good movie about the California Gold Rush would have been equally appropriate here, but there are none.

On August 19, 1848, the New York Herald was the first major newspaper on the East Coast to report the discovery of gold. On December 5, 1848, President James Polk confirmed the discovery in an address to Congress. An overwhelming number of gold-seekers and merchants began to arrive from virtually every continent. The earliest were called "forty-niners" (referring to 1849 when most arrived). The first from Europe, reeling from the effects of the Revolutions of 1848 and with a longer distance to travel, began arriving later in 1849, mostly from France, with some Germans, Italians, and Britons. Forty-niners also came from Latin America, particularly from the Mexican mining districts near Sonora, and from Asia, primarily from China, where California was given the name Gum San ("Gold Mountain").

There was no easy way to get to California; forty-niners faced hardship and often death en route. From the East Coast, a sailing voyage around the tip of South America would take five to eight months, and cover some 18,000 nautical miles. Alternatives included: sail to Panama, cross it through jungle, and wait on the Pacific side for a ship sailing for San Francisco; or cross Mexico starting at Veracruz; or go overland across the continental United States. Each of these routes had its own deadly hazards.

In San Francisco, ships' captains found that their crews deserted to go to the gold fields so that the bay became a forest of masts from hundreds of abandoned ships. Enterprising San Franciscans turned the abandoned ships into warehouses, stores, taverns, hotels, and one into a jail.

Providing goods for the California Gold Rush stimulated economies around the world. The return of large amounts of California gold to pay for these goods raised prices, stimulated investment, and created jobs. Gold worth tens of billions of today's dollars was recovered, which led to great wealth for a few. Recent scholarship confirms that merchants made more money than most miners. For example, there was Levi Strauss. In 1853 he began selling to miners in San Francisco sturdy denim overalls that would eventually become the most stylish pants for generations the world over, and his company would eventually become the largest clothing manufacturer in the world.

Other businessmen, through good fortune and hard work, reaped great rewards in retail, shipping, entertainment, lodging, or transportation. Boarding-houses, food preparation, sewing, and laundry were highly profitable businesses often run by women (married, single, or widowed) who realized men would pay well for a service done by a woman. Brothels also brought in large profits, especially when combined with saloons and gaming houses. Few women arrived during the early years, only 700 in 1849. In 1850, women made up only 8 percent of California's population. In mining areas, they made up less than 2 percent. They held various roles including prostitutes, single entrepreneurs, and wives (poor and wealthy). The reasons they came varied: some came with their husbands, refusing to be left behind to fend for themselves; some came because their husbands sent for them; and others came (singles and widows) for the adventure and economic opportunities.

At first, the gold nuggets could be picked up off the ground, in some cases, thousands of dollars worth each day. Even ordinary prospectors averaged daily gold finds worth 10 to 15 times the daily wage of a laborer on the East Coast. A person could work for six months in the gold fields and find the equivalent of six years' wages back home. The value of real estate exploded and is a good indicator of the rate of inflation generally. A lot in San Francisco purchased in 1847 for $16.50 sold for $6,000 in the spring of 1848 and was later resold for $48,000.

It is estimated that over 300,000 miners found a total of more than $200 million in gold in the five years of the California Gold Rush. On average, about half the gold-seekers made a modest profit after expenses. However, most, especially those arriving later, made little or even lost money. Miners lived in tents, wood shanties, or deck cabins removed from abandoned ships. With names like Rough and Ready and Hangtown, each mining camp usually had its own saloon and gambling house and brothel. In San Francisco alone, there were more than 500 bars and 1,000 gambling dens. In the span of 18 months, the city burned to the ground six times.

There were a thousand murders in San Francisco during the early 1850s, but only one conviction. These highly male, transient communities with no established institutions were prone to high levels of violence, drunkenness, and greed-driven behavior. Each camp had its own rules and often handed out justice by popular vote, sometimes acting fairly and sometimes giving Indians, Mexicans, and Chinese the harshest sentences.

Faced with gold increasingly difficult to retrieve, Americans began to drive out foreigners to get at the gold that remained. The new California State Legislature passed a foreign miners tax of twenty dollars per month and American prospectors began organized attacks on foreign miners, particularly Latin Americans and Chinese. Several hundred Chinese arrived in San Francisco in 1849 and 1850 and by 1852 more than 20,000 had landed. Their distinctive dress and appearance was highly recognizable in the gold fields and created animosity.

In Chapter Nine, we will focus on the specifics of the effect of the Gold Rush on California Native Americans. Gold mining damaged California's rivers, lakes, and even some mountains, which were washed away by hydraulic mining. In 1846, about 10,000 Californios lived in California, primarily on cattle ranches in what is now the Los Angeles area. A few hundred foreigners were scattered in the northern districts, including some Americans. It is estimated that approximately 90,000 people arrived in California in 1849, about half by land and half by sea. Of these, perhaps 50,000 to 60,000 were Americans, and the rest were from other countries. Between 1847 and 1870, the population of San Francisco exploded from 500 to 150,000.

In the midst of the Gold Rush, towns and cities were chartered, a state constitutional convention was convened, a state constitution written, elections held, and representatives sent to Washington, D.C. to negotiate the admission of California as a state. California experienced such rapid growth in a few short months that it was admitted as the 31st state in the Compromise of 1850 without the normal intermediate phase of being a territory.

Soon gold was discovered in Colorado, Utah, Arizona, New Mexico, Idaho, Montana, and South Dakota. The discovery of the Comstock Lode, containing vast amounts of silver, resulted in the Nevada boomtowns of Virginia City, Carson City, and Silver City. The wealth from silver, more than from gold, fueled the maturation of San Francisco in the 1860s and helped the rise of some of its wealthiest families, such as that of George Hearst.

In 1869 with the completion of the First Transcontinental Railroad, travel that had taken months could now be accomplished in days, so hundreds of thousands of U.S. citizens came west. Californians were discovering that land in the state, if irrigated during the dry summer months, was extremely well suited to fruit cultivation and agriculture in general. Vast expanses of wheat, other cereal crops, vegetable crops, cotton, and nut and fruit trees were grown (including oranges in Southern California). The foundation was laid for the state's prodigious agricultural production in the Central Valley and elsewhere. Agriculture was California's second gold rush.

Overnight California gained the international reputation as the "golden state" and quick success in a new world became known as the "California Dream." California was perceived as a place of new beginnings, where great wealth could reward hard work and good luck. It was America's America. Historian H. W. Brands noted:

> The old American Dream . . . was the dream of the Puritans, of Benjamin Franklin's 'Poor Richard' . . . of men and women content to accumulate their modest fortunes a little at a time, year by year by year. The new dream was the dream of instant wealth, won in a twinkling by audacity and good luck. [This] golden dream . . . became a prominent part of the American psyche only after Sutter's Mill."

The 1850s Gold Rush is still seen as a symbol of California's economic style, which tends to generate technology, entertainment, and social trends in booms and busts. Miners, farmers, oil drillers, movie makers, airplane builders, and dot-com entrepreneurs have each had their boom times.

Attracted to the mild Mediterranean climate and wide variety of geography, filmmakers established the studio system in Hollywood in the 1920s. Today entertainment is the U.S.'s second most profitable export, and with the Hollywood movie, the U.S. has, in the words of German filmmaker Wim Wenders, "colonized the subconscious" of the world.

A couple of decades after the founding of Hollywood, Stanford University and its Dean of Engineering, Frederick Terman, began encouraging faculty and graduates to stay in California and develop a high-tech region in the area now known as Silicon Valley. As a result, California is a world center of technology, engineering, and the aerospace industry. Just before the "Dot Com Bust" of 2000, California had the 5th largest economy in the world among nations. It is home to an eighth of the population of the US.

The period of our film was also a period of intellectual ferment in America. Transcendentalism was a philosophical and literary movement that developed around Concord, Massachusetts, and flourished from about 1836 to 1860. Transcendentalists advocated a faith centering on the divinity of humanity and the natural world and they signaled the emergence of a new national culture based on native materials and not an imitation of Europe. The Transcendentalists were a major part of the American Renaissance in literature, roughly from 1850 to 1855, during which many American literary classics were produced, including Ralph Waldo Emerson's *Representative Men* (1850), Nathaniel Hawthorne's *The Scarlet Letter* (1850), Herman Melville's *Moby-Dick*

(1851), Henry David Thoreau's *Walden* (1854), and Walt Whitman's *Leaves of Grass* (1855).

Most people know that the two art forms in which the U.S. was dominant in the world in the Twentieth Century were movies and pop music. But far fewer know about the other art form in which the U.S. was dominant in the Twentieth Century: poetry. That dominance started with Walt Whitman. He personified that new actor on the stage of history: the American. From his free-verse form, to the use of himself as his primary subject matter, to an erotic-mystical religiosity and an unshakable faith in democracy, he was unique and unprecedented. He was also not-quite-openly gay.

Transcendentalism was such a deep expression of the American character that it returned to the stage of history in the 1960s reincarnated in the Counter Culture. Transcendentalism and the Counter Culture shared mystical aspects influenced by Indian and Chinese religions, both experimented with communal living, and the Transcendentalists were abolitionists while members of the Counter Culture fought for civil rights. After the Summer of Love of 1967 in San Francisco, the Counter Culture spread around the world becoming the biggest cultural transformation of the second half of the twentieth century.

The promise of free land in the "New Territories" caused mass migration across the continent throughout the 19th Century by new immigrants and native-born Americans alike, which we will focus-on in Chapter 9. But the "New Territories" also caused the Civil War, the apocalypse of the nineteenth century. It is considered the first modern war and the prelude to the global catastrophes of the world wars. We will use two movies for it: Chapter 7 will be *Gettysburg* and Chapter 8, *Lincoln*.

Mexican War Era Timeline

1835 Texas Revolution began
1836 Battle of the Alamo
    -Texan victory in Battle of San Jacinto ends Texas Revolution
    -Samuel Colt invented the revolver.
    -The original "Gag Rule" was imposed in Congress, a bar on
    even a discussion of antislavery petitions.
    -Martin Van Buren was elected President.
    -Panic of 1837: financial crisis built on a speculative fever
    followed by a five-year depression, with the failure of banks
    and record-high unemployment levels.
1838 The "Trail of Tears," forced removal of the Cherokees from
    the Southeast, led to thousands Native American deaths.
1839 United States v. The Amistad was decided.
1844 James K. Polk elected President of the United States.
1846 Mexican–American War began.
1848 Mexican–American War ends with the Treaty of Guadalupe
    Hidalgo

-Zachary Taylor elected President.
-California Gold Rush began.
1850 California became the 31st state.
1858 The first transatlantic telegraph cable was laid.

Recommendations

There are no other movies that come close to the U.S.–Mexican War (which tells you something right there about public opinion of it), but there have been numerous films about the Alamo, the most famous battle of the Texas war of independence. The most recent is 2004's *The Alamo* starring Randy Quaid, Billy Bob Thornton, and Jason Patric as Sam Houston, Davey Crockett, and Jim Bowie respectively. More than just the battle of the Alamo, it covers the high points of the Texas Revolution including the climactic Battle of San Jacinto.

Billy Bob Thornton steals the movie with his Davy Crockett, a case study in the snares of celebrity, which existed even then. It is (relatively) fair to the Mexicans. Plus it has gorgeous cinematography, rousing patriotic oratory, and of course, choreographed slaughter. This recent version was vastly better than the consensus of its reviews, as Roger Ebert pointed out. But since it tried to be all things to everybody, it wasn't enough for anybody, and consequently, was one of the all time box office bombs.

It is much more accurate than John Wayne's 1960 version though. That was a standard Wayne product, in this case directed by him, with him starring as Davy Crockett. The battle sequences are impressive with uniformed extras seemingly in the numbers of the actual armies. At the very end, the loyal black slave of Jim Bowie (who was a slave trader) sacrifices his life to protect his master. Of course, neither version of the Alamo mentions that one of the sacred rights Texans were fighting for was the right to own slaves, which was illegal under Mexican rule.

There are no movies about the California Gold Rush, except one from the Thirties with Edward G. Robinson called *Barbary Coast*, about Gold Rush San Francisco. But there are a couple of excellent films about Old West mining towns. There is an independently produced gem and a minor classic, from 1991, *Thousand Pieces of Gold*. Based on a true story, and starring future Oscar-winner Chris Cooper, it features life in a 19th century Idaho mining town, plus Chinese female sex slavery, a credible romance, and even a plausible happy ending. *The Hanging Tree* (1959), in color, with Gary Cooper, is a very good movie loaded with period detail and set in a gold mining town in Montana late in the 19th century.

Into the West (2005) was a 12 hour TV miniseries produced by Steven Spielberg. It followed two families, one Indian, one white, from 1825 to 1891 and touched on the first mountain men, the Gold Rush, the wagon trains, the Transcontinental Railroad, and the Wounded Knee Massacre, which ended the

Plains Indian Wars. So, *Into the West* should be just right for us, but most of the characters are one-dimensional, and though there are excellent sections of some episodes, most of the miniseries is a plodding meandering soap opera. It got 16 Emmy nominations, virtually all of them technical and not one for direction, writing, or acting. That pretty much says it all.

There is a minor American classic about Emiliano Zapata, the great Mexican peasant general of the 1910-20 Mexican Revolution. *Viva Zapata!* (1952) was based on an original script, which was in turn based on original research, by Nobel Prize winner John Steinbeck, and it was directed by multi-Oscar winner Elia Kazan. Both were at the height of their powers, as was the star, Marlon Brando, and co-star Anthony Quinn, who won his first Oscar for playing Zapata's brother. The film won the Grand Prize at the Cannes Film Festival that year.

More recently, HBO produced *And Starring Pancho Villa as Himself* (2003), starring Antonio Banderas as the other great general of that revolution, former peasant and outlaw, Pancho Villa. At the time of production, this was the most expensive 2-hour television/cable movie ever made, with a budget of over $30 million. It tells the true story of the filming of *The Life of General Villa* (which was shot in 1914), the very first feature length movie, in which Pancho Villa played himself. Banderas is a credible Villa and the film is a good representation of the Revolution.

Most of the other Hollywood films on the Mexican Revolution are quite bad. *The Old Gringo* (1989) stars Gregory Peck, Jane Fonda, and Jimmy Smits and is based on a novel of the same name by the famed Carlos Fuentes, but it was a disaster, at the box office and esthetically. We don't get to see much of the revolution because all the action is on one hacienda and the tacked-on bodice-ripper is forced and trite in the context. *Villa Rides* (1968) has Yul Brynner portraying Pancho Villa as if he were a haughty Eastern European aristocrat.

But there is *The Professionals* (1966), which is in a class by itself. It meets all the box office action requirements; that is, the Americans bag a high body-count of dispensable ethnics. But in addition, *The Professionals* has much rumination on Life and Revolution. Star and producer Burt Lancaster's character says "Maybe there's only one revolution... since the beginning. The good guys against the bad guys. Question is... who are the good guys?" The four Americans, revolutionaries-turned-mercenaries, then go on a killing rampage, working their way across northern Mexico in order to commit a kidnapping. And they would have remained the bad guys except for an implausible ending. The film was made by auteur Richard Brooks who, like his mentor John Huston, specialized in literary adaptations. *The Professionals* is based on a novel and Brooks' script and direction were nominated for an Oscar. (He won one for his script of *Elmer Gantry* [1960].) Like most of Brooks' films, *The Professionals* has spectacular art direction; that is, this one is redolent of the look-and-feel of the

Mexican Revolution. Here's how authentic this Hollywood film is: the Mexicans speak Spanish to each other.

The Mexican Revolution was a favorite setting for some of those campy, stylized, revenge epics of the Sixties and Seventies, "Spaghetti Westerns." Some were made by Italian communists who were attracted to the stark poor-vs-rich morality of the Mexican Revolution. There was even a subgenre known as the "Zapata Western," an excellent but under appreciated example of which is also the only one of the subgenre directed by the legendary Sergio Leone, *Duck You Sucker!* (1970). It is technically very well made and it too has much rumination on Revolution. It features something not usually seen in foreign films about the Mexican Revolution, urban intellectual revolutionaries.

Two of the most famous of those are the focus of the extraordinary *Frida* (2002). It is about the life and loves of artists Frida Kahlo and her husband Diego Rivera, and it is visually stunning and dramatically powerful. It provides insight into the intellectual and artistic ferment following the Mexican Revolution. It was directed with characteristic flair by Julie Taymor in one of the best fusings ever of visual art with narrative cinema.

The definitive documentary on our subject is PBS's *The U.S.-Mexican War 1846 -1848* (2009). For the Gold Rush and the early years of the American West, there is Ken Burns' masterful *The West*, which we will return to in more detail in a later chapter. Plus PBS' The American Experience series has the doc *The Gold Rush* (2006). The History Channel's *Gold Fever* (2013) pushes the limits of the docudrama form. Following the fortunes of an assortment of historical characters, the film covers the Gold Rush as a documentary, with talking heads, narrator, etc., but the reenactments are so detailed and cohesive as to almost form a self-contained narrative movie within the doc. It's all quite good despite too many stagey action-formula touches.

Out of Ireland: the Story of Irish Immigration to America (1995) is a documentary that details the history of Irish immigration to America using archival and contemporary footage, readings from correspondence, and expert analysis of the potato famine, Irish folk traditions, Catholicism, and political oppression.

Of course, Irish immigration to the States continues today and there is a minor classic about that. *In America* (2002) has a semi-autobiographical screenplay by the director, six time Oscar nominee Jim Sheridan, and two of his daughters. The film follows the struggles of a poor immigrant Irish family in 1982 New York City. The film was nominated for three Academy Awards including Best Original Screenplay, Best Actress for Samantha Morton, and Best Supporting Actor for Djimon Hounsou, the star of *Amistad*, as a neighbor and an African immigrant dying of the then-new disease AIDS.

At www.escalloniapress.com, there are free recommendations of the best books - histories, biographies, memoirs, and even novels - related to the subjects of this chapter.

Ch. 7 – Gettysburg

Before

Movie critic Gene Siskel dubbed this 1993 movie, "bloated Southern propaganda." The Confederate parts are unquestionably that, but we are going to use that flaw as a teaching opportunity. Plus the film is more than just propaganda: through meticulous attention to historical detail, it is unequalled for giving a sense of the Civil War battlefield; it was filmed on the actual Gettysburg battlefield using five thousand enthusiastically authentic reenactors; the battle depicted was the pivotal battle of the war, the bloodiest battle of the war, and the biggest battle ever on American soil. In this chapter, we'll deal mainly with the military aspects of the Civil War, and in the next chapter, with the politics.

In the middle of the film, on day two of the three-day battle, is one of the most stirring scenes of all the films in this book or in film history. The scene has one of those true melodramatic devices that good fiction would not dare invent: the fate of this battle, of the Union, and, what was ultimately at stake in the war, of democracy itself, fell squarely on the shoulders of a young abolitionist professor from Maine. Sometimes in history, the participants know exactly what is at stake historically in their actions, and he knew exactly what was at stake. He was a colonel but a military amateur, who at times in this battle faced an enemy ten times his size, and who, when his men ran out of ammunition, came up with a brilliant surprise maneuver.

He was Joshua Lawrence Chamberlain (1828–1914) and it was the Battle for Little Round Top. Because of this movie, tourists at the Gettysburg Battlefield now rank the monument to Chamberlain's 20th Maine Regiment as their most important stop. His story is in the middle of Confederate propaganda because this film is based on the novel, *The Killer Angels* (1974), winner of a richly deserved Pulitzer Prize. The book was backed up with seven years of meticulous research. "I have not consciously changed any fact," author Michael Schaara claimed.

Most of the film's dialogue is dialogue and narration from the novel. Rarely has a novel been so thoroughly filmed, but unfortunately, writer-director Ronald Maxwell eschews the even-handed perspective of the book. Kurosawa once said you could give a first rate script to a third rate director and still have a good movie, but you could not give a first rate director a third rate script and have a good movie. Here we have a third rate director with a second rate script with some first rate sections.

Maxwell is a member of the Cult of the Confederacy, or more traditionally, the Lost Cause Cult; indeed, this film is a cinematic monument to the Cult. The Cult has had members as illustrious as Nobel laureate William Faulkner and former Democratic Senator and Navy Secretary (also a novelist) Jim Webb, who was briefly considered as a running mate for Obama in 2008. Then it came out Webb was a vocal defender of the Confederacy.

In order to be romanticized, all that Confederate honor and valor cannot have been spent on an evil cause, so right after the end of the war, the earliest Cultists concocted "states' rights" as the cause of choice to replace discredited slavery. But according to James M. McPherson, Pulitzer Prize winner and dean of Civil War historians, writing in the April 12, 2001 issue of *The New York Review of Books*, "Since the 1950s most professional historians have come to agree with Lincoln's assertion that slavery 'was, somehow, the cause of the war.' Outside the universities, however, Lost Cause denial is still popular, especially among Southern heritage groups that insist the Confederate flag stands not for slavery but for a legacy of courage and honor in defense of principle."

In that article, McPherson also reviewed a book by Charles Dew, passionate Cultist and historian. McPherson calls Dew's *Apostles of Disunion* "an eye-opening study of the men appointed by seceding states as commissioners to visit other slave states... in order to persuade them also to leave the Union and join together to form the Confederacy... Dew was 'stunned' to discover that protection of slavery from the perceived threat to its long-term survival posed by Lincoln's election in 1860 was, in fact, the dominant theme in secessionist rhetoric."

In other words, this is what the Confederate leadership was telling itself was the cause of the war. Dew wrote, "Defenders of the Lost Cause need only read the speeches and letters of the secession commissioners to learn what was really driving the Deep South to the brink of war in 1860–61."

Mississippi's Declaration of Secession says, "Our position is thoroughly identified with the institution of slavery--the greatest material interest of the world." South Carolina's "Declaration of the Immediate Causes Which Induce and Justify the Secession of South Carolina from the Federal Union," the very first secession document, actually opposes states' rights. The Slave Power, as the Confederacy was called before the war, conspired to get a Supreme Court decision nullifying the rights of Northern States to ban slavery, thus allowing slave owners not only to take their slaves into the New Territories (the land taken from Mexico) but anywhere in the Union.

So, the Cult of the Confederacy, like creationists and climate change deniers, stands against the unanimity of the experts. Yet the Cult has penetrated even to the US Immigration and Naturalization Citizenship Test which accepts "slavery or states' rights" as the correct answer to the question: "The Civil War was fought over what important issue?" The Cult has had remarkable success in Hollywood as well, making the sufferings of white Southern civilians the dominant theme by far of American movies about the Civil War. More on that in the Recommendations section.

Actually, the number of slaves, 4 million, divided by the number of Civil War dead, 750,000, means approximately 5.3 slaves were freed for each soldier killed. The old estimate for Civil War dead was 620,000 but that has been revised upward after a recent study of census data by J. David Hacker, a demographic historian. The revised number of military casualties exceeds those of all our other U.S. wars put together. This new figure is about 2.4 percent of the American population, white and black, of 31.5 million in 1861. The same percentage would translate into almost 7.5 million dead in the United States of today. Historian John Huddleston estimates that 30% of all Southern white males aged 18–40 died and 10% of all Northern males 20–45 years old.

But if the Confederates were defending slavery and not states' rights, and the vast majority of Southern soldiers did not own slaves, why did they allow themselves to be slaughtered on such a scale? Honor or, perhaps even more, dread of dishonor, was a major factor in keeping soldiers at the front on both sides. Frequently, they fought in hometown units made up of relatives and lifelong friends.

There are two scenes in *Gettysburg* that touch on Confederate motives for the war. The first gives voice to the common Confederate soldier's reasons for fighting. In *The Killer Angels*, it is an almost comic scene involving Chamberlain's younger brother Tom, who is told by a Confederate prisoner that he, the prisoner, is fighting for his "rats" (rights). Tellingly, the film leaves out the follow up question in the book. "I asked this fella," Tom tells his brother in the book, "what rights he had that we were offendin', and he said, well, he didn't know, but he must have some rights he didn't know nothin' about." The filmmakers replace that exchange with a more coherent plaint from the Confederate, "Why is it you folks cain't live the way you wanna live and let us live the way we do. Live and let live I hear say." Of course, he doesn't mention letting slaves live the way they want.

The second scene touching on Confederate motives comes almost an hour and a half into the movie, at the end of the first day. It follows the scene in the book where a frustrated Southern politician goes on a tirade about the government in Washington being a tyrannical foreign government. The tirade is meant to convince a British military observer that Britain should ally with the Confederacy. When the Brit points out slavery prevents that, the filmmakers invented an ending that has the politician saying: "Always the darkies. Nuthin' but the darkies." Slavery, what a nuisance!

Confederate soldiers fought to protect family, community, region, and, most importantly, race, from invasion by the forces of what they saw as evil and ruin. The fear of racial "mongrelization" and more specifically of black sexuality are evident in the frequent Confederate portrayals of Lincoln and the "black republicans" as having a secret agenda of forced marriages between southern white women and black men (an inversion of the power relationship that already existed between white men and black women). This is an example of a political style of hysterical hyperbole that continues to this day.

Such is the pathology of racism that the Southerners convinced themselves they were racially superior to even the white Northerners. A pet theory of some Confederates was that the whites of the South were descendants of the (French) Normans who conquered and ruled England for centuries, and the whites of the North were descendants of the Anglo-Saxons, who were serfs, or modified slaves, of the Normans.

At the center of the Confederate part of this film is Martin Sheen's somnolent portrayal of Robert E. Lee (1807 – 1870). Lee was the son of Revolutionary War officer Henry "Light Horse Harry" Lee III, a friend and favorite of George Washington. A top graduate of the United States Military Academy, Robert E. distinguished himself as an exceptional officer and combat engineer in the United States Army for 32 years including service in the Mexican-American War. He married Martha Washington's great granddaughter. When Virginia declared its secession from the Union in April 1861, Lee chose to follow his home state, despite his personal desire for the country to remain intact and despite the fact that Lincoln offered him command of a Union Army. Lee then shocked the world with a string of battlefield victories against five consecutive Union commanders who had much larger armies.

Lee of course is a saint to the Cult. As late as 1989, the Encyclopedia Americana declared that he was "one of the greatest, if not the greatest, soldier who ever spoke the English language." The journalist-historian Douglas Southall Freeman, whose four-volume biography of Lee won the Pulitzer Prize in 1935, declared: "His character offers historians no moral flaws to probe."

Some recent historians take a different view. They point out that instead of conserving manpower and making selective counterattacks against targets of opportunity, wearing down the will of the enemy as George Washington did, Lee had a romantic obsession with winning the war in a single, climactic battle. Therefore, he repeatedly attacked and invaded, sacrificing his limited manpower until forced to surrender. Lee could have lost most of his battles but won the war, like Washington, instead he won most of his battles and lost the war. Of all army commanders on both sides in the Civil War, Lee's troops suffered the highest percentage of casualties.

Tom Berenger is back after *One Man's Hero*, this time as General James Longstreet (1821 – 1904). Despite a beard distractingly phony in some scenes, Berenger does a more convincing job than Sheen. Longstreet was one of the foremost Confederate generals of the war and the principal subordinate to Lee, who called him his "Old War Horse." He served under Lee as a corps commander for many of the famous battles.

The best acting among the Confederate officers comes from Stephen Lang who plays George Pickett (1825 –1875). Pickett was a career Army officer who became a general in the Confederate Army and who admits in the film that he graduated last in his class at West Point. Saying more than he intends, he then quips, "The Yankees got all the brains."

If the filmmakers have caressed the Confederacy, they have nevertheless still been fair to the Union. Crusty old last-of-the-breed Western actor Sam Elliott is superb as Major General John Buford (1826–1863). As was the case with many of his West Point classmates on both sides, Buford had to choose between North and South, and he had ample reason to join the Confederacy. He was a native Kentuckian, son of slave-owners, and the husband of a woman whose relatives would fight for the South, as would some of his own. Plus the Governor of Kentucky promised him "anything he wanted." But he stayed with the Union Army.

We meet him in the movie on July 1st, 1863, the first day of the battle, when he first sees rebel infantry approaching the town of Gettysburg. Buford immediately understands its strategic significance and what Lee is planning. Going back to ancient times, fighting from the high ground was an enormous advantage for an army, and on the first day at Gettysburg, Buford just wants to hold the high ground until reinforcements arrive.

On the second day, Joshua Lawrence Chamberlain must hold the highest ground, Little Round Top, without reinforcements. Trusty old Jeff Daniels is back after his deft rendition of George Washington in *The Crossing*. He does every bit as well with Chamberlain. As with Washington, Daniels has a vague resemblance to Chamberlain and the mustache is an exact copy. Something not in Daniel's portrayal, nor in the novel, is the speech impediment from which Chamberlain suffered his whole life.

He entered Bowdoin College in Brunswick, Maine, in 1848, after teaching himself to read Ancient Greek in order to pass the entrance exam. He eventually went on to teach every subject in the curriculum except science and mathematics. He was fluent in nine languages besides English, and in 1861, he was appointed Professor of Modern Languages at Bowdoin. He married Fanny Adams, adopted daughter of a local clergyman, in 1855, and they had five children, three of whom died in infancy.

If the filmmakers have allowed an abolitionist speech from Chamberlain, they won't let the word "abolitionist" anywhere near him in the script, but the word describes him perfectly. He was a friend of Harriet Beecher Stowe, wife of a fellow Bowdoin professor and author of the abolitionist novel *Uncle Tom's Cabin* (1852), an international sensation. Lincoln said when meeting Stowe, "So this is the little lady who started the big war."

In the movie, Chamberlain's younger brother Tom seconds his brother's abolitionist motive in that conversation with the Confederate prisoner where Tom mentions freeing the slaves and saving the Union. Most Union soldiers however were not fighting to free the slaves but only to preserve the union. The Union was seen as a transcendent bond among all of the American people, not a voluntary association of states that could be disbanded by any one or several of them. The people of the United States as a whole, rather than the people of each individual state, were sovereign under the Constitution, which was adopted to form "a more perfect union" by "We the People." This was the constitutional theory on which Lincoln denied the right of secession, and on which the North fought the war.

When the war began, U.S. Grant wrote to a friend that from henceforth there were only two kinds of Americans: patriots and traitors. Union soldiers saw themselves as facing an army of traitors out to destroy the country. When Sherman's Union Army marched into South Carolina, after devastating Georgia, the soldiers proclaimed, "This is where treason began and this is where it will end." Even Chamberlain wrote to Maine's Governor, "I fear, this war, so costly of blood and treasure, will not cease until men of the North ... defend the national existence against treachery."

The treachery began after Lincoln's election, when on December 20, 1860, South Carolina seceded from the Union, hence its being the birthplace of treason. Mississippi, Florida, Alabama, Georgia, Louisiana, and Texas followed it in the coming months. Lincoln made it clear he would not threaten slavery where it already existed but he would not accept secession, and when on April 12, 1861, Confederate shore batteries fired on the federally-held Ft. Sumter in Charleston harbor, South Carolina, Lincoln declared it a national insurrection and the war had begun.

The Civil War is the central event in American history. It was the largest military conflict in the Western world between the Napoleonic Wars of the early 1800s and World War I. Three and a half million men fought in the Civil War. Extensive use of railroads, the telegraph, steamships, and mass-produced weapons made it the earliest truly industrial war. The mobilization of civilian factories, mines, shipyards, banks, transportation, and food supplies all foreshadowed World War I. While the North had advantages in technology, finance, and transportation plus a much larger population, it had to invade, conquer, and hold Southern territory. The South, on the other hand, had to keep the invaders at bay and inflict enough punishment so that the North would grow

weary and negotiate a peace treaty recognizing the Confederacy's independence.

The first major land battle was the Battle of Bull Run on July 21, 1861,
during which the Union army was completely routed and fled back to nearby
Washington, D.C. Lincoln then put General George McClellan in command of
the Army of the Potomac, as the Union Army in the east was called. McClellan
attacked Virginia in the spring of 1862 in the "Peninsula Campaign" and was
soundly defeated by Robert E. Lee and retreated. In late August 1862, Lee
defeated General John Pope at the Second Battle of Bull Run ceding the
Confederacy almost total control of Virginia.

Remember that the success of the American Revolution required an
alliance with a superpower, in that case France. The Confederacy, too, hoped
for a saving foreign alliance, specifically with England and France, whose textile
industries were so dependent on Southern cotton. The Union's naval blockade
crippled a Southern economy completely dependent on cotton exports.

In September 1862, Lee, **emboldened by recent victories**, launched a
daring offensive into Maryland, hoping a major victory on northern soil would
secure that foreign alliance. Lee then met McClellan at the Battle of Antietam in
what would be the single bloodiest day in American history. Lee suffered 11,000
killed or wounded and McClellan, 13,000, but Lee was forced to retreat, allowing
the North to declare victory. That in turn provided Lincoln with the political cover
to issue a preliminary Emancipation Proclamation, freeing slaves in the
rebellious states.

Lincoln's biggest problem for most of the war was reluctant and/or
incompetent generals. He taught himself military strategy and he knew that, to
overcome the South's strategically defensive position, the North had to take
advantage of its superior numbers by launching numerous simultaneous attacks
that would prevent the enemy from consolidating its forces. But Lincoln was
frustrated by generals who, though often trained in those elementary precepts at
West Point, nonetheless failed to act on them. Frustrated by McClellan's timidity,
Lincoln replaced him with Ambrose E. Burnside (1824-1881). In December
1862, at the Battle of Fredericksburg, in Virginia, Burnside suffered nearly
13,000 casualties, twice the number suffered by Lee's men, severely damaging
Northern morale. Lincoln then replaced Burnside with Joseph Hooker (1814-
1879) who, at the Battle of Chancellorsville, in Virginia, in May 1863, was also
routed. But in that battle, a Confederate sentry accidentally killed the
Confederate General Stonewall Jackson, Lee's "right hand." Lee bemoans the
loss in the movie.

Then in June, 1863, Lee invaded Pennsylvania. His goal was again a
decisive victory on Northern soil that would deal the deathblow to Northern
morale while gaining European recognition of the Confederacy. When Lee's
forces drove northward into Pennsylvania, he assumed, mistakenly, that the
Union forces were still in Virginia. When he learned that instead they were in

close pursuit, he ordered his forces, strung out from Maryland to Harrisburg, Pennsylvania, to converge at Gettysburg, Pennsylvania, a hub for several important roads.

Before they fought Lee's army at Gettysburg, Joshua Lawrence Chamberlain's 20th Maine fought it in the Battle of Fredericksburg. They suffered relatively few casualties but were forced to spend a night on the freezing battlefield among the wounded from other regiments. Chamberlain had to use bodies of the fallen for shelter and through the night listened to bullets striking the corpses. The 20th Maine missed the Battle of Chancellorsville, the other major battle just before Gettysburg, due to an outbreak of smallpox in their ranks.

At four hours and fourteen minutes, this movie is one of the longest ever released by a Hollywood studio. There are vast stretches of dramatic swamp here, so we will only use the first two and a half hours, ending with Chamberlain's performance on Little Round Top. I will describe in the After section what you missed if you don't finish the film.

Remember as you are being force-fed the camaraderie of the adorable Confederate officer corps that they were defending one of the great evils of all time. "The greatest wrong inflicted on any people," as Lincoln described it. The ante-bellum ("before the war") Old South was a tradition-bound criminal conspiracy to steal the labor of its victims, a particularly pure form of kleptocracy.

Jim Webb has complained of the "nazification" of the Confederacy, referring to the historians who have noted the unavoidable parallels between the two regimes. The fascist political parties that swept through most western and some Asian countries in the 1920s and 1930s had an American counterpart, the Ku Klux Klan. It had arisen to terrorize and murder blacks in the South after the Civil War and had practically disappeared when it got a second life through the overwhelming popularity of the first Hollywood epic, *Birth of a Nation* (1915). Directed by D.W.Griffith, Kentucky-born son of a Confederate colonel, the film featured the heroic KKK saving white women from animalistic black rapists (white actors in black face). Through that movie, the KKK rose to the prominence of a minor political party in the 1920s with membership in the millions and electing governors and senators.

The most prominent and successful of those fascist political parties that swept over Europe was the Nazi Party. Just as the leaders of the Old South did eighty years before, the Nazis romanticized war and led their society to destruction. Just like the German Army during World War II, which was never defeated on the ground by another army the same size or smaller, the Confederate Army fought better and their generals were more brilliant. Just like the Allies in World War II, the Union Army won because it was bigger and it had greater industrial resources.

Explaining why during World War II he wrote a novel about post-Civil War Reconstruction, our old friend Howard Fast wrote, "In the oppression of the American Negro I saw blueprinted and limned in fierce bright light the essence of the horror we fought in Europe." In the 1950s and 1960s, the membership of the KKK and the American Nazi Party certainly saw the similarities between their groups, because frequently the same people were in both, even in the leadership.

An inability to face the truth about their war is something the South shares with another World War II enemy. Some Japanese live in a similar coma of denial about their country's role in that war. A couple times a decade, whenever new Japanese textbooks came out, there used to be riots in China and Korea and other parts of Asia over self-serving distortions.

After

"The President of the United States of America, in the name of Congress, takes pleasure in presenting the Medal of Honor to Colonel Joshua Lawrence Chamberlain, United States Army, for extraordinary heroism on 2 July 1863, while serving with 20th Maine Infantry, in action at Gettysburg, Pennsylvania, for daring heroism and great tenacity in holding his position on the Little Round Top against repeated assaults... "

That was his reward for what you just saw him do. But that wasn't the end of his service and sacrifice for his country. At the Siege of Petersburg, in June of 1864, Chamberlain was shot through the right hip and groin, the bullet exiting his left hip. Despite the injury, he stuck his sword into the ground to hold himself upright while he waved his men on to a charge, and then he collapsed. Grant promoted Chamberlain to Brigadier General on the battlefield. Chamberlain's incorrectly recorded death was then reported in the Maine newspapers. Later, although many, including his wife Fanny, urged Chamberlain to resign, he served through to the end of the war.

During the final advance that would finish the war, he sustained another wound (in the chest and left arm, which was almost amputated), and was nearly captured. Nevertheless, afterwards, Lincoln made him a Brevet Major General. In all, Chamberlain served in 20 battles and numerous skirmishes, was cited for bravery four times, had six horses shot from under him, and was wounded six times. At the surrender ceremony of Robert E. Lee at Appomattox, Virginia, Chamberlain was given the honor of commanding the Union troops.

To review what we have seen: on July 1, 1863 most of Lee's army of 75,000 reached Gettysburg, as did the 90,000-man Union army. On July 2, Lee tried to attack Union positions, including Little Round Top, from the left and right flanks, but northern troops repelled the attack.

If you didn't watch the movie to the end: On the third day, Lee launched a frontal assault against the center of the Union lines, a well-fortified position on a low hill. 15,000 Confederate troops, led by General George E. Pickett, marched three-quarters of a mile across open ground into withering Union rifle and artillery fire. Known as "Pickett's Charge," it is generally considered the high water mark of the Confederacy; that is, its last best chance at winning the war. Instead, Picket retreated with 50% casualties, and when Lee urged him to reform his division for an expected Union counter attack, Pickett replied, "General, I have no division."

When Lee's army headed back to Virginia the evening of the following day, July 4th, it was clear that the Confederacy had suffered a disastrous defeat. Nearly 25,000 Confederate soldiers were killed, wounded, or missing in action at the Battle of Gettysburg. Lee was never able to mount another major offensive and the Confederacy never received that saving foreign recognition.

Something left out of the novel and the movie is the vital and heroic contribution of one of the Union's youngest generals, a twenty-three year old who would later become very famous for an historical defeat, George Armstrong Custer. At Gettysburg, on the second day, Lee sent cavalry out to protect his rear and Custer, immediately upon spotting them, led a reckless but effective cavalry charge against them.

The Union Army of the Potomac and the Confederate Army of Northern Virginia fought each other to a bloody stalemate across a two hundred mile front for almost four years. During that same time, Union armies in the West, the area between the Appalachian Mountains and the Mississippi River, marched victoriously through 1,200 miles of enemy territory, 7 Confederate states, destroying farms, railroads, and other infrastructure.

On that same July 4th as the Union victory at Gettysburg, Vicksburg surrendered to U.S. Grant, giving the Union control over the entire Mississippi River and splitting the Confederacy in two. Grant was the Union's key strategist and tactician in the West. He won victories at Forts Henry and Donelson; the Battle of Shiloh; and the Battle of Vicksburg, considered one of the turning points of the war. At the Third Battle of Chattanooga, Grant drove Confederate forces out of Tennessee and opened a route to Atlanta and the heart of the Confederacy.

At the beginning of 1864, Lincoln made Grant a Lieutenant General, a rank last held by Washington, and commander of all Union armies, which were over 533,000 strong, the largest army in the world. Only three years before Grant was distinguished only for the unrelenting failure of everything he attempted, from career soldier through a series of failed businesses, plus farming, bill collecting, and a job in a leather tannery. Years earlier, he had distinguished himself for bravery in the U.S.–Mexican War where he was uncommonly cool and clear-headed in combat.

Grant, along with his close friend General William Tecumseh Sherman, and President Lincoln, all believed that only total war, the utter defeat of Confederate armies in the field and the destruction of their economic base, would end the war. This was total war not in terms of deliberately killing civilians, as in World War II, but rather in terms of destroying the homes, farms, and railroads sustaining the enemy army.

Grant and Robert E. Lee first fought each other on May 7, 1864, in an unusually dense forest called "The Wilderness," the site of a Lee victory over the same army, under Hooker, only a year before. The night before Grant's battle, Union soldiers camped on the Chancelorsville battleground where recent rains had opened up graves and strewn skeletons around them. In a war distinguished for gruesome battles, the Wilderness was appalling. At one point, the woods caught on fire. Then wounded men stranded in no man's land caught on fire, and through the night, soldiers on both sides listened to their screams.

At the Wilderness, Grant lost 17,000 men and gained not a thing. After the last day of the three-day battle, he wept uncontrollably all night in his tent, but the next morning he did what no previous general did who had been defeated by Lee, Grant advanced. And everyone knew that Lincoln had finally found his man. Grant had told Lincoln, "No matter what happens, there will be no turning back." "That man Grant will fight us every day and every hour of every day until the end of the war," Grant's old prewar friend Confederate General Longstreet said.

Thus began Grant's "Overland Campaign," battles of attrition, 30 days without let up, from the Wilderness to Spotsylvania to Cold Harbor. 30 days in which the two armies lost more men than both sides had lost in the previous three years. At Spotsylvania, it was the most intense exchange of gunfire in history up to that point. So many bullets hit some men that their bodies fell apart. At Cold Harbor, Grant lost 7,000 in less than an hour.

After seven weeks, he suffered 65,000 casualties, but he never stopped pressing Lee's Army of Northern Virginia, through a series of flanking maneuvers, backward toward the Confederate capital, Richmond, Virginia. Finally, Grant pinned Lee down in the Siege of Petersburg, Richmond's central railroad hub. Once Grant and Lee came to grips in the Wilderness, the two armies were never again out of contact with each other for the next eleven months. There was continuous relentless fighting, marching, digging, day after day, month after month with no letup. For over nine months, the two armies fought from thirty miles of trenches, presaging the same trench warfare stalemate of World War I Europe.

As the horrendous casualty numbers increased, Lincoln's chances for re-election in the upcoming 1864 election began to dim, and with them the possibility of Union victory and the survival of democracy.

The same day Grant started for the Wilderness, General William Tecumseh Sherman left Chattanooga, Tennessee, for Atlanta, Georgia, with three armies under him totaling almost a hundred thousand men. When Lincoln put Grant in charge of all the Union armies, Grant gave Sherman Grant's former command of Union troops in the Western theater.

Sherman graduated near the top of his West Point class three years ahead of Grant who graduated in the middle of his class. Theirs was a famous, unlikely, and vitally important friendship; indeed, a recent book about it was titled *Grant and Sherman: The Friendship That Won the Civil War* (2005). (It's overripe for a good movie.) The Union victory can be traced back to a two-day strategy session Grant and Sherman had in March 1864 in a room of the Burnet House, a Cincinnati hotel. Considering how much personal and professional failure and humiliation these two men had endured up to that time, those were a redemptive two days as well.

When he was bored or missing his wife too much, Grant was prone to drink. When someone complained about Grant's drinking problem, Lincoln retorted, "Find out what he drinks and send a case of it to each of my other generals." Meanwhile, due to a "melancholy insanity," as his wife described it, that ran through Sherman's family, the pressure of command caused him to a have mental breakdown and be relieved of duty in December 1861. He was back within weeks however, and by March 1862, serving under Grant.

A Northern newspaper complained that the long and complicated Vicksburg Campaign was "... under the leadership of a drunkard, whose confidential adviser was a lunatic." Indeed, Sherman famously said, Grant "stood by me when I was crazy, and I stood by him when he was drunk; and now, we stand by each other always." Theirs was an unlikely friendship because they were polar opposites. Grant was reserved, undemonstrative, taciturn, and rumpled (he wore a corporal's uniform in part as protection from snipers but it also became a symbol of his humility). Sherman was nervous, talkative, effusive, and volatile.

After he left Chattanooga, Sherman defeated Confederate generals Joseph E. Johnston and John Bell Hood on the way to Atlanta outside of which he eventually stalled just like Grant at Petersburg. But on September 2, 1864, the city finally fell to Sherman, in the process guaranteeing Lincoln's reelection. To deny the Union Army supplies, the Confederates burned down much of the city (memorably depicted in *Gone with the Wind*). Sherman then began his famous "March to the Sea," the purpose of which he told Grant in a letter was " to make Georgia howl," which he did by destroying 20% of its farms and causing $100 million worth of damage. Followed by 25,000 freed slaves, he reached the Atlantic Ocean at Savannah in December and then turned north and inflicted the same devastation on South Carolina.

At about the same time, diminutive Union General Philip Sheridan was sent into the Shenandoah Valley of West Virginia by Grant with the charge to "Do all the damage to railroads and crops you can."

Eventually, Grant forced Lee, his army shrunk by desertions and casualties, to abandon Petersburg and Richmond. Traditionally the fall of the capital means defeat, and the Civil War was no different. Lee soon surrendered to Grant on April 9, 1865, at Appomattox Court House, Virginia.

After the war, Lee became president of what is now Washington and Lee University, as well as the greatest Southern hero of the war and an icon of the Lost Cause cult.

Longstreet enjoyed a successful post-war career working for the U.S. government as a diplomat, civil servant, and administrator. However, his conversion to the Republican Party and his cooperation with his old prewar friend, President Ulysses S. Grant, as well as critical comments in his memoirs about General Lee's wartime performance, made him anathema to the Lost Cause cult.

Due to his immense popularity, Joshua Lawrence Chamberlain served four terms as Governor of Maine. He then served on the faculty, and as president, of his alma mater, Bowdoin College.

When Grant became president, he appointed Sherman Commanding General of the United States Army. One of Sherman's main concerns was protecting the construction and operation of the railroads from hostile Indians. After the 1866 Fetterman Massacre in Wyoming, in which Sioux and Cheyenne wiped out an entire command of eighty one, Sherman wrote Grant that "we must act with vindictive earnestness against the Sioux, even to their extermination, men, women and children." After Custer's defeat at Little Bighorn, Sherman wrote that "during an assault, the soldiers can not pause to distinguish between male and female, or even discriminate as to age." But despite his harsh treatment of the warring tribes, Sherman spoke out against the unfair way speculators and government agents treated the natives within the reservations. The Plains Indian Wars are covered in detail in Chapter 9.

Ulysses S Grant was the 18th president of the United States (1869–1877). His presidency was marred by his defense of corrupt appointees and by a deep economic depression (called the Panic of 1873). But he also led the Radical Republicans in their efforts to eliminate the last vestiges of Confederate nationalism and slavery, protect African American citizenship, and defeat the Ku Klux Klan. Unfortunately, as he left the White House in March 1877, many of his policies were being undone. Grant had the strongest civil rights record of any president between Abraham Lincoln and Lyndon B. Johnson.

Next, we devote an entire movie and chapter to the 16th president and likely the only genius to occupy the White House, Abraham Lincoln.

Civil War Battle Timeline

1861

Feb 4 After Lincoln is elected President, representatives from six seceding states adopt a Confederate constitution in Montgomery, Ala. Five days later, they chose Jefferson Davis, a former Senator from Miss., as the president of the Confederate States of America.

Apr 12 At 4:30 a.m., Confederate guns fired on Fort Sumter, a federal installation in South Carolina's Charleston harbor. The fort surrendered after 34 hours of bombardment.

Apr 14 Lincoln calls for 75,000 volunteers to put down the insurrection and the Civil War begins.

Apr 18 Virginia's Robert E. Lee rejects Lincoln's offer of command of a Union army.

Apr 19 Lincoln orders the blockade of ports in Confederate states.

Jul 21 In Virginia, the Battle of Bull Run, or First Manassas as the Confederates called it, is a humiliating route of the Union.

1862

Mar 9 The Battle of the Ironclads, the Confederate Merrimack vs. the Union Monitor, at Hampton Roads, Virginia, is a draw.

Apr 7 Battle of Shiloh, first major battle in the Western theater, in Tennessee, was a victory for U.S. Grant.

Apr 24 In the Battle of New Orleans, Union Admiral David Farragut's naval squadron forced New Orleans to surrender.

Jun 25 Union General George McClellan's "Peninsula Campaign" fails to take the Confederate capitol Richmond, Virginia.

Aug 30 The Battle of Second Bull Run or Second Manassas was another costly and humiliating defeat for the Union.

Sept 17 Battle of Antietam, near Sharpsburg, Maryland, is the bloodiest day in U.S. history. Confederates withdrew so the Union claimed victory.

Dec 13 The Battle of Fredericksburg in Virginia in which Lee trounced Ambrose Burnside with Union casualties almost twice those of the Confederacy.

1863

Apr 21 May 11 The Battle of Chancellorsville is another stunning Lee victory though his "right arm," General "Stonewall" Jackson, is accidentally killed by his own sentry.

May 19 In three weeks, Grant's marches 180 miles through Mississippi, wins five battles, and settles into a siege of Vicksburg.

Jul 1-3 The Battle of Gettysburg in Pennsylvania.

Jul 4 Grant's Siege of Vicksburg in Mississippi ends in Union victory.

Jul 18 54th Massachusetts Colored Infantry (of the movie *Glory*) attacked Battery Wagner at Charleston Harbor, South Carolina, losing over a third of its men.

Sept 20 The Battle of Chickamauga Creek in Georgia, another Union defeat.

Nov 25 The Battle of Chattanooga in Tennessee is another victory for Grant.

1864

Mar 2 U.S. Grant named General-in-Chief of Union armies.

Apr 12 At Fort Pillow, Tennessee, on the Mississippi River, Confederates massacre 431 black soldiers after they surrendered.

May 4 Grant's "Overland Campaign" begins, a month long series of battles against Robert E. Lee that will end with a siege of the Confederate capitol Richmond, Virginia.

May 4 General Sherman's "Atlanta Campaign" begins in which he defeats successive Confederate armies, striking through the Confederate heartland and ending in a siege of Atlanta, Georgia.

May 5-7 Grant vs. Lee at the Battle of the Wilderness

May 8-21 Grant vs. Lee at the Battle of Spotsylvania Court House

May 31 - Jun 12 Grant vs. Lee at the Battle of Cold Harbor

Jun 9   Grant begins Siege of Petersburg, Virginia, the main supply base and rail depot for the entire region

Jul 18 - Sept 3 Sherman's Siege of Atlanta ends with Union capture of the city.

Nov 15 - Dec 21 After his destructive "March to the Sea" from Atlanta, Sherman captures Savannah, Georgia.

1865

Feb   Sherman marched north from Georgia through South Carolina, again destroying everything in his path.

Apr 3 - 4 Grant's nine month siege finally forces Lee and the Confederate government to abandon the Confederate capitol Richmond, Virginia.

Apr 9 – Lee surrenders to Grant at Appomattox Courthouse, Virginia.

Recommendations

Esthetically, *Glory* (1989) is an incomparably superior film to *Gettysburg* and it is *Gettysburg's* indispensable corrective. *Glory's* battles are every bit as stirring. It begins with Antietam and the climax at Fort Wagner is stunning and gut-wrenching. The film won Academy Awards for sound and cinematography, and Denzel Washington won his first Oscar, in this case for Best Actor in a Supporting Role.

Indeed, *Glory* is esthetically the best film ever made about the Civil War, but it has flaws. It tells the story of the all-black 54th Massachusetts Volunteer Infantry which was lead by the white abolitionist Colonel Robert Gould Shaw. He was an exceptionally decent and courageous man, and Matthew Broderick does a fine job portraying him. But *Glory* is another instance of something we saw in *Amistad*: the earnest young white liberal and his moral struggles taking up far too much screen time, especially when the black actors are burning holes in the screen.

The real 54th Massachusetts was made up mostly of free blacks not ex-slaves, and as the model black regiment, they received adequate supplies and equipment. However, the shortages in the film illustrate the racism so prevalent in the Union Army as well in the North generally. Ironically, this Hollywood movie left out a romantic angle that would have been very appropriate: Shaw had only spent a week with his new bride before he led the suicidal charge against Fort Wagner.

John Huston, the most literary of directors, became interested in the classic Civil War novel *The Red Badge of Courage* while he was serving in World War II. When he made the movie in 1950, as mentioned before, he chose the most decorated American soldier of World War II, Audie Murphy, to play Henry Fleming, the novel's cowardly hero. Bill Mauldin, the most famous editorial cartoonist of World War II, did fine in another featured role. Plus the film boasts a roster of some of the best character actors of the period. It is likely many of the actors and extras were themselves only five years from a World War II battlefield.

A complaint against the novel is that it is more about war in general and not specific enough about the Civil War (author Stephen Crane wasn't even born at the time of the war). That definitely is not true of the film, which is rich with the look-and-feel of camp life, soldier relations, and of course the battlefield.

Huston thought it could have been his best film but after poor audience test screenings, the studio, also fearing the film was too anti-war, cut it to 70 minutes. Ever since, it has been considered a mutilated masterpiece, but however great it might have been, it is still great enough as it is to be a minor American classic and a close second to *Glory* esthetically.

Friendly Persuasion (1956) tells the story of a pacifist Quaker family living on an idyllic farm in southern Indiana during the Civil War. Directed by three-time Academy Award winner William Wyler and starring two-time Oscar winner Gary Cooper, the film itself didn't win any Oscars but it did win the Palm d'Or, the top prize at the Cannes Film Festival. Smarmy and sentimental in parts, it is also gripping in parts, and it is ideal for our purposes because it so accurately and thoroughly presents this quintessential American community of radical religious dissenters. The Quakers were also the leading abolitionists, though the word, still offensive in the 1950s, is nowhere in the script. Nevertheless, the film is a rare big-budget major studio sponsorship of that perspective.

Friendly Persuasion was made when the numbing carnage of World War II was still a fresh memory and while the country was coming to terms with the new apocalyptic threat of the Cold War. This film reasonably addresses the issue of whether or not, among the many things Hitler destroyed forever, pacifism is one of them. This is dramatized effectively when a Confederate army invades the Quaker family's community and eventually even their own farm. The film was released without a screenwriting credit because the screenwriter had been blacklisted in the anti-communist witch-hunts of the 1950s. In the 1980s, President Ronald Reagan, whose first intellectual reference was always Hollywood, made a gift of the film to Soviet Premier Mikhail Gorbachev at one of their summit meetings, suggesting the film was symbolic of the need to find an alternative to war.

I have to mention another big-budget major studio film about an Indiana abolitionist, in this case played by Montgomery Clift, who marries a Southern cracked belle, played by Elizabeth Taylor. *Raintree County* (1957) is a godawful mess but it does have a rare extended sequence in which the main character fights with Sherman across Georgia, plus there is Liz's Oscar-nominated impersonation of Scarlett O'Hara overdosed on gothic delirium because she might have a black ancestor.

Shenandoah (1965) stars James Stewart as an antislavery Virginia patriarch who also opposes the war though from political and not religious convictions. It has some choice anti-war lines, such as: "It's like all wars, I suppose. The undertakers are winning." Nevertheless, the issues aren't developed, slavery and blacks are marginal, and the family drama, romance, and action are all canned and trite.

The Horse Soldiers (1959) was directed by John Ford and stars John Wayne and William Holden. Behind a contrived formula romance and contrived clashes between the protagonists, it is unusually fair to the Union. It is based on the true story of a daring Union raid hundreds of miles behind enemy lines during the Siege of Vicksburg.

There are two made-for-TV movies worth note. *Ironclads* (1991) is another Ted Turner production and actually a highly watchable movie. It concerns the Battle of the Monitor and Merrimack, the first meeting in combat of ironclad warships and arguably the most important naval battle of the American Civil War. It was fought near Chesapeake Bay in Virginia and was part of the effort of the Confederacy to break the stranglehold of the Union blockade. The duel ended indecisively after about three hours, with neither being able to inflict significant damage on the other. The ships did not fight again and the blockade remained in place. The battle received worldwide attention though, causing Britain and France to immediately halt construction of wooden-hulled ships and begin building ironclads.

Andersonville, yet another Turner production, won the 1996 Emmy for director John Frankenheimer (one of four in a row he would win in the Nineties). He was already the director of some of the best movies of the Sixties.

A little background info is in order now. Because the Confederacy refused to stop murdering unarmed black troops after they surrendered, Grant suspended the system of prisoner exchange in an effort to force the Confederacy to treat black and white prisoners the same. The Confederate leadership refused, and as a result, prisons North and South become overcrowded, and in the South, they became nightmares. Andersonville in Georgia was the worst Confederate prison camp of all. It was overcrowded to four times its capacity, with an inadequate water supply, no sanitation, and reduced food rations. Of the 45,000 Union prisoners held there, nearly 13,000 died. The camp commandant, Captain Henry Wirz, was the only soldier tried and executed for war crimes during the Civil War.

Two TV miniseries tried to encompass the whole Civil War. They had a similar structure: two families, or two sides of the same extend family, on opposite sides of the war. In *The Blue and the Gray* (1982), the main character is a journalist who witnesses many of the important events of the Civil War. Unfortunately, the lead actor, in his first and last starring role, was an unmitigated disaster. This put a hole in the heart of the 8-hour series, despite a stellar cast and a story concept by Pulitzer Prize-winning Civil War historian Bruce Catton.

North and South was actually three miniseries broadcast in 1985, 1986, and 1994, one set before, one during, and one after the war. They are based on the 1980s trilogy of novels North and South by John Jakes. The first installment remains the seventh-highest rated miniseries in TV history and the second had a similar success. North and South too had a stellar cast and included as characters many of the top historical figures from both sides of the war. The vast far-fetched plot, a lot of restirred clichés, centers on best friends at West Point who find themselves and their families on opposite sides of the war. One family is slave-owning rural planters and the other lives by manufacturing in a small Northern mill town. They reflect some of the divisions between North and South that eventually led to the war.

As for movies that take the Southern side, we don't need to search for them, we can't avoid them. As already mentioned, the Cult of the Confederacy has had remarkable success in Hollywood, reaching back to the beginning of motion pictures and the influential first movie epic, *Birth of a Nation* (1915). It was the biggest grossing film until *Gone with the Wind* (1939), which is the top-grossing film of all time, adjusted for inflation, according to the website Box Office Mojo. Based on the Pulitzer Prize winning novel of 1937, *Gone with the Wind* established the movies' dominant version of the Civil War: invaded suffering white Southerners who were benign slaveholders with content loyal slaves. The *Gone with the Wind* version was corrected by the revisionism of the 1960s.

Then in 1976, the Cult struck back with Clint Eastwood's mega hit *The Outlaw Josie Wales*. It was based on a novel by a speechwriter for Alabama Governor George Wallace, the single most notorious segregationist during the Civil Rights Era. The film has a psychotic fantasy of a "Union atrocity" in which unarmed surrendering Confederate soldiers are mowed down by a Gatling gun (early machine gun).

Even when Hollywood finally got around to showing black Civil War soldiers in *Glory* (1989), the filmmakers felt they had to show some irrelevant and, compared with the structural criminality of the Confederacy, negligible Union criminality. But then the technical advisor was Southern historian Shelby Foote, a well-known Cult member. Another cultist, media mogul Ted Turner, financed *Gettysburg* and *Gods and Generals*, both box office mega disasters.

One of the more ridiculous scenes in *Gone with the Wind* has a slave telling Miss Scarlett, as he marches to the front, "Don't you worry, we'll stop them Yankees." That scene is echoed in Ang Lee's *Ride with the Devil* (1999), which is unapologetically pro-Confederate throughout and has the preposterous and pathetic spectacle of a black man voluntarily fighting for the Confederacy. The producers may have duped the Taiwanese immigrant Lee.

In 2003, a heaping helping of good ol' Southern fried white suffering arrived in theaters complete with an eighty million dollar budget and a roster of top stars. *Cold Mountain* is wall-to-wall Southern white suffering with a few slaves in the background, without a single line of dialogue, a matter of art direction. Based on a National Book Award winning novel, it includes another

"Union atrocity:" gang rape of a mother and abuse of her baby. The film begins with the Battle of the Crater during the Siege of Petersburg, Virginia, and while it does show Confederate soldiers gleefully shooting trapped Union soldiers, it leaves out the part in that battle where the Confederates killed black soldiers after they surrendered, while Robert E. Lee was nearby and did nothing to stop the slaughter.

In *Cold Mountain*, the filmmakers needed a morally neutral background against which to set a soppy clichéd bodice-ripper. That particular background seems morally neutral because we have seen it so often that it must be at least acceptable, and because Southern whites really did suffer. However, their suffering is vastly over weighted in the movies compared with the lives of millions upon millions destroyed over centuries by Southern slavery. Plus, of course, the suffering of Southern whites was the just punishment for slavery, or as Lincoln put it in the Second Inaugural Address, "the woe due to those by whom the offense came... and... every drop of blood drawn with the lash shall be paid by another drawn with the sword..."

Ronald Maxwell's skills as a filmmaker did not improve when a decade later he did *Gods and Generals* (2003), the prequel to *Gettysburg*. It is just another Confederate wax museum of a movie, this one focused a lot on a saintly Stonewall Jackson. This movie too is dramatically shapeless with even more speeches full of Southern nobility. In a phony bid for "balance," it includes scenes of Jeff Daniels as Joshua Lawrence Chamberlain before and during the Battle of Fredericksburg. There are a couple black characters, loyal slaves of course. In one scene, the camera lingers on a black man cheering the rebels as they march off to war. Rotten Tomatoes gave the film a whopping 9% positive reviews.

Among the countless documentaries about the Civil War, one towers above the rest: Ken Burns' *The Civil War*. When it was first broadcast on PBS on five consecutive nights in September of 1990, it was a huge national event, with an audience of about 40 million, making it the most-watched PBS program ever. Full of groundbreaking technical and stylistic innovation, it received more than 40 major television and film honors. Watching it in its more than 10 hour entirety might be as good as a one-semester course at a community college.

Ken Burns' brother Ric produced *Death and the Civil War* (2012) for PBS. It was based on the book *This Republic of Suffering: Death and the American Civil War* (2008) by Drew Gilpin Faust, which focused on how the unprecedented carnage altered the character of the republic and the psyche of the American people.

At www.escalloniapress.com, there are free recommendations of the best books - histories, biographies, memoirs, and even novels - related to the subjects of this chapter.

Chapter 8 - Lincoln

Before

The opening scene of this movie is the obscure and minor Battle of Jenkins Ferry on April 30, 1864, in Arkansas. It is the only scene of actual killing in this war movie so it should be gruesome and it is. Knee-deep in mud, black Union soldiers and white Confederates are fighting with unusual ferocity hand-to-hand and with bayonets. These Confederates have recently killed unarmed black prisoners after they surrendered. After a century of Hollywood's pro-Confederate bias, this scene and the immediately following description of the battle by participants, announces that in this movie the Confederates are not gallant idealists defending states' rights but war criminals who are paying for their crimes.

On at least half a dozen battlefields, Confederates killed unarmed black soldiers after they surrendered. The most notorious incident was the Fort Pillow Massacre on the Mississippi River on April 12, 1864, when Confederate troops under General Nathan Bedford Forrest (founder of the Ku Klux Klan) killed hundreds of unarmed black captives. In Forrest's own words, "The river was dyed with the blood of the slaughtered for two hundred yards. The approximate loss was upward of five hundred killed, but few of the officers escaping. My loss was about twenty killed." Forrest doesn't mention what James Loewen mentioned in his ground-breaking *Lies My Teacher Told Me* (1995), that Forrest's men "crucified black prisoners on tent frames and then burned them alive." As already mentioned, because the Confederacy refused to stop killing unarmed black prisoners of war and their white officers, prisoner exchanges were suspended, and instead thousands of POWs, both Union and Confederate, died in fetid and overcrowded prison camps.

Inspite of all the talent involved in this film, it stutters a bit at the beginning, and as a consequence, it has four different consecutive beginnings. The Battle of Jenkins Ferry segues into a scene with, at first, two black soldiers talking about that battle to President Lincoln at night in the Washington Naval Yard. Then two white soldiers join the conversation, and we have begun our story with a demonstration of the tremendous love the Union troops felt for the leader they called "Father Abraham." Their votes were crucial to his reelection in 1864.

However, it's unlikely random Union soldiers would have memorized the Gettysburg address, like these, (it only became revered decades after the war), and even less likely the soldiers would be that informal with their president. This scene ends with a close shot of the famous profile as if from the shoulder of the statue in the Lincoln Memorial in Washington D.C., or the head on Mt. Rushmore, complete with glowing white steam for the clouds below his god-like perspective.

Then we take a surprising plunge into the depths of Lincoln's psyche. In an eerie indistinct animated sequence, we see Lincoln standing on top of a rushing ship, while in voice-over, he is describing to his wife Mary, as he often did, one of the numerous recurring dreams he had during those years.

Screenwriter Tony Kushner then has Lincoln quoting Shakespeare, as he will numerous times in the film, reminding us of the Shakespearean dimensions to Lincoln's story. Also, the quotes are often pithy comments on the scene in which they are delivered; to wit, when he has a comical and fictitious (and implausible) meeting with some shady political operatives, Lincoln starts the conversation with a quote from the comical reprobate Falstaff in *Henry IV, Part II*. Lincoln often attended Shakespeare productions and even exchanged letters with famous actors about the plays. His favorites were *King Lear, Richard III, Henry VIII, Hamlet*, and especially *Macbeth*. "I think nothing equals 'Macbeth,' " Lincoln said.

According to his secretary John Hay, Lincoln read more Shakespeare than all other authors combined. This is appropriate for the president who was arguably the finest writer to occupy the White House, and more than any other, owed his presidency to his writing skills. The King James Bible and the poets Robert Burns and Lord Byron also influenced him. Lincoln incorporated these influences into his own unique rhetorical gift for making closely reasoned argument ring with religious urgency.

That Shakespeare quote after the dream sequence ushers us into the fourth beginning, in the First Lady's White House boudoir, where we listen-in on a late middle-aged couple, with decades of marriage, unburdening at the end of the day. This is a very political marriage, as we will be reminded throughout the film. At the end of this scene, Mary guesses that the ship in the dream, which we naturally assumed to be the war, is actually Lincoln's approaching political campaign to pass the Thirteenth Amendment, which would remove constitutional protection for slavery and finally ban it. Kushner isn't equating the war with the amendment but suggesting the enormity of the political battle to get the amendment through Congress. Especially since it requires a two thirds majority and it already failed to pass the year before.

The dream actually comes from an entry in the diary of Navy Secretary Gideon Welles. The entry describes the president telling his cabinet on the day that he was assassinated of a dream where "he seemed to be in some singular, indescribable vessel, and that he was moving with great rapidity towards an indefinite shore." Lincoln claimed that he had this dream before "nearly every great and important event of the War."

This movie is the collaboration of three artists each of whom is in the top ranks of his respective art form in his generation. For his stage epic, *Angels in America* (1993), screenwriter Kushner won the Pulitzer Prize, two Tony Awards, and an Emmy for its screenplay. President Obama awarded him the National Medal of Arts in 2013. Kushner is openly gay, far left politically, Jewish, and Southern. He is also an overtly political playwright and one of the shrewdest and subtlest political analysts around. Before September 11, 2001, he wrote a play, *Homebody/Kabul* (2001), set in Afganistan and with the Taliban as the villains. So, Kushner is ideal for the subject of this movie.

Like Arthur Miller was, Kushner is also a "public intellectual" and occasional center of controversy. His criticism of Israel created opposition to his receiving an honorary doctorate in 2006 at Brandeis University. The same reason was cited when, on May 2, 2011, the Board of Trustees of the City University of New York (CUNY) voted to remove Kushner's name from the list of people invited to receive honorary degrees. On May 6, three previous honorees threatened to return their degrees, and the board of trustees reversed its decision.

Through many drafts of this script, Kushner checked every word for its appropriateness to 1865. He proves himself a poet of vintage slang, gems of which are scattered all over *Lincoln*. In the earliest scene in the First Lady's boudoir, he has Lincoln use "shindy" and "flubdub." Here's a gorgeous line of Lincoln's from later in the film, "You grousel and heckle and dodge about like pettifogging Tammany Hall hucksters!" This mixes the archaic, the still-current, and even the invented; Kushner was inspired to coin his own Lincolnese, "grousel" being an example.

Daniel Day-Lewis, as mentioned in Chapter Two, is the son of a British Poet Laureate and son-in-law of Arthur Miller. He won his third Best Actor Oscar for his Lincoln, making him the only male actor in history to garner three wins in the lead actor category.

Steven Spielberg is ... uh, well, Steven Spielberg: an American institution, the Disney of his generation, and a director with extraordinary technical skills. He is the recipient of two Academy Awards for Best Director. *Lincoln* (2012), Spielberg's fourth dramatic foray into American history, received widespread critical acclaim and was nominated for twelve Academy Awards and won Best Production Design and Best Actor. Day-Lewis's performance was the first directed by Spielberg to win an Academy Award.

Their subject is straight out of central casting. What kind of man should he be who has been chosen America's greatest president in poll after poll of historians and the public? Lincoln is better than could have been invented. The folkloric image of a plowboy who reads at night in front of the fire in a log cabin is romanticized, of course, but in Lincoln's case, it was also true. So, he is revered not just for captaining the country through its worst crisis but also as a powerful symbol of Americans' most cherished belief about their country, the rags-to-riches "American dream." Plus, he was a paragon of political acumen and moral integrity ("Honest Abe"), not to mention the wit (emphasized in our film). By the way, the log cabin symbol was an embarrassment that he tolerated as a presidential campaign gimmick.

He was born in 1809 in Kentucky to farmers who were anti-slavery and knew prosperity and poverty and who kept moving west. His mother died when he was 9 but he bonded well with a loving stepmother. He may have had only a year or so of formal schooling, but the "Rail Splitter" (as he was called in his first presidential election) eventually acquired wealth through a career as one of the top lawyers in Illinois, appearing in court against corporations about as often as for them. Lincoln and his partner handled about two hundred cases a year concerned with debt, foreclosure, ejectment, slander and libel, divorce, and occasionally murder.

Starting in 1834, Lincoln served four successive terms in the Illinois House of Representatives and became a leader of the Illinois Whig party. He served one term in the U.S. House of Representatives from 1847 to 49 when the dominant issue was the U.S.-Mexico War. As already mentioned, he took an unpopular anti-war position that some considered political suicide, and indeed, it haunted the rest of his political career. Nevertheless, he won the ultimate political prize.

Before he reached the White House, he had a four-year-old son die, then while running the war, an eleven-year-old son died, Willie, his favorite. And through the war, his wife gradually went mad with grief. Then there is the ending of Lincoln's story: martyrdom for democracy at the moment of triumph. Celebrity actor John Wilkes Booth assassinated him in a theater on Good Friday, causing comparisons to Christ of course. Certainly, Lincoln suffered and died for our sins, and that we are capable of producing a leader of his quality, redeems us somewhat as a nation. Leo Tolstoy described him as "a Christ in miniature, a saint of humanity."

Almost two hundred statues of Lincoln decorate the American landscape. Plus there are more abroad. According to the Smithsonian Institution's inventory of American sculpture, of the more than six hundred memorials and statues of American presidents almost one third commemorate Lincoln. In DC, George Washington's monument is an obelisk but Lincoln's demands the man. So, in the neoclassical Lincoln Memorial, he sits like a gigantic Greek god in its temple, majestic and fierce on his marble throne, with a face as handsome as they could make it and still be recognizable. Walt Whitman, who saw Lincoln often, said he was so ugly he was beautiful.

During the central event in the history of America, its greatest crisis, American democracy produced a genuine "philosopher-king." However, among his legal associates, Lincoln was known less for intellectual brilliance than thoroughness. With a political issue, he would spend weeks, months, even years taking its measure, jotting down his musings, refining his opinions, and finally, honing his rhetoric. In the speeches, public letters, memos, and other writings, often he is the brilliant lawyer presenting his case to the jury on the important national issues using finely-calibrated, irrefutable logic.

Such was the quality of his intellect that an old lawyer friend, Leonard Swett, said Lincoln could "state the case of his adversary better and more forcefully than his opponent could himself." Jeffrey Rosen, legal affairs editor at *The New Republic*, wrote in the May 10, 2004 issue of that magazine, "Lincoln led by the force of his argument and by the conveyed sense of irreducible conviction behind the argument. What is striking about Lincoln's achievement is that he did not rely on others to provide constitutional justifications for his actions after the fact; he justified them himself, with such analytical precision and legal sophistication that, even in retrospect, his own constitutional account of his actions surpasses any other."

It has been claimed that there are 16,000 different books about Lincoln (that number probably includes pamphlets, articles, essays, etc.). This would seem to imply there is nothing new to say, yet, and it is a manifestation of how endlessly fascinating he is, there continues to be a cottage industry of Lincoln popular history. One of the most successful of its products is the basis for our film: the bestseller *Team of Rivals: the Political Genius of Abraham Lincoln* (2005) by Doris Kearns Goodwin, twice winner of the Pulitzer Prize for history.

Her book focuses on Lincoln's cabinet which was dominated by three men he had just defeated for the 1860 Republican presidential nomination: Attorney General Edward Bates, Secretary of the Treasury Salmon P. Chase, and Secretary of State William H. Seward. By the time of our movie, early 1865, of the original three only Seward is left in the cabinet, with whom Lincoln formed a genuine friendship. Lincoln relied on his cabinet, in ways that Kearns Goodwin presents in great detail, but his hardest decisions were made alone; such as the decision to not abandon Ft. Sumter, after the Confederates demanded it, and risk starting a war. The cabinet was almost unanimously for abandoning it and he against, so they didn't abandon it.

From Kearns Goodwin's book, Spielberg chose the subject of the passage of the Thirteenth Amendment and Kushner dramatized it. There is a palpable tension in this film between the highly intellectual playwright and the highly Hollywood director. Spielberg seems to have made his peace with intellectuals, who pummeled his movies for decades, after he forced an intellectual to carry a typewriter through World War II combat in *Saving Private Ryan* (1996). Still, you can feel Spielberg teasing Kushner's script toward Frank Capra feel-good, or perhaps, toward a Spielbergian version of John Ford's masterful mythical *Young Mr. Lincoln* (1939). (Capra never made a Lincoln film, but reverential retreats to the Lincoln Memorial sustain the beleaguered everyman hero of *Mr. Smith Goes to Washington* [1939].)

Kushner's script is a reconstitution of the political maneuvering necessary to get Congress to pass a constitutional amendment; in this case, at the risk of prolonging a war. His script is intricate, meticulously detailed, and full of documentary grit; however, it covers only ten pages of Kearns Goodwin's book. An even bigger source for the script is probably Michael Vorenberg's *Final Freedom: The Civil War, The Abolition of Slavery, and the Thirteenth Amendment* (2001). Kushner sort of admitted this, however he did it reluctantly, because it is Kearns Goodwin's name that is in the movie's credits.

If this narrow subject fails to exploit the full potential of a movie about Lincoln, it is ideal for presenting the politics of slavery. The Thirteenth Amendment was the climax and culmination of the long political history of slavery. In the U.S. Constitution slaves counted as three-fifths of a person in terms of population numbers for Congressional representation, so the elite planter class had long held power in Congress out of proportion to the total number of white Southerners.

The following timeline is more useful here than at the end of the chapter.

Timeline for the Politics of Slavery

1787
- The Northwest Ordinance of 1787 banned slavery north of the Ohio River establishing it as the boundary between free and slave territories. This division set the stage for national competition over admitting free and slave states into the Union, the most contentious political issue before the Civil War.

1820
- The Missouri Compromise prohibited slavery north of 36 degrees, 30 minutes north latitude and admitted Missouri as a slave state and Maine as a free state.

1846
- Rep. David Wilmot submits an amendment to a military appropriations bill prohibiting slavery in any territory acquired from Mexico. The Wilmot Proviso passes the house twice but is defeated in the Senate.

1848
- The Free Soil party is formed, opposing the expansion of slavery into the western territories.
- The Treaty of Guadalupe Hidalgo ends the Mexico War. The U.S. acquired California, Nevada, Utah, New Mexico, and parts of Arizona, Colorado, Kansas, and Wyoming.

1850

-Congress adopts the Compromise of 1850, which admits California to the Union as a free state, but does not forbid slavery in other territories acquired from Mexico. It also includes a Fugitive Slave Law requiring all law-enforcement officials to hand over any black to anybody claiming to be their owner, with imprisonment and heavy fines for anyone aiding a runaway slave.

1852

-Harriet Beecher Stowe publishes *Uncle Tom's Cabin* (1852), which sells a million copies in 16 months.

1854

-Sen. Stephen Douglas introduces the Kansas-Nebraska Act, which repealed the Missouri Compromise and allowed for "popular sovereignty," settlers deciding for themselves if their states would be slave or free. In the Kansas election, in which some 6000 votes were cast even though only 2000 voters were registered, pro-slavery forces won. By the end of the war of reprisals in "Bleeding Kansas," 200 were dead.

1856

Abolitionist Sen. Charles Sumner of Massachusetts denounces "The Crime Against Kansas" and pro-slavery Representative Preston Brooks beats Sumner with a cane on the chamber floor, leaving him disabled for three years.

1857

In the case of Dred Scott Decision, the Supreme Court ruled that African Americans had no rights under the Constitution, and that neither the federal government nor the territorial legislatures could exclude slavery from the new western territories.

1860

Jun 23 Northern Democrats in Baltimore nominate Stephen Douglas for the presidency.

Jun 28 Southern Democrats nominated John C. Breckinridge as their presidential candidate.

Nov 6 Abraham Lincoln is elected president with less than 40%, and no votes from the South, but an overwhelming Electoral College victory.

Dec 20 South Carolina votes to secede from the Union.

1863

Jan 1 President Abraham Lincoln signed the Emancipation Proclamation It was an executive order based on the president's constitutional authority as commander in chief, not a law passed by Congress. It proclaimed the slaves free in the ten states in rebellion, denying those states an indispensable labor source. It applied to 3 million of the 4 million slaves.

1864

Apr 8 The Senate passed the Thirteenth Amendment to the Constitution abolishing "involuntary servitude."

1865

Jan 31 The House passed the Thirteenth Amendment.

Dec 6 After ratification by the requisite three quarters of the states, the Thirteenth Amendment was adopted.

After his single term in the U.S. House of Representatives ended in 1849, Lincoln attended to his law practice. But the Kansas-Nebraska Act stirred his moral aversion to slavery and re-awakened his political aspirations. He was instrumental in the creation of the new Republican Party, and at its 1856 national convention, Lincoln placed second in the contest to become the party's nominee for vice president. In 1858, Lincoln was the Illinois Republican nominee for the U.S. Senate running against Stephen A. Douglas. Lincoln lost the election, but his performance in the famous "Lincoln-Douglas Debates" plus his speeches, brought him national attention. That, and being a moderate from a swing state, eventually brought Abraham Lincoln the presidency, and the country, civil war.

"I never, in my life, felt more certain that I was doing right, than I do in signing this paper," Lincoln said as he became the "Great Emancipator" and signed the Emancipation Proclamation. The Proclamation also provided for the recruitment of ex-slaves: 74% of military age blacks volunteered; 179,000 served, forming nearly 10% of the Union Army; over 30,000 died.

When the unprecedented casualty numbers of Grant's 1864 military campaigns unnerved the Northern people and produced a movement for peace negotiations, Lincoln refused to drop emancipation as a precondition for peace, even though this refusal threatened his own reelection. "The promise being made, must be kept..." said Lincoln. "Why should [black Union soldiers] give their lives for us, with full notice of our purpose to betray them? I should be damned in time and eternity for so doing. The world shall know that I will keep my faith to friends and enemies, come what will."

By making the freeing of the slaves an explicit goal of the Union war effort, the Proclamation also swung public and government opinion to the Union in France and England and prevented them from recognizing the Confederacy.

Lincoln's reelection was in doubt through much of the summer and fall of 1864, but after Union victories in Atlanta and Mobile Bay, he won 55 percent of the vote. During the period covered in our movie, early 1865, victory is in sight and the Union and democracy likely saved, but the lawyer in Lincoln has alerted him to possible future legal challenges to what he considers his greatest achievement, the Emancipation Proclamation. It can only be safeguarded by a Constitutional amendment. In the first cabinet meeting in the film, Lincoln introduces the subject in an aria of subtlest legal reasoning.

The film will focus on the process of passing the amendment in Congress with a special emphasis on political chicanery. It is the film's main insight, not particularly original or profound, that Lincoln was capable of using dirty politics. Actually, the trading of appointments for votes here is minor compared with, for instance, what he did during the dicey 1864 election when he gave leave to soldiers from strongly pro-Lincoln districts so they could go home and vote for him.

It was this practical politician in Lincoln that frustrated abolitionists, like the black soldier in the second beginning of the film. But "had [Lincoln] put the abolition of slavery before the salvation of the Union," leading abolitionist Frederick Douglass conceded after the war, "he would have inevitably driven from him a powerful class of the American people and rendered resistance to rebellion impossible. Viewed from the genuine abolition ground, Mr. Lincoln seemed tardy, cold, dull, and indifferent; but measuring him by the sentiment of his country, a sentiment he was bound as a statesman to consult, he was swift, zealous, radical, and determined."

James M. McPherson is the dean of Civil War historians, a Pulitzer Prize winner, and author of three books on Lincoln. One of them is a superb mini-bio (under a hundred pages), *Abraham Lincoln*, which was published by Oxford University Press in 2009, the second centennial of Lincoln's birth. In it McPherson wrote: "Only after years of studying the powerful crosscurrents of political and military pressures on Lincoln did I come to appreciate the skill with which he steered between the numerous shoals of conservatism and radicalism, free states and slave states, abolitionists, Republicans, Democrats, and border-state Unionists to maintain a steady course that brought the nation to victory—and the abolition of slavery—in the end."

The practical politician is the main focus of our film, but there is of course more than politics to the man and that is present in the film too. Evidence is thin concerning the inner workings of Abe and Mary Lincoln's family. None of the family members kept diaries. Hardly any of the family correspondence remains. Immediately after Abe became president, Mary deliberately burned most of the correspondence that existed at that time. Almost all of our information about their relationships derives from second- or third-hand accounts, usually recollected after the war.

In an interview in the Nov. 2, 2012 issue of the *Wall Street Journal*, Tony Kushner said: "Mary knew within an hour of meeting him, as she told a cousin, 'He's the greatest man of the 19th century and he's going to be president of the United States,' when he was just this country lawyer who couldn't dance. She was from a political family and was incredibly smart and ambitious." She was also self-absorbed, exasperating, and sometimes unhinged, and capable of causing him grief in public as well as in the White House family quarters, as we witness in the film. As First Lady, she accepted bribes, padded expense accounts and payrolls, appropriated wages from White House servants, tried to raid the stationery fund, disguised personal expenses in government bills, helped peddle cotton trading permits, and engaged in other illegal activities.

In December 1839, in Springfield, Illinois, Abraham Lincoln met Mary Todd, who was from a wealthy slave-holding family in Lexington, Kentucky. A wedding set for January 1, 1841, was canceled at Lincoln's initiative. In addition to his mother and his first love, Ann Rutledge, he had lost his sister when he was 19, so perhaps he feared the loss of yet another loved one; in any case, he fell into months of black depression. Abe and Mary later met at a party and married on November 4, 1842, in the Springfield mansion of Mary's married sister. Mary was 23 years old and Abe was 33. While preparing for the nuptials and feeling anxiety again, Lincoln, when asked where he was going, replied, "To hell, I suppose."

In a scene of the movie in Mary's boudoir, when she and Abe are arguing over whether their son Robert should join the army, she mutters at one point: "You've always blamed Robert for being born, for trapping you in a marriage that's only ever given you grief and caused you regret." She's mentioning the belief of some biographers that she trapped Abe into marriage. Friends of both said as much. Robert was born less than nine months after the wedding, which took place after one day's notice. This should in no way devalue her. She was, after all, the woman for whom all three of the leading contenders in the 1860 Presidential contest were former beaux: Stephen A. Douglas, John C. Breckenridge, and Abe.

In that same *Wall Street Journal* interview, Kushner explained, "I think he ran away from Mary because he knew if he married her that she was going to insist that he become who he became. By the 1830s... everybody saw a crisis coming. He knew he was somebody who could step into a position of leadership, and I think it terrified him, as it should have... He had a marriage that was genuinely based on love. He was married to a difficult but enormously impressive woman who adored him and contributed to his life and his success." Many marriages fail after the death of even one child. This marriage survived the deaths of two.

Later in life, Mary struggled with the stresses of losing her husband and 3 of her 4 sons (Tad died at 18 from heart failure). Eventually, Robert Lincoln committed her briefly to a mental asylum in 1875. Kushner and Spielberg have a wonderful scene in which we see how the war president handled the grief over the loss of his favorite son. Abe already had chronic bouts of severe depression, "the hypo," as he called it. When first love Ann Rutledge died of typhoid fever, his resulting depression was so great that friends feared he was suicidal. Like Abe, Mary also lost her mother while still a child, but she hated her stepmother.

The Mary of two time Oscar winner Sally Fields easily measures up to Day-Lewis' Lincoln. Fields and Mary share the same round-faced, worn, plain-prettiness. For faces this familiar it's important the actors have at least a vague resemblance to their characters. David Strathairn has a remarkable resemblance to Secretary of State William Seward, a prosthetic nose would have made them almost indistinguishable. And Bruce McGill is almost as close to the bespectacled, long-bearded Secretary of War Edwin Stanton. Jared Harris actually resembles Sherman more than Grant but Harris is especially fine conveying Grant's gravitas.

Ironically, the biggest disappointment in this area is Day-Lewis. Kushner has him say an actual comment of Lincoln's, "Some weariness has bit at my bones," but we don't see in Day-Lewis that emaciation of the late photographs, the weight of the war manifest in his Lincoln's body. His stoop was so great, though he was only 56, that he joked about becoming "a student of the earth." This lapse on Day-Lewis' part is especially odd in an era when gaining and shedding poundage for a role seems de rigeur for the serious film actor.

In many scenes of this political drama, you are going to hear about Democrats and Republicans. The roles of the Democrats and Republicans have been reversed in our time from what they were then. Just as Southern whites voted solidly against it, black people voted solidly for Lincoln's Republican Party until the 1930s, when Franklin Roosevelt started wooing blacks to the Democrats. Lyndon Johnson's 1964 Civil Rights Act cinched it, so today about 95% of black people vote Democratic.

In the late 1960s, Richard Nixon began implementing the Republican's "Southern Strategy," which took advantage of the white backlash to the Democrats' civil rights reforms. Ronald Reagan continued this strategy when he officially began his 1980 presidential campaign in Philadelphia, Mississippi, an insignificant small town known for only one thing, the torture-murder of three civil rights workers in 1964. The "Southern Strategy" was so successful that today 90% of white Southerners vote Republican. Indeed, the Deep South, the old Confederacy, is the core constituency of today's Republican Party.

And that's how the party of Lincoln became the party of the Confederacy.

After

One of the most damning pieces of evidence for Abraham Lincoln's racism is a quote from one of the late debates with Stephen Douglas, after Douglas had pummeled Lincoln with race baiting. "I am not, nor ever have been, in favor of bringing about in any way the social and political equality of the white and black races," Lincoln said. On the same topic he later wrote: "My own feelings will not admit of this; and if mine would, we well know that those of the great mass of white people will not. Whether this feeling accords with justice and sound judgment, is not the sole question.... A universal feeling, whether well or ill founded, cannot be safely disregarded." He was pushed to say these things, and in the latter quote, one can sense his reluctance, but there is no reason not to take him, of all people, at his word. Kushner overtly and courageously brings up Lincoln's racism near the end when Lincoln, stunningly, mentions extending the vote to "some colored men, the intelligent, the educated, and veterans."

Historian Garry Wills, whose *Lincoln at Gettysburg* (1993) won the Pulitzer, wrote "Abraham Lincoln was born into a racist family, in a racist region of our country, during a racist era of our history. It would have been amazing if he had not begun his life as a racist... He did not really know any educated blacks until he became acquainted, near his death, with Frederick Douglass... [Lincoln] became less and less racist, ending up almost entirely free of prejudice by his death."

Lincoln twice invited Douglass to the White House for private consultations and also invited him to tea at the Lincolns' summer cottage. Douglass wrote that in these meetings he discovered "a deeper moral conviction against slavery than I had ever seen before in anything spoken or written by him... In his company I was never in any way reminded of my humble origin, or of my unpopular color." At the Second Inaugural Ball, Douglass was barred from entering because of his race. When Lincoln found out about it, he got him in. Douglass then entered the East Room, and as he approached Lincoln, the latter said loud enough so all could hear, "Here comes my friend Douglass!" When they shook hands, Lincoln asked Douglass what he had thought of Lincoln's speech earlier in the day. Lincoln added, "There is no man in the country whose opinion I value more than yours."

Another scene in our movie that touches on Lincoln's racism is his conversation with Mrs. Keckley, the ex-slave who was Mary Lincoln's dressmaker and confidante (and the founder of the Contraband Relief Association which helped ex-slaves and wounded soldiers). This scene is ill conceived and makes Lincoln far too evasive and hesitant about accepting black people after final emancipation. That conversation with Mrs. Keckley would have been only weeks from the above scene with Frederick Douglass at the Inaugural Ball.

In the climactic scene concerning Lincoln's racism, there is no mention of black people at all. It is instead an impromptu late night lecture on Euclid to two young telegraphers, who are as bewildered by it as we are at first. What we are witnessing in this scene is Lincoln grappling with his own racism, using his own iron-jawed logic (symbolized by the incontrovertible axioms of Euclid, "mathematical reasoning" as Lincoln calls it). "Things which are equal to the same thing are equal to each other," Lincoln vehemently declares. He doesn't explain himself because he is talking out loud to himself. Nevertheless, we know in this context what the things are that "are equal to each other." Another clue is Lincoln's comment in the same scene, "Euclid says this is 'self-evident.' " Like the truths the Declaration of Independence calls "self-evident," such as "that all men are created equal." This scene is a brilliant and subtle set piece, a triumph of the playwright over the screenwriter. When Lincoln rode the judicial circuit, he carried a copy of Euclid in his saddlebags for sharpening his logic.

Lincoln was always the political chess master; his true motives for anything could be mixed and/or highly calculated. Friend and Illinois Senator Lyman Trumbull observed that Lincoln "communicated no more of his own thoughts and purposes than he thought would subserve the ends he had in view." Lincoln's secretaries Nicolay and Hay (both omnipresent in the movie but in the background) once observed that "to measure right [Lincoln's] utterances ..." the surrounding "conditions ... must continually be kept in mind." An example is the time Lincoln invited a committee of free blacks from the District of Columbia for a meeting at the White House, where he lectured them, blunt to the point of rudeness, about the virtues of colonization abroad for freed slaves.

This would have been uncharacteristic and unconscionable except that the black leaders were not the real audience of his lecture, indeed they were just props. Lincoln had also invited a stenographer from the *New York Tribune* to record his words knowing they would be published around the country. Lincoln was using racism strategically to prepare public opinion for the Emancipation Proclamation, which he had decided on but hadn't announced. Promoting colonization he believed was the best way to defuse anti-emancipation sentiment.

Our film explores new territory for Hollywood not only by dramatizing the minutiae of Congressional politics in that era but also the gradations and variations of Northern racism in that era. Remember in the movie Mr. and Mrs. Jolly of Jefferson City, Missouri, who visited Lincoln in his office? The Jolly's scene is wholly invented, as is their congressman, "Beanpole" Burton. At one point in the scene, Seward exclaims, "The people!" and that of course is exactly who the Jollys represent, the real target audience of Lincoln's meeting with that committee of free black leaders.

We get a good dose of the Jollys' racism in their concerns about freed slaves: "some Alabama coon" coming north and stealing chickens and jobs. Alexis de Tocqueville observed that "the prejudice of race appears to be stronger in the states which have abolished slavery than in those where it still exists; and nowhere is it so important as in those states where servitude never has been known."

Probably the worst outbreak of Northern racism ever was the New York City Draft Riots of July 13–16, 1863. Working-class Irish immigrants were reacting to a new draft law. They resented that wealthy men could hire a draft substitute for $300 ($5,555 in 2014 dollars) and they resented fighting to free slaves. Soon this anti-draft protest turned into a racist white mob attacking blacks wherever they could be found. At least 11 black people were killed. Public buildings were destroyed, plus two Protestant churches, and the homes of abolitionists and black people. The Colored Orphan Asylum was burned to the ground. The army restored order.

Lincoln had to always be cognizant of that racism so dominant in the Northern electorate. That racism was also highlighted in the scene in our film where Thaddeus Stevens made an agonizing concession to it in Congress, disavowing racial equality, of the kind we take for granted today, in order to pass the amendment killing slavery. Stevens is a link between this film and its predecessor of almost a century, the viciously racist *Birth of a Nation* (1915), in which Stevens is a villain. Spielberg and Kushner make him a pragmatic radical whose position is celebrated, turning *Lincoln* into an overt repudiation of *Birth of a Nation*. One of Stevens' last lines in *Lincoln*, "The greatest measure of the nineteenth century was passed by corruption, aided and abetted by the purest man in America," is an actual quote attributed to Thaddeus Stevens though by a dubious source. However, it is an excellent distillation of the story in the movie.

Historians were all over this movie like ants on jelly. Rather than quote from all of the upset historians, we'll just quote one of the most eminent, Eric Foner, whose *The Fiery Trial: Abraham Lincoln and American Slavery* won the 2011 Pulitzer Prize, the Bancroft Prize, and the Lincoln Prize. He said of the film, "Emancipation—like all far-reaching political change—resulted from events at all levels of society, including the efforts of social movements to change public sentiment and of slaves themselves to acquire freedom... The film grossly exaggerates the possibility that by January 1865 the war might have ended with slavery still intact. The Emancipation Proclamation had already declared more than three million of the four million slaves free."

None of the congressional floor exchanges from the movie match the official record. There is one scene that needs special mention because of how grossly it violates the historical record as well as logic, and that is when Lincoln slaps his son in full view of busy Washington sidewalks. The Lincolns were notorious as parents for *not* disciplining their children, and Robert had a reputation for being deferential and respectful toward his parents. But the President of the United States loses his self-control on a public thoroughfare and nobody notices? Just as the Thirteenth Amendment has to carry the symbolic flag in the film for Lincoln's lifelong quest to end slavery, so the arguments of this one married couple over whether their child should fight in the war crystallizes the fears of a generation. Lincoln awkwardly alludes to this in that same scene in which Robert is slapped.

The film has it right that Robert was present, as a member of Grant's staff, for Lee's surrender at Appomattox. He would later serve as Secretary of War in two Republican administrations, and though he was not present for his father's, Robert was present for the assassinations of both Presidents Garfield and McKinley. At age 79, he spoke at the dedication ceremonies for the Lincoln Memorial in 1922.

Those three political operatives under Secretary of State Seward were known as the "Seward Lobby." They were not the shady characters they are in the film, and rather than buying the votes of lame-duck Democrats with patronage in Washington, they spent most of their time in New York, trying to persuade the editors of influential Democratic newspapers and the state's Democratic governor to send signals that would allow wavering lame-duck Democrats to switch their votes. Also, the First Lady was not sitting in the gallery during the final vote on the amendment, or at any other time for that matter.

The Constitution stipulates that after amendments have been passed by the U.S. Congress, they must be passed by the state legislatures, twenty of which acted immediately in passing the Thirteenth Amendment. By the end of 1865, the requisite three quarters of the states had finally and forever closed the door on American slavery.

Near the end of the film, there is a scene with Lincoln slowly riding horseback with a Union cavalry detachment across a battlefield immediately after a battle. He is on his way to meet Grant at Petersburg, just outside Richmond, Virginia, the Confederate capitol, which will fall later that day, April 3, 1865, signaling the end of the war, as the fall of a capitol usually does. In this battlefield scene, Spielberg is leading us back to the opening scene of the film and to the reality behind the previous two hours of political wrangling: heaped bodies of young men and boys who suffered horribly then died.

What the Union soldiers died for, ultimately, was democracy itself, the success of the American experiment, proof that a democratic government was viable. That was the meaning of Lincoln's obsession with saving the Union. Saving the Union was saving democracy itself. That is the stirring conclusion of his and the country's most famous speech, the Gettysburg Address. "We here highly resolve... that government of the people, by the people, for the people, shall not perish from the earth." In a message to Congress, he declared, "We shall nobly save, or meanly lose, the last, best hope of earth."

At a time when the U.S. was the only true democracy in the world, it was also the largest slaveholding country in the world. "The monstrous injustice of slavery," Lincoln had said back in 1854, "deprives our republican example of its just influence in the world—enables the enemies of free institutions, with plausibility, to taunt us as hypocrites." A Union sergeant from Ohio wrote in his diary that the war must be prosecuted "for the great principles of liberty and self government at stake, for should we fail, the onward march of Liberty in the Old World will be retarded at least a century, and Monarchs, Kings, and Aristocrats will be more powerful against their subjects than ever."

Regarding the historical accuracy of *Lincoln*, Kushner said, ""The rule was that we wouldn't alter anything in a meaningful way from what happened... None of the key moments of that story—the overarching story our film tells—are altered." As mentioned before, filmmakers are constantly balancing the demands of visual story telling with those of historical accuracy, and our film ends on a particularly potent example.

In *Lincoln*, photographer Alexander Gardner has loaned Lincoln's young son Tad glass negatives of photographs of slaves, some of whom have been brutalized and are scarred. Critical historians have pointed out that Gardner did not take those particular photos, and besides, he wasn't likely to risk damage to or loss of irreplaceable glass negatives by loaning them to a child. However, in exchange for these minor historical and logical infractions, Kushner and Spielberg are able to introduce into a movie that takes place mainly in the White House and the halls of Congress, the gruesome reality of slavery, in the most indelible manner possible under the circumstances and using actual artifacts.

The images on the glass negatives are discussed once but shown twice: the first time, when Lincoln holds them up to the flames in a fireplace, and the second time, when Tad holds them up to a candle flame. Much later, an extreme close-up of a candle flame transitions us from the deathbed scene to the film's last scene, the Second Inaugural Address. Previously, a candle flame backlit images of black people as property, now, with victory in sight and the Thirteenth Amendment passed, we see scattered among the crowd on the platform behind the president, black people, no longer property but Americans. In reality, there were no black people on that platform, though they were present in large numbers among the audience of 40,000. By fading on the Second Inaugural Address, Kushner and Spielberg end bringing us full circle from another one of the beginnings of the film, that conversation between Lincoln and Union soldiers that highlighted the Gettysburg Address. Those are the two speeches on the walls of the Lincoln Memorial.

It's pretty hard to be an American and not revere Lincoln, so it isn't too surprising that in *Birth of a Nation* he is a sympathetic character. It was part of Lost Cause mythology that if he hadn't been assassinated he would have prevented the "excesses" of the abolitionist radicals in Congress during Reconstruction. Ironically, there is some truth to that.

Reconstruction policy was the greatest cause of division among Republicans in early 1865, not the Thirteenth Amendment, as in the movie. Conservatives were pitted against radicals regarding not only the future of ex-slaves but also ex-Confederates. Lincoln held a moderate view of Reconstruction, as we see in that scene where he and Thaddeus Stevens have their secret meeting in the White House kitchen, and Stevens begins by laying-out his radical vision of Reconstruction, which Lincoln challenges.

Reconstruction was the period from 1865 to 1877 during which the states that had seceded were "reconstructed" by the federal government before being readmitted to the Union. In some respects, Reconstruction was the continuation of the politics of slavery post-abolition. The image of Reconstruction pro-mulgated in *Birth of a Nation* was the accepted one for most of the twentieth century: an orgy of black misrule and exploitation of victimized Southern whites. The research of recent decades has turned all that on its head.

Just before the war ended, Congress created the Freedmen's Bureau to aid ex-slaves and white refugees by providing food, clothing, and fuel. It also taught ex-slaves to read and write, helped locate lost family members, and advised them on negotiating labor contracts. Without deference to a person's color, the Bureau leased and sold parcels of confiscated land.

Immediately after the end of the war, the all-white state governments of the former Confederacy tried to reintroduce slavery in all but name with laws called "black codes" that greatly restricted freedmen's rights. By fall 1865, the new Democratic President Andrew Johnson declared the war goals of national unity and the end of slavery achieved and reconstruction completed, but Republicans in Congress rebelled.

The black codes and Southern violence against ex-slaves seemed to be making a mockery of the sacrifice of Union sons, so the election of 1866 gave the Radical Republicans veto-proof majorities in both houses of Congress and this began what is called "Radical Reconstruction." Congress put the former Confederacy under the rule of the U.S. Army, which conducted new elections in which the freed slaves voted and in which former Confederate leaders could not run for office. During this period also, Congress initiated impeachment proceedings against Andrew Johnson for his obstructionism and failed by only one vote to remove him from office.

In nearly all the Southern states, biracial state governments were formed by coalitions of ex-slaves, plus recent black and white arrivals from the North (called "carpetbaggers" by white southerners), and white Southerners who supported Reconstruction ("scalawags"). Those biracial state governments introduced various Reconstruction programs including: the South's first public schools, new charitable institutions, they raised taxes, and improved railroads.

Conservative opponents called the biracial governments corrupt and began committing acts of terrorist violence against supporters of those governments such as beatings, shootings, burnings, and lynchings. Much of the violence was carried out by members of the Ku Klux Klan, a mounted death squad in mardi gras costumes. The KKK was only one of numerous terrorist organizations entrenched in nearly every Southern state by 1870; such as, the White League, the Red Shirts (presaging the Black and Brown Shirts of 1920s European Fascism), and the Knights of the White Camellia. The latter killed, in Louisiana alone, more than two thousand people, most of them black, during the three years between the war's end and Grant's election to the presidency.

In 1870 and 1871, Congress enacted laws to enforce the provisions of the Fourteenth Amendment (which gave citizenship to ex-slaves) and Fifteenth Amendment (which gave them the vote). President Grant enforced these laws with federal marshals and federal courts backed by federal troops when necessary. Federal grand juries handed down more than three thousand indictments. Only a few hundred of the guilty thousands were convicted and punished, but that was enough to hold down the Klan for a while. As a consequence, blacks voted in solid numbers, and the 1872 election was the fairest and most democratic presidential election in the South until 1968.

The fate of Reconstruction had always depended heavily and ultimately on popular support in the North, which was gradually dwindling. In 1873, violence flared up across the South again. A backlash in the exhausted electorate to Reconstruction and to an economy in depression following the Panic of 1873, gave Democrats control of the U.S. House of Representatives in the election of 1874. White Democrats, calling themselves "Redeemers", gradually regained control of the South state by state, frequently using fraud and violence to control elections.

Then, in the 1876 presidential election, Democrat Samuel J. Tilden won the popular vote but Republican Rutherford B. Hayes won in the Electoral College. In a backroom deal, Hayes promised to withdraw troops from the South in exchange for the Democrats accepting a Republican victory. Thus the "Compromise of 1877" ended Reconstruction and left in place a racist Southern terror state that would survive into the 1960s. In practical terms, the end of Reconstruction meant the former slaves lost all civil and political rights for nearly a century, and economically were placed in a more efficient form of slavery called "sharecropping," in which farmers paid rent with a percentage of their harvest and were never out of debt to their employers.

Eric Foner maintains that the driving force behind Reconstruction was not vengeance against former Confederates as the latter contended, but a "utopian vision," and that Reconstruction was "a massive experiment in interracial democracy without precedent in the history of this or any other country." Also, Reconstruction defined the federal government's role in protecting and promoting civil rights, which would be important during the civil rights movement of the 1950s and 60s, sometimes referred to as the Second Reconstruction.

The Civil War wiped out two thirds of the assessed wealth in the Confederacy, most of it in human beings. Two fifths of Confederate livestock were killed and more than half of its farm machinery destroyed, not to mention the destruction of railroads, bridges, factories, and even cities. Plus one quarter of the Confederacy's white men of military age were dead. From 1860 to 1870, while Southern wealth decreased by more than 60 percent, Northern wealth increased by 50 percent.

During the war, the absence in the U.S. Congress of obstructionist Southern conservatives made possible a whole host of accomplishments, which were enough to make Lincoln an important president aside from the Civil War. He signed the Homestead Act in 1862, making millions of acres of government land in the West available for purchase at little or no cost. The Morrill Land-Grant Colleges Act, also signed in 1862, provided government grants for agricultural colleges in each state. The Pacific Railway Acts of 1862 and 1864 granted federal support for the construction of the United States' first transcontinental railroad.

Also, Lincoln signed the Revenue Act of 1861, creating the first U.S. income tax, and the National Banking Act, which created a system of national banks. Lincoln is largely responsible for the institution of the Thanksgiving holiday. In June 1864, he approved unprecedented federal protection for the area now known as Yosemite National Park.

The Homestead Act and the Pacific Railway Acts also were major contributing factors to the creation of the mythical "Wild West," the setting for our next movie, *Little Big Man.*

Reconstruction Timeline

1863
Jan 1 Emancipation Proclamation is signed
1865
Mar 3 Freedmen's Bureau is established
Apr 9 Lee surrenders at Appomattox
Apr 14 John Wilkes Booth shoots President Lincoln, Andrew Johnson becomes
the 17th president.
Nov 1 Southern legislatures begin drafting "Black Codes" to reestablish white
supremacy.
Dec 1 President Johnson declares the reconstruction process complete.
Outraged Radical Republicans in Congress refuse to recognize new
Southern state governments.
Dec 18 13th Amendment is ratified by the states, prohibiting slavery.
Dec 24 Ku Klux Klan begins; the first of many secret terrorist organizations in
the South for reestablishing white supremacy.
1866
Apr 9 Congress passes a Civil Rights Bill over Johnson's veto.
May   For three days in Memphis, Tennessee, white mobs killed 48 people,
nearly all black, and injured many more, plus destroyed hundreds of
black homes, churches, and schools.
July 30 In New Orleans, a white mob attacks blacks and Radical Republicans
attending a black suffrage convention, killing 40 people.
Nov   Republicans win well over a two-thirds majority in the House of Repre-
sentatives and the Senate. The election is seen as a popular referendum
on the widening divide between Johnson and the Radicals.
1867
Mar 2 Congress passes the first series of Reconstruction Acts and
Congressional, or "Radical" Reconstruction, commences.
Mar 23 Under the Second Reconstruction Act, Army commanders in each
Southern district register all qualified adult males to vote regardless of
race.
1868
May 16 President Andrew Johnson avoids removal from office by one vote in
Senate impeachment proceedings.
Jul 28 The Fourteenth Amendment is ratified, granting citizenship to ex-slaves.
Aug 11 Thaddeus Stevens dies and at his own request is buried in
an African American cemetery.
Sep 28 In the Opelousas Massacre in Louisiana, 200 to 300 black
Americans are killed.
1869
Freedmen's Bureau creates the first public school system in the
South with nearly 3,000 schools serving over 150,000 students.
1870
Feb 3 The Fifteenth Amendment to the Constitution is ratified guaranteeing
universal male suffrage is now the law of the land.
1871
Apr 1 Congress passes the Ku Klux Klan Act, the first time that specific crimes

141

committed by individuals are deemed punishable by federal law.

1872

Nov 1 Landslide reelection of U. S. Grant. He invites black people
to the inaugural ball for the first time in American history.

1873

"Panic of 1873" is a financial panic and depression after 89 of the
country's 364 railroads go bankrupt. 18,000 businesses fail in the
next two years.

1874

Democrats gain control of the U.S. House of Representatives and
several governorships of northern states.

1877

Inspite of losing the popular vote, Republican Rutherford B. Hayes
wins presidential election through a backroom deal with Southern
Democrats. Almost immediately, Hayes withdraws federal troops
from the South, ending Reconstruction.

Recommendations

Spielberg's *Lincoln* is unquestionably the best film about Lincoln, but there are two other notable films both of which focus on the years before the presidency, so they somewhat complement our movie.

Young Mr. Lincoln (1939) is a cinematic folk song. It was directed by John Ford and starred a young Henry Fonda, and within a year of its completion, Ford and Fonda would be working together on one of the crowning achievements of American cinema, *The Grapes of Wrath* (1940) (with its title from the abolitionist marching song, "Battle Hymn of the Republic"). Russian director and film theorist Sergei Eisenstein wrote of *Young Mr. Lincoln* in 1945, "It immediately enthralled me with the perfection of its harmony, and the rare skill with which it employed all the expressive means at its disposal." Cahiers du Cinéma, the leading French film magazine, devoted an entire issue to the film in 1970.

Young Mr. Lincoln is Lincoln Hollywoodized (right down to a comical sidekick, standard issue for the cowboy movie hero at the time). Nevertheless, the main characters are all there from Lincoln's early manhood in 1830s Illinois, and the film is set against a richly detailed mural of American society in that era including omnipresent alcoholism. The latter is memorably highlighted by a trial judge's demand of the spectators, "Put them jugs away!!" The murder trial takes its plot and crucial details from an actual case in which Lincoln was attorney for the defense, and which he won, as in the movie, using an almanac to discredit a key witness. However, he was not at the beginning but many years into his career and marriage. Also, in the film, he takes a few coins from the poor mother of the defendant, but in life, he refused payment from her.

But did Lincoln stand in a jailhouse door single-handed against a mob trying to lynch innocent boys? And did he then disarm the mob with his wit? Well sir, no, not exactly... but his Secretary of the Treasury, Salmon P. Chase, did once brace himself in a doorway and face down a pro-slavery mob trying to get at an abolitionist editor. 'Zat close enuff fer ya?

Abe Lincoln in Illinois came out in 1940 after WWII had already started in Europe. The film is based on White House speech writer Robert Sherwood's popular and critical Broadway success of the same name, which won the Pulitzer Prize. The play was written during a period of rising Nazi aggression in Europe, so for 1930s audiences the Slave Power was, appropriately enough, a stand-in for Nazi Germany. Raymond Massey, for whom Sherwood had written the title role, told an interviewer in the Thirties, "If you substitute the word 'dictatorship' for the word 'slavery' throughout Sherwood's script, it becomes electric for our time."

It's not a very good film. Nevertheless, it presents some crucial and reasonably accurate scenes of the life and the political career: from the characterization of the parents to the Ann Rutledge affair, and from his first campaign speech to the Lincoln-Douglas Debates. The latter are especially well-handled, though some of Lincoln's lines are from speeches and not the debates. Still slavery is front and center, while in *Young Mr. Lincoln,* it is only mentioned once and fleetingly. The banners, placards, and songs of the presidential campaign in *Abe Lincoln in Illinois* are accurate. There is even a short sympathetic scene of a surrendering John Brown linking him to Lincoln.

Raymond Massey would later play an unsympathetic John Brown in two other movies. Massey's Lincoln in this movie is stiff, stilted, and gloomy, and his wit has none of Lincoln's bite (Kushner's Lincoln is actually very funny). Mary is given the right degree of intellect and ambition, at least until after the marriage, after which she is trivialized into a pathological shrew. His lack of ambition is probably the single biggest flaw in the Lincoln of *Abe Lincoln in Illinois*. Billy Herndon, his last law partner and a major character in this film, said, "[Lincoln's] ambition was a little engine that knew no rest." This movie's Lincoln is reluctantly dragged by Mary's ambition when in fact his easily matched hers.

In 1988, TV attempted a short mini series (three hours), *Gore Vidal's Lincoln,* based on Gore Vidal's novel *Lincoln* (1984), discussed in detail on escalloniapress.com. This film provides the fullest cinematic presentation yet of the presidency and is a faithful and skillful adaptation of the novel, with its flaws, too cynical, and it virtues, subtle political understanding. It is a big sprawling nineteenth century novel wound around the Lincoln marriage and presidency with historical characters and historical events, many of which, though integral to the novel, feel tacked-on and extraneous in the movie because they are not developed enough.

Robert Mulligan as Seward is fine, as is the redoubtable James Gammon (Zachary Taylor in *One Man's Hero*) as Grant, and John Houseman, head embedded in white whiskers, is awesome as the elderly General Winfield Scott. But too much of the rest of the acting is just industrial-strength TV and worse. Sam Waterston, a fine actor, was horribly miscast as Lincoln. He's far too spry;

though he was close to Lincoln's age, he looks and moves as if ten years younger. He can't settle on an accent, and though he has the folksy charm down, he is completely devoid of the single most important characteristic, gravitas. Mary Tyler Moore's Mary is better, but still woefully short of Sally Fields'. Indeed, Spielberg's *Lincoln* makes an already disappointing *Gore Vidal's Lincoln* look even worse.

Robert Redford directed but did not appear in *The Conspirator* (2010), about the plot to assassinate Lincoln, and the plot's only female member, Mary Surratt. The film looks good, the period detail is fine, and the acting and the script are sound; however, the film asks us to sympathize with someone who may not have known about the conspiracy unfolding around her, but given her sympathies, not knowing about it was almost a technicality. After her execution, the Supreme Court held that her Constitutional rights were violated because she was tried by a military tribunal and not a civilian court. While there are no small breaches of the Constitution, in the context of the Lincoln assassination, does this particular breach deserve its own movie?

As for movies about Reconstruction, *Sommersby* (1993) is more Southern white suffering but with a unique and welcome twist. It's partially based on a French film, which was based on a true story, of a returning soldier who poses as someone with whom he shared a cell in a military prison. Our film has reworked the story for the South in the early hopeful years of Reconstruction, so it features scenes of Eric Foner's "utopian vision" of biracial cooperation. There is even a black trial judge played by the venerable James Earl Jones.

The film has plenty of the racist reaction to that utopian vision, from the first minutes, when we see the feet of two lynched blacks and transfixed children staring up at them. Plus, there is a late night visit from the already-mentioned Knights of the White Camellia, guilty of thousands of racist murders. As he is dragged from the witness stand, a White Camellia member says to the black judge, "In two years when the Yankees are gone, you'll be back in the field where you belong." The period detail is excellent as are the direction and much of the acting. The core of the film is a love story featuring a luminous Jodie Foster opposite Richard Gere (also the film's producer).

Unfortunately, by the time of the clever but unconvincing court-room climax, all logic and plausibility have long departed the convoluted plot, so we feel cheated of our time. Plus the title character is not sufficiently explained. How did a con man and thief become a sensitive, liberal, visionary businessman willing to sacrifice his life for others? We haven't a clue. A better actor than Gere could have suggested a depth and mystery that would have helped. The film has the feel, in part at least, of a Gere vanity project.

The made-for-TV movie *Freedom Road* (1979) was based on a 1944 novel of the same name by our old friend Howard Fast, author of *The Crossing* about George Washington. *Freedom Road* is the best novel by far about Reconstruction. The movie was directed by Czechoslovak exile and Oscar winner Jan Kadar, a former professor of film in Prague, who trained most of the directors of the famous Czechoslovak New Wave of the 1960s. But the film's biggest draw is its star: boxing champion Muhammad Ali. And he is also its biggest drawback. It's not just his zombie-like walk-through as the main character but his familiar face is a distraction. With a good actor at its center, this might have been a good film, but as it is, it's unwatchable.

You have just watched a movie about congressional political machinations, now just for grins, watch a movie about the same thing set a century after the events in *Lincoln*. In *Advise and Consent* (1962) the movie is contemporaneous with the period in which the novel and movie were made. The subject is congressional approval of a Secretary of State and not the passage of a law; nevertheless, the contrast would be instructive. It is a showcase of the top acting talent of the time, plus it is based on the Pulitzer Prize-winning novel of the same name by Allen Drury. The movie won the top prize, the Palme d'Or, at that year's Cannes Film festival.

There are numerous fine documentaries about Lincoln. From the American Experience series comes PBS's *The Assassination of Abraham Lincoln (2009)*. It focuses mainly on Booth and his accomplices but there is an excellent thumbnail sketch of the Lincoln presidency at the beginning. Of course, Lincoln is the central character of Ken Burns' *Civil War*, which also contains an excellent thumbnail biography.

For the marriage, however, there is one towering giant among docs, *Abraham and Mary Lincoln: A House Divided* (2001). It is sublime. Part of PBS' the American Experience series also, it was co-written by Geoffrey Ward who co-wrote Ken Burns' *Civil War*. Its narrator is historian David McCullough, who narrated Burns' *Civil War*, and it uses Burns' technique of actors in voice over fleshing-out the principals' quotes, in this case David Morse as Abe and Holly Hunter as Mary, both of whom are extraordinary. Besides presenting a more balanced and detailed picture of the marriage than our movie, it also provides a handy abbreviated version of the war itself. Also, the beginning of the last episode has an excellent encapsulation of the events in Spielberg's *Lincoln*, such that, this section in the 2001 documentary could have been in part an inspiration for the 2012 movie.

For Reconstruction we have *Reconstruction: The Second Civil War* (2005), also part of PBS' American Experience series. Besides providing an overview of the period, it adds to the usual cast of politicians and generals several extraordinary ordinary Americans – ex-slaves turned politicians, ex-Union veterans in the South, former slaveholders, etc. -- and recounts their experiences during Reconstruction.

At www.escalloniapress.com, there are free recommendations of the best books - histories, biographies, memoirs, and even novels - related to the subjects of this chapter.

Chapter 9 – Little Big Man

Before

Little Big Man (1970) is perfect for our purposes. It is based on a novel of the same name which was a post-modernist take on the American genre of the Old West Tall Tale. Author Thomas Berger said he read seventy books on the Old West and then went into a trance to create our hero and narrator, Jack Crabb. It's a tall tale because the fictitious Crabb interacts with many of the famous historical figures of the American Old West. The novel was also a take on the "captivity narrative," stories told by former Indian captives, men and, particularly, women. It was a traditional genre so popular that some books were invented for profit. *Little Big Man* is also a classic "picaresque;" that is, a story depicting in realistic, often humorous detail the adventures of a roguish hero of low social degree living by his wits in a corrupt society.

Jack Crabb will move between the Indian and white world not feeling completely at home in either but feeling the attractions of both. As he moves between these worlds, besides encountering famous historical figures, we will get to see him in the roles of most of the Old West archetypes: pioneer, Indian, cavalry scout, snake-oil salesman, merchant, husband to an immigrant, destitute alcoholic, crazed hermit-trapper, and that most imposing of them all, gunslinger. All of which makes *Little Big Man* perfect for our purposes.

Eyebrows may be raised because of the film's broad humor and sharply critical attitude toward what has been traditionally viewed as a great triumph, "the winning of the west," and also because of some characterizations that verge on cartoonish, Custer's for instance. But *Little Big Man* provides a reasonably accurate feel for the actual historical West, and at the same time, a critical perspective on the mythological West as promulgated by Hollywood, most of which was fictitious, as we will see.

This movie has one of the best performances by one of the all time best American film actors, Dustin Hoffman. He is in every scene and he sets the tone of the movie. Often with no more than his posture, he plays a hapless innocent reminiscent at times of the great silent movie comedians.

This is also one of those rare times when the screenplay improves on the book, in this case a very good book, a minor classic. This movie is also the cinematic masterwork of one of the best practitioners of that craft, director Arthur Penn. And it is one of the quintessential Sixties revisionist movies. Only 8 years before, there was a big epic full of the top stars of the day called *How the West was Won* (1962), an excellent film actually and especially useful for us. Nevertheless, the title expresses the traditional Hollywood attitude of chest-thumping triumphalism which was reinforced by narrator Spencer Tracy's reference to the land being "won ... from primitive man."

Like some other movies in this book, *Little Big Man* itself made history. It was the first sympathetic and historically accurate portrayal of Native Americans that wasn't also overly romanticized. Also, the key character, Old Lodge Skins, was played by an actual Native American, Chief Dan George, a chief of the Tsleil-Waututh Nation of Vancouver. He was nominated for an Academy Award and a Golden Globe.

Our movie premiered in 1970, just two years after U.S. troops massacred possibly as many as 504 unarmed civilians in the village of My Lai during the Vietnam War. The movie's depiction of the Seventh Cavalry's victory at the "Battle of the Washita River" as a massacre of women and children was intended as a comment on My Lai. Jack's Cheyenne wife Sunshine was deliberately cast to look Vietnamese and the ranting lunatic Custer was a comment on the defenders of the Vietnam War.

The film also makes a direct appeal to the hippies, then at their peak, who idolized Native Americans and their culture. The repeated scenes of Jack Crabb seated at the feet of his wise old Indian grandfather, like a disciple with his guru, reflected the spiritual pursuits of the hippies.

There was a print found on the walls of many American homes in the first half or so of the twentieth century titled "The Last Warrior" (there are actually several versions). A dying Indian brave on his pony, both slumped in exhaustion and defeat, are set against a sunset. The print symbolized relief for the removal of this centuries-old mortal threat and guilt for ruthlessly displacing and destroying this noble ancient culture.

There is one big fact you need to know about the history of the indigenous peoples of the U.S.: the U.S. government signed nearly four hundred treaties with the Indians and broke every single one without exception. But then you have known this since early grade school. Out on the playground what did you call someone who took back a gift? Indian giver.

Our story begins in 1859 (a hundred and eleven years before the movie's premiere) when our 121 year old narrator was ten and surprisingly the film opens on a classic scene of the massacre by bloody-thirsty savages of peaceable pioneers crossing the Great Plains. The scene features freshly bleeding corpses, buzzing flies, and burning conestoga wagons (also known as "prairie schooners"). Remember the "New Territories," taken from Mexico in the

U.S.- Mexico War, that caused the Civil War? Well they also caused a westward migration of hundreds of thousands who wanted a free piece of those territories.

The "yeoman farmer" ideal of Jeffersonian democracy was still a powerful influence in American politics during the 1840s–1850s, with many politicians believing a homestead act would help increase the number of "virtuous yeomen." The Free Soil Party of 1848–52, and the new Republican Party after 1854, demanded that the new lands opening up in the west be made available to independent farmers, rather than wealthy planters who would develop it with the use of slaves forcing the yeomen farmers onto marginal lands. Southern Democrats had continually fought (and defeated) previous homestead law proposals, as they feared free land would attract European immigrants and poor Southern whites to the west. As already mentioned, after the South seceded and their conservative delegates left Congress, it passed the Homestead Act of 1862. Anyone who had never taken up arms against the U.S. government and was at least 21 years old or the head of a household (including freed slaves), could file an application to claim a federal land grant. The occupant had to reside on the land for five years and show evidence of having made improvements.

It took Americans a century and a half to expand as far west as the Appalachian Mountains, a few hundred miles from the Atlantic coast. It took another 50 years to push the frontier to the Mississippi River. By 1830, fewer than 100,000 pioneers had crossed the Mississippi. But, from the early to mid 1830s, and particularly through the epoch years 1846–1869, the Oregon Trail and its many offshoots were used by about 400,000 settlers, ranchers, farmers, miners, and businessmen and their families. From the Missouri River, they covered 2,000 miles in six months following the main rivers and crossing mountains to finally arrive in the valleys in Oregon and California. The settlers moved in large groups under an experienced wagon master, bringing their clothing, farm supplies, and animals.

The most famous wagon train, and a monument to the hazards of the westward migration, was the Donner Party, a group of 87 American pioneers who in 1846 set off from Missouri in a wagon train headed west for California, only to find themselves trapped by snow in the Sierra Nevadas. The subsequent casualties resulting from starvation, exposure, disease, and trauma were extremely high, and many of the survivors resorted to cannibalism.

After that opening scene, we see a ten year old orphaned Crabb get adopted by the Cheyenne Indians and finding it idyllic. If that seems romanticized remember that, as mentioned earlier, the Puritans felt threatened enough by the phenomenon of whites joining Indians that they made it a capital offence. Speaking of Puritans, you'll meet a type of Indian called a "heemanay," what we would call a drag queen. He represents Indian acceptance of homosexuality, an attitude of these heathens that still hasn't reached vast sections of America today.

Our film takes place during what were called the Plains Indian Wars which occurred from 1862 to 1890, the last phase of a conflict going back, as we saw in *The New World*, to Jamestown in 1607. This film climaxes with the most famous battle of and the Indians' greatest victory in the Plains Indian Wars, the Battle of Little Big Horn, "popularly known as 'Custer's Last Stand' " as Jack Crabb puts it. Conflicts between Indians and Europeans are generally separated into two categories: the Indian wars east of the Mississippi River and the Indian wars west of the Mississippi. Our film and this chapter will deal mostly with the latter.

Those east of the Mississippi began with white migration into the Southeastern United States in the 1820s to the 1830s. The new Democratic Party of President Andrew Jackson demanded removal of the Indians out of the southeastern states into new lands in the west, and the party prevailed and that caused the "Trail of Tears" that we learned about it in Chapter Five.

West of the Mississippi, in the Apache Wars, Colonel Christopher "Kit" Carson, one of the most famous names of the Old West, forced the Mescalero Apache onto a reservation in 1862. In 1863-1864, Carson used a scorched earth policy in the Navajo Campaign, burning Navajo fields and homes, and capturing or killing their livestock. In the Red River War of 1874-75, the U.S. army forced the Comanche to return to their reservation by killing their horses. The last Comanche war chief, Quanah Parker, surrendered in June 1875.

Red Cloud's War was led by the Lakota (Sioux) chief Red Cloud against the military who were erecting forts along the Bozeman Trail. It was the most successful campaign against the U.S. during the Indian Wars. In the Treaty of Fort Laramie (1868), the U.S. granted a large reservation to the Lakota, without military presence; it included the entire Black Hills. But the land would be taken from them as soon as gold was discovered on it.

In 1877, the Nez Perce under Chief Joseph, unwilling to give up their traditional lands and move to a reservation, undertook a 1,200 mile fighting retreat from Oregon to near the Canadian border in Montana. Numbering only 200 warriors, the Nez Perce battled some 2,000 American regulars and volunteers of different military units, together with their Indian auxiliaries of many tribes, in a total of eighteen engagements, including four major battles and at least four fiercely contested skirmishes. The Nez Perce were finally surrounded at the Battle of Bear Paw and surrendered.

Many of the Apache had been at war with the Spanish and Mexicans for almost three centuries when the US annexed present-day Arizona and New Mexico in 1848. The U.S. finally induced the last hostile Apache band under Geronimo to surrender in 1886.

Captain Jack was a chief of the Modoc tribe of California and Oregon, and was their leader during the Modoc War. With 53 Modoc warriors, Captain Jack held off 1,000 men of the U.S. Army for 7 months.

In the opening scene of *Little Big Man*, the treatment of the Indians by the U.S. is characterized by the historian interviewing Jack Crabb as "genocide ... the extermination of an entire people." That extermination was incremental, atrocity-by-atrocity, and this was nowhere more apparent than at the end of the westward migration in California.

The human and environmental costs of the Gold Rush were substantial. Native Americans, dependent on traditional hunting, gathering, and agriculture, became the victims of starvation, as gravel, silt, and toxic chemicals from mining operations killed fish and destroyed habitats. Starvation often provoked the Native tribes to steal or take by force food and livestock from the miners, increasing miner hostility and provoking retaliation against the Indians.

As they did everywhere else in the hemisphere, Native Americans in California also succumbed in large numbers to introduced diseases such as smallpox, influenza and measles with some estimates as high as an 80–90% mortality rate. But the Gold Rush also produced an unprecedented amount of casual violence practiced on California Indians by miners and settlers. Sexual assaults on Native women were quite common. Retribution attacks on solitary miners would result in large scale massacres of Indian populations without regard for age or sex. These "attacks of reprisal" often targeted tribes or villages completely innocent of the original act. When Europeans had finally made it across the continent, that "extermination" had become recreational genocide.

Peter Burnett, California's first governor, declared that California was a battleground between the races and that there were only two options for California Indians, extinction or removal. Northern California newspapers openly called for extermination. The Act for the Government and Protection of Indians, passed on April 22, 1850 by the California Legislature, provided the basis for the enslavement and trafficking in Native American labor, particularly that of young women and children, which was carried on as a legal business enterprise. Native American villages were regularly raided to supply the demand, and young women and children were carried off to be sold, the men and remaining people often being killed. The State of California also paid out $25,000 in bounties for Indian scalps with varying prices for adult male, adult female, and child sizes.

The Native American population in California, estimated at 150,000 in 1845, had dropped to less than 30,000 by 1870. (The pre-European population of Native Americans, estimated at 300,000, had already been decimated due to diseases carried by Spanish settlers.) An estimated 4,500 were murdered. As evidence of how much attitudes have changed in rural Northern California over a century, in two separate incidents in the late 1980s and early 1990s, two Native American men with criminal records killed on-duty sheriff's deputies, and after a change of venue, had initial convictions reversed in retrials.

It is a measure of the fairness and even-handedness of this movie that it opens with a classic example of "Indian savagery." It doesn't deny that the

Indians were capable of savagery, it just balances things out with the savagery of the whites. The latter occurs fairly early in the movie when the Cheyenne find a village that has been wiped out by the U.S. Army and the Cheyenne chief, Old Lodge Skins, declares that they "must teach a lesson to these white savages." But that massacre by the U.S. Army is a minor prelude to the real and famous one that bends the movie in half.

The movie's portrayal of the "Battle of Washita River," a Custer-led massacre of women and children in the snow, is accurate right down to the tune played by the regimental band, "Garry Owen," (armies liked to carry along their own live sound track in those days).

George Armstrong Custer was once convicted of desertion and mistreatment of soldiers, and suspended from rank and command for one year. Ten months into his punishment, in September 1868, General Philip Sheridan (Union hero of the Civil War and author of the famous dictum, "The only good Indian is a dead Indian") reinstated Custer in order to lead a campaign against the Cheyenne who had been making raids in Kansas and Oklahoma that summer.

Custer, born in 1839, graduated last in his class at West Point. But, as Jack Crabb explains to his Cheyenne Grandfather about Custer, "in the war of the whites to free the black men," Custer earned a reputation for reckless bravery and became one of the heroes of the Union army. He fought at Gettysburg and was present at Robert E. Lee's surrender at Appomattox. After the Civil War, Custer was dispatched to the west to fight in the Indian Wars.

On a November dawn in 1868, Custer attacked a large village of Cheyenne encamped near the Washita River. Custer did not attempt to identify which group of Cheyenne was in the village, or to make even a cursory reconnaissance of the situation. Had he done so, Custer would have discovered that they were peaceful people and the village was on reservation soil, where it was guaranteed safety. There was even a white flag flying from one of the main dwellings, indicating that the tribe was actively avoiding conflict.

Outnumbered and caught unaware, scores of Cheyenne were killed in the first 15 minutes of the "battle." Though a small number of the warriors managed to escape to the trees and return fire, within a few hours, the village was destroyed--the soldiers had killed 103 Cheyenne, including the peaceful Chief Black Kettle and many women and children.

The same year as *Little Big Man, Soldier Blue* came out, a slight film except for an ending that gave it some notoriety because it depicts with gory detail of a massacre of Cheyenne similar to the "Washita Massacre." The "Sand Creek Massacre" occurred four years before the Washita Massacre and also involved the hapless Chief Black Kettle. On November 28, 1864, Colonel John Chivington, "the Fighting Parson," ordered his 800 troops, who had drunk heavily along the way, to attack a Cheyenne band at their winter camp on Sand Creek. One officer, Captain Silas Soule, refused to follow Chivington's order and told his men to hold fire. Other soldiers in Chivington's force, however, immediately attacked the village. An estimated 200 Indians were killed and mutilated, mostly women, children, and elderly men. Chivington and his men decorated their weapons, hats, and equipment with scalps and other body parts, including fetuses and male and female genitalia. They also publicly displayed these battle trophies in the Apollo Theater and saloons in Denver.

Fifteen U.S. soldiers were killed in the attack and more than fifty wounded, mostly by friendly fire from drunk fellow soldiers. There was public outcry and congressional investigations but nothing came of it. The story of Indian mistreatment was not just a story of white savagery but of civilized whites not taking that savagery seriously enough to force a stop to it. Incidentally, there is also an unnamed massacre in *Little Big Man* besides that on the Washita River. That has been mistaken for Chivington's "Sand Creek Massacre," but it is simply supposed to be a generic white massacre of Indian civilians.

The "Battle of Washita River" was hailed as the first substantial American victory in the Plains Indian Wars. However, Custer's habit of boldly charging Indian encampments of unknown strength would eventually lead him to his death at the Battle of the Little Bighorn. That battle was part of The Great Sioux War of 1876-77 conducted by the Lakota under Sitting Bull and Crazy Horse. The conflict began after repeated white violations of the Treaty of Fort Laramie (1868) once gold was discovered in the Black Hills.

Remember at both Sand Creek and the Washita River, the Indians were where the government wanted them and where they had been guaranteed safety. But as Jack Crabb so poetically puts it: "Sometimes grass don't grow, the wind don't blow, and the sky ain't blue." Now watch the movie and see what he is talking about.

After

Edwin S. Porter's *The Great Train Robbery* (1903) was the very first movie to tell a story, plus it gave birth to the Western genre, plus it is credited with establishing the movies as a commercially viable entertainment medium. Until 1970, 25% of all Hollywood movies were Westerns, and in 1958 (the Fifties were the golden age of the TV Western), there were thirty-one TV Westerns running in prime time each week. French director and film theorist Jean-Luc Godard called the Western "the most cinematic of cinematic genres."

Almost all those TV shows and movies climaxed with the the hero and villain(s) in a quickdraw showdown of the type at which Wild Bill Hickcock and the Soda Pop Kid appeared to be so proficient. The quickdraw gunslinger is brilliantly satirized in the movie, especially that pseudo-zen bit about shooting the gun before you touch it. In the real Old West, however, the quickdraw showdown never happened. Not one time. That was not how they did it.

That seems tantamount to saying they didn't ride horses then, but you don't have to take my word for it, take the word of Larry McMurtry, Pulitzer Prizing winning novelist of the Old West, winner of the Spur Award for Best Western Novel, and the bomb-throwing co-producer and Oscar winning co-screen writer of the homosexual cowboy romance, *Brokeback Mountain.*

In the March 24, 2005 *New York Review of Books*, McMurtry wrote about the most famous of all gun fights, between the Earp brothers plus Doc Holliday and members of the criminal gang known as the Cowboys: the Gunfight at the O.K. Corral. "When Virgil, Wyatt, and Morgan Earp started their many-times-filmed walk toward the O.K. Corral, Wyatt and Morgan had their pistols in their hands," McMurtry wrote. Wyatt later claimed in a court document "that when [Sheriff] Johnny Behan told him that he had disarmed the cowboys, [Wyatt] relaxed and stuck his pistol in his coat pocket." In other words, the good guys did not face the bad guys waiting for the latter to make the first move toward their holstered guns.

"When it came to gunfights, displaying your weapon was the first move, not the last, of anyone who was seriously interested in surviving," McMurtry maintains. "The quick-draw holster, invented in Hollywood as a movie prop, would have been worse than useless in real life." Note: Wyatt returned his pistol to his "coat pocket."

"Wyatt Earp, far from being draped with holsters and gun belts, was often not armed at all ... Their pistols were most often used as clubs," McMurtry adds. Though Earp doesn't appear in the movie *Little Big Man*, he is in the novel, and there he does to Jack Crabb what Earp was best known for doing to miscreants, not shooting them, but whacking them over the head with the butt of his gun. This isn't to say that the Old West wasn't very dangerous. But typically, gunfights were spontaneous with alcohol usually involved.

The mythologizing of the Old West began while it was still happening, in the dime novels, which sold in the millions, while some of their heroes were still alive. The mythologizing continued through the Wild West Shows, the most famous being Buffalo Bill Cody's. In 1903, Owen Wister published *The Virginian*, a novel romanticizing cowboy life in the Wyoming cattle country of the 1870s, and introducing the strong, silent hero, his pretty school marm sweetheart, and the climactic showdown.

Then, in the 20th century, the mythologizing continued through Hollywood movies and TV series and even cigarette commercials. The cowboy hero in his simple morality tale was the Six-Gun Galahad, the medieval knight errant of the Arthurian Romances transposed to the Old West, a nomadic wanderer on horseback, fighting villains, bound only by his own code of honor (such as giving your opponent a chance to draw his gun before you drew yours), often rescuing damsels or other victims in distress. The cowboy hero became the embodiment of American identity and manhood in the Twentieth Century, and he still is for millions of Americans. Indeed the psychological roots of our contemporary "gun culture" are in this mythological archetype. This chapter is important not only because it covers a critical part of American history but also of American psychology.

But of course, these icons of heroism and rectitude had no more reality than "the Soda Pop Kid." Wyatt Earp, the most famous real life lawman of the Old West, was a professional gambler and sometime brothel bouncer married to a prostitute and opium addict.

The term "cowboy" was used during the American Revolution to describe someone who opposed independence and who fought for the British. In Tombstone, Arizona, in the 1880s, it was an insult to call someone a "cowboy," as it suggested he was a horse thief, robber, or outlaw. The San Francisco Examiner editorialized, "Cowboys [are] the most reckless class of outlaws in that wild country...infinitely worse than the ordinary robber." The activities of the Cowboys of Tombstone ultimately ended with the Gunfight at the O.K. Corral and the resulting Earp Vendetta Ride. "Cowboy" as an adjective for reckless, irresponsible, or heedless, developed in the 1920s, and has been used most recently to describe the foreign policy of George W. Bush.

The influence of the cowboy icon would seem to have faded, but know that as late as 2005, the United States Senate declared the fourth Saturday of July as "National Day of the American Cowboy." And know too that there will always be, down in Southern California, a statue in eternal bronze of the ultimate screen cowboy, John Wayne, in his movie costume, standing before the airport named after him.

In *John Wayne's America* (1997), Pulitzer Prize winning historian Garry Wills writes, "One becomes American by going out. We are a people of departures, not arrivals. To reach one place is simply to catch sight of a new Beyond. Our basic myth is that of the frontier. Our hero is the frontiersman. To become urban is to break the spirit of man. Freedom is out on the plains, under endless sky. A pent-in American ceases to be American. In his 1844 lecture on 'The Young American,' Emerson said that Americans need the boundless West in order to become themselves.

"The Western can deal with the largest themes in American history— beginning with the 'original sin' of our country, the seizing of land from its original owners. It deals with the waves of emigration west—trappers, miners, herders, ranchers, farmers. It tracks the racing, overlapping new technologies— the stagecoach, the Conestoga wagon, the telegraph, the cavalry, the railroads, barbed wire, successively improved firearms, new breeds of horse. It explores the relations of people with the land, of the individual with the community, of vigilante law to settled courts."

The fictional Soda Pop Kid's friend Wild Bill Hickock (1837–1876) really did exist. Hickock fought for the Union during the Civil War, went to the West as a fugitive from justice, worked as a stagecoach driver, as a scout for Custer, a lawman, a gambler, and a stage actor in a production created by Buffalo Bill called *The Daring Buffalo Chasers of the Plains*. Like Earp, Hickock's law-enforcement duties and gambling easily overlapped. He was the first "dime novel" hero of the western era, but it is difficult for historians to separate the truth from fiction about Hickok, since most of the stories about him were greatly exaggerated or fabricated by both the dime novel writers and Hickcock himself.

In our movie, his friendship with Jack and his death, like Custer's, are turned into superb comic bits. Hickock was involved in several famous gunfights and he was shot and killed while playing poker in a saloon in Deadwood, Dakota Territory (now South Dakota), sitting uncharacteristically with his back to the door and holding a pair of aces and a pair of eights which became known ever after as the "dead man's hand."

Though we don't see much of him in the movie, we do see "Buffalo Bill" Cody (1846 – 1917) from a distance supervising the stacking of valuable buffalo hides. He acquired his moniker providing buffalo meat for the construction of the railroads. He fought for the Union (he came from an abolitionist family), was an army scout in the West, and achieved fame as the result of a dime novel loosely based on his life that was published in 1869 and was adapted into a stage melodrama in 1871. But most famously, he created "Buffalo Bill's Wild West," a circus-like show that featured Indian attacks on wagon trains, stagecoach robberies, a cyclone, a prairie fire, and even Custer's Last Stand. It employed actual historical figures like Sitting Bull, and toured the U.S. and Europe for more than thirty years. The show influenced many 20th-century portrayals of "the West" in cinema and literature. Larry McMurtry believes that at the turn from the 19th to the 20th century, Buffalo Bill Cody was the most recognizable celebrity on earth.

The rise of the cattle industry and the cowboy as cattle herder is directly tied to the demise of the huge herds of buffalo. Near the end of the film, while both of them are watching Buffalo Bill, Allardyce T. Merriweather, trying to get Jack to go buffalo hunting with him, says, "There's a world of money chewing grass on those plains Jack .... The buffalos are gettin' scarce..." As Larry McMurtry wrote in yet another *New York Review* essay, "There were so many buffalo—fifty million, by some estimates—that no one could really envision their disappearance, yet it took barely twenty years to eliminate them." They were a vital resource of food, clothing, and shelter for the Plains Indians. Loss of habitat, disease, and over-hunting reduced the herds through the 19th century to the point of near extinction. By 1890 there were only 750 left. Conservationists lobbied Congress to establish public bison herds in several national parks and by 2003 the bison population reached 500,000.

The end of the bison herds opened up millions of acres for cattle ranching, which the Spanish had introduced to the Southwest in the 17th century using longhorn cattle. The earliest cowboys in Texas learned their trade, adapted their clothing, and took their jargon from the Mexican vaqueros or "buckaroos." Chaps, the heavy protective leather trousers worn by cowboys, got their name from the Spanish "chaparreras," and the rope, or lariat, was derived from "la reata".

After the American Civil War, some veterans who returned home and found no future there went west and became cowboys. Some were Blacks, Hispanics, Native Americans, and even Britons. Nearly all were in their twenties or teens. It was very hard work for little pay and few stayed with it long.

Also after the Civil War, Texas ranchers raised large herds of longhorn cattle. The nearest railheads were 800 or more miles north in Kansas. The ranchers and their cowboys drove over 1.5 million head of cattle between 1867 and 1871 north along the Western, Chisholm, and Shawnee trails. A typical drive would take three to four months and contained two miles of cattle six abreast usually with one cowboy for every 250 cattle. By the 1870s and 1880s, cattle ranches expanded further north into new grazing grounds and replaced the bison herds in Wyoming, Montana, Colorado, Nebraska, and the Dakota Territory, using the railroads to ship to both coasts.

Anchoring the booming cattle industry in Kansas and Missouri were the lawless cattle towns of Abilene, Kansas City, Dodge City, and Wichita. For the cowboy arriving with money in hand after two months on the trail, the cattle town was exciting. Like the mining towns in California and Nevada, cattle towns experienced a short period of boom and bust lasting about five years. However, unlike the mining towns which in most cases became ghost towns and ceased to exist after the ore played out, cattle towns often evolved from cattle to farming and continued on after the grazing lands were exhausted.

During hard times in the cattle industry a few cowboys turned to banditry. The legendary outlaws of the Old West, including Jesse James, Billy the Kid, the Dalton Gang, Black Bart, Butch Cassidy and the Wild Bunch and hundreds of others, preyed on banks, trains, and stagecoaches. Frank and Jesse James, and Cole and Jim Younger, used the hit-and-run tactics they learned in the Confederate Quantrill's Raiders. Many outlaws were just misfits and drifters who roamed the West avoiding the law. Their names and exploits are a part of American folklore, and their guns and costumes achieved the ultimate mythological imprimatur: they became children's toys.

The most enduring fashion adapted from the cowboy, popular nearly worldwide today, are "blue jeans", originally made by Levi Strauss in San Francisco in 1850 for miners. It was the cowboy hat, however, that came to symbolize the American West. Today of course the whole cowboy outfit is as likely to appear on a dentist or a banker as on a working cowboy.

By the way, cowboys rarely fought Indians. It was the army that did that. As for the fate of the Plains Indians after Little Bighorn, Old Lodge Skins was right when he told Jack, "We won today, we won't win tomorrow." (Incidentally, the Little Bighorn battle scenes in our movie were filmed in Montana near the actual battle site.) After the battle, Indian scouts reported that a large contingent of U.S. troops was still active in the area, so the Sioux and Cheyenne packed up their camps, and within 48 hours of their victory, they had dissolved into the wilderness.

"Little Bighorn is one of the most-written-about battles in world history," wrote Larry McMurtry in that same Wyatt Earp essay. Besides Custer, two of his brothers, a nephew, and a brother-in-law were killed at Little Bighorn. Five of the Seventh Cavalry's companies were annihilated. The total U.S. casualty count, including scouts, was 268 dead. When news of it arrived in the East, the U.S. was observing the centennial of its independence, and it shocked a people accustomed to battlefield victories and increasingly convinced of their inherent superiority and their claim to manifest destiny. From the Indian perspective, it was the beginning of the end and has even been referred to as "the Indians' last stand."

Afterwards, the U.S. Army mounted an aggressive campaign to force the remaining free Indians onto reservations. Within a year, nearly all the Plains Indians had been confined there. As for the Black Hills (what the fight at Little Big Horn was about), the Sioux were forced to cede the land to United States government or it would cease to supply rations to the reservations.

The end of the Plains Indian Wars came on December 29, 1890, on the Lakota Pine Ridge Indian Reservation in South Dakota, in what is known as the Wounded Knee Massacre. On the morning of that day, troops of the Seventh Cavalry went into a camp to disarm the Lakota. A scuffle ensued, a shot was fired, and the 7th Cavalry (yes, Custer's outfit) opened fire indiscriminately from all sides, including their four Hotchkiss guns (a small rapid-fire cannon), killing men, women, and children. By the time it was over, at least 150 men, women, and children of the Lakota Sioux had been killed and 51 wounded, some of whom died later. Some estimates placed the number of dead at 300. 31 troopers also died, many victims of friendly fire. At least twenty troopers were later awarded the Medal of Honor. This was the last "battle" of the American Indian Wars.

According to the U.S. Bureau of the Census (1894), "The Indian wars under the government of the United States have been more than 40 in number. They have cost the lives of about 19,000 white men, women and children, including those killed in individual combats, and the lives of about 30,000 Indians."

Something else ended with the Plains Indian Wars: the frontier. When the eleventh U.S. Census was taken in 1890, the superintendent announced that there was no longer a clear line of advancing settlement, and hence no longer a frontier in the continental United States. Historian Frederick Jackson Turner used the statistic to announce the end of the era in which the frontier shaped the American character.

In a scholarly paper in 1893, "The Significance of the Frontier in American History," Turner put forth his "Frontier Thesis" which fashioned scholarship for three or four generations and appeared in practically all American textbooks. He believed the spirit and success of the United States was directly tied to the country's westward expansion. The West, not the East, was where distinctively American characteristics emerged. As each generation of pioneers moved 50 to 100 miles west, they abandoned useless European practices, institutions, and ideas, and instead found new solutions to new problems created by their new environment. Over multiple generations, the frontier produced characteristics of informality, violence, crudeness, democracy, and initiative that the world recognized as "American".

Then in 1901, an authentic cowboy and historian of the West took up residence in the White House, someone who made "cowboy" internationally synonymous with the brash aggressive American. Theodore "Teddy" Roosevelt (1858 – 1919) was the 26th President of the United States (1901–1909). He is noted for his exuberant personality, range of interests and achievements, and his leadership of the Progressive Movement, as well as his "cowboy" persona and robust masculinity. Roosevelt's achievements as a naturalist, explorer, hunter, author, and soldier are as much a part of his fame as any office he held as a politician. Roosevelt was 42 years old when sworn in as President of the United States in 1901, immediately after President McKinley was assassinated, making Roosevelt the youngest president ever.

Born into wealth, Roosevelt was a sickly child who suffered from asthma and stayed at home studying natural history. To compensate for his physical weakness during childhood, he embraced a strenuous life during adulthood. In 1884, after his wife and his mother died on the same day, he left politics and went to the frontier, becoming a rancher in the "Badlands" in the Dakotas. When the Spanish–American War broke out in 1898, Roosevelt formed the Rough Riders, a volunteer cavalry regiment that fought in Cuba. The Cuban war hero was elected governor of New York in 1898 and in 1900 became vice president.

For his aggressive attacks on trusts over his two terms, he has been called a "trust-buster." A trust is what we call now a cartel, corporations that group together for the purpose of monopolizing a given industry to reduce competition and control prices. The predatory tendencies of unregulated capitalism, always present in the American economy, by the last quarter of the 19th century resulted in an unprecedented concentration of wealth and abusive political power in a group called the "Robber Barons." A small number of their giant corporations controlled major sectors of the nation's economy, including banking, manufacturing, meatpacking, oil refining, railroads, and steel. Theirs was an era of political scandals and unethical business practices that Mark Twain dubbed the "Gilded Age" and it stuck.

The building of the Transcontinental Railroad provided a golden opportunity for the Robber Barons. Built between 1863 and 1869, joining the eastern and western halves of the United States, its construction was one of the greatest American technological feats of the 19th century. The Union Pacific Railroad built the eastern half and it depended on Irish immigrants for labor and for know-how on ex-Army engineers who had kept the trains running during the American Civil War. The Union Pacific Railroad laid on average a mile of track per day while a foot a day was what the Central Pacific Railroad averaged, at some points, while going east through the granite of California's Sierra Nevada mountains. Facing a labor shortage in the more sparsely-settled West, the Central Pacific Railroad relied mainly on Chinese immigrants working three shifts around the clock, drilling holes into which they packed black powder and later nitroglycerine.

At ceremonies connecting the two halves on May 19, 1869, at Promontory Point, Utah, the President of the Central Pacific Railroad, Leland Stanford, was supposed to drive in a gold spike but he missed and some workman had to drive it in for him. Historian Wendell Huffman said, "The transcontinental railroad was the technological manifestation of manifest destiny." There are no reliable records of deaths during construction. Estimates range from thousands to less than a hundred.

Now passengers and freight could reach the west coast in a matter of days instead of months at one-tenth the cost while western agricultural products, coal, and minerals could move quickly to the east coast. It opened up vast regions of the North American heartland for settlement, and made the stagecoach lines and wagon trains obsolete.

Yet, three years after the completion of the transcontinental railroad, the Union Pacific was facing bankruptcy, inspite of its success and millions in government subsidies. The founders of the company had set up another company called Crédit Mobilier of America, to which the Union Pacific subcontracted the actual track work and which charged Union Pacific often twice or more the customary cost. President Lincoln asked Massachusetts Congressman Oakes Ames, who was on the railroad committee, to clean things up. Ames instead gave stock options to other politicians, in addition to cash bribes, while at the same time continuing the lucrative overcharges. When it all came to light, Crédit Mobilier became the biggest scandal of the Gilded Age.

Remember in the movie, before the Battle of Little Big Horn, when Custer (beautifully played by the redoubtable Robert Mulligan) was ranting about "Gr-r-rant!! ... Sitting up there in the White House..."? Well, that was Ulysses S. Grant that he was railing against, the winner of the Civil War, one of America's greatest generals, and one of its worst presidents. Though he was honest, he surrounded himself with scoundrels in the White House making his one of the most corrupt and scandal-ridden of presidencies, and his biggest scandal was Crédit Mobilier.

It made it into the press during Grant's reelection bid in 1872, but the crimes had been committed under Johnson, so Grant won. There was a congressional investigation that implicated both his first and second term vice presidents and future President James Garfield, among other politicians. It ended with Oakes Ames' death three months into the investigation.

The unprecedented corruption of the Grant administration even reached into the Bureau of Indian Affairs, of course. Millions were lost in kickbacks which often meant rotten food on the reservations, when there was any food at all.

Eventually the Union Pacific was picked up cheap by one of the top robber barons, Jay Gould. The son of a poor farmer, he made millions selling shoddy blankets to the Union Army, then through stock manipulation and bribery gained control of several railroad companies. His attempts to manipulate the gold market helped set off a depression in 1869.

Robber baron J.P. Morgan was a financier and banker born into great wealth who made it greater by loaning money to France during the Franco-Prussian War. In the depths of the Panic of 1893, the Federal Treasury was nearly out of gold so Morgan and the Rothschilds supplied the U.S. Treasury with enough gold to restore the treasury surplus in exchange for a 30-year bond issue. The Panic of 1907 was a financial crisis that almost crippled the American economy and that put major New York banks at risk of bankruptcy. There was no financial mechanism to rescue them, so Morgan stepped in, took charge, and resolved the crisis. The Federal Reserve System was created as a solution for similar problems in the future.

Between 1890 and 1913, forty-two major corporations were organized by, or their securities were underwritten, in whole or part, by J.P. Morgan. In 1892, Morgan arranged mergers that created General Electric. By 1900, he controlled half the train tracks in the country and his friends controlled most of the rest. They created a trust and fixed freight prices exorbitantly high. In 1901, he met steel magnate Andrew Carnegie at a party where they created U.S. Steel, the first billion dollar corporation.

Carnegie was a poor Scottish immigrant who first worked in a cotton factory, then in a telegraph office, and then for the Pennsylvania Railroad where he rose to an executive position. He invested in railroads, railroad sleeping cars, bridges and oil derricks, and built further wealth as a bond salesman raising money for American enterprise in Europe. He eventually built Carnegie Steel Company, and using an improved production technique, revolutionized American steel production and ruthlessly took over the steel market.

An even bigger robber baron, the first American worth more than a billion dollars, and, adjusting for inflation, the richest person in history, was John D. Rockefeller. He was the founder of the Standard Oil Company, which was the first great business trust. Rockefeller revolutionized the petroleum industry and defined the structure of modern philanthropy.

So America during the Gilded Age was like a lawless Old West cattle town, and when "that damn cowboy," as Teddy Roosevelt's political enemies called him, arrived in town, he aimed to clean things up with Progressive reforms. Before him there were some modest attempts at reform such as the Sherman Anti-Trust Act, which was supposed to protect trade from "unlawful restraints," (the author of the law was a friend of Rockefeller) but a conservative Supreme

Court wound up actually using it against striking railway workers who the Court claimed were "restraining trade."

Teddy used it against "trusts," large corporations conspiring together to control prices and eliminate competition, such as the beef trust and the American Tobacco Company. He also strengthened the Interstate Commerce Commission (which regulated rail rates), created the Department of Labor and Commerce (later separated), and oversaw passage of the Pure Food and Drug Act.

The Gilded Age also saw a plethora of important inventions. English immigrant Alexander Graham Bell invented the telephone in that fateful year of 1876. George Eastman invented the box camera in 1888 bringing photography to the masses. But the greatest inventor of that age was the "Wizard of Menlo Park," Thomas Alva Edison (1847 – 1931). Born poor and nearly deaf as a boy, he would eventually hold more than a thousand patents. The key to Edison's fortunes was telegraphy. From years of working as a telegraph operator, he gained knowledge of the basics of electricity. He then developed many devices that greatly influenced life around the world, including the phonograph; the motion picture camera; a long-lasting, practical electric light bulb; a stock ticker; a mechanical vote recorder; and even a battery for an electric car. Edison developed the system of electric-power generation and distribution to homes, businesses, and factories that is the heart of the modern industrialized world.

Another engineering feat of the Gilded Age was the Brooklyn Bridge. Designed and built by a pair of German immigrants, the Roeblings, father and son, between 1869 and 1883, the former died from an injury and the latter suffered from a crippling and excruciating case of the bends (nitrogen in the blood) from working too long in the airtight, pressurized underwater chambers of the foundation. Contemporaries marveled at what technology was capable of and the Brooklyn Bridge became a symbol of the optimism of the time. The first steel frame skyscraper, the Home Insurance Building went up in Chicago, Illinois in 1885. It was only ten stories high but nevertheless was also a marvel of its day.

I have only mentioned the most famous robber barons here but there were dozens, and they all were opposed to unions and had no qualms about using violence even murder to suppress the union movement. That is the theme, among many, of our next film, which brings us into the twentieth century, and it is the favorite movie of history teachers and a minor American classic, and one that climaxes with one of the most authentic shoot-out scenes on film.

Last Quarter of the 19th Century Timeline

1872 Credit Mobilier Scandal
1876 The National League of baseball was founded.
    -Battle of Little Bighorn

-Wild Bill Hickok was killed by a shot to the back of the head
 by Jack McCall while playing poker in Deadwood, South Dakota.
-Alexander Graham Bell invented the telephone.
-U.S. celebrates first centennial
1879 Thomas Edison invented the light bulb.
1881 Gunfight at the O.K. Corral in Tombstone, Arizona Territory.
-James Garfield inaugurated as President, soon assassinated, and
 Chester A. Arthur becomes President.
-Outlaw Billy the Kid was shot and killed by Sheriff Pat Garrett.
1882 The Chinese Exclusion Act-passed prohibiting both immigration from
 China and the naturalization of Chinese immigrants already here.
-Jesse James was shot and killed by Robert and Charlie Ford.
1883 Buffalo Bill Cody debuted his Wild West Show.
-The Brooklyn Bridge, a technological wonder of its time, opened.
1885 The first steel frame skyscraper, the Home Insurance Building, went up in
 Chicago, Illinois.
1887 The Dawes Act passed, imposing a system of private land ownership on
 Native American tribes. Indian landholdings were reduced from 138
 million acres in 1887 to only 48 million acres in 1934. And with their land,
 many Native Americans lost a fundamental structuring principle of tribal
 life since communal land ownership had been a centuries-old tradition.
1890 The Sherman Antitrust Act was passed prohibiting business activities
 deemed anticompetitive by federal regulators and requiring the federal
 government to investigate and pursue trusts or monopolies.
-Wounded Knee Massacre
1892 General Electric was founded.
-The Sierra Club was founded by pioneering naturalist John Muir.
1896 Supreme Court decision Plessy v. Ferguson affirmed the legality of
 "separate but equal" public facilities (racial segregation).
1900 The United States population exceeded seventy-five million.

Recommendations

How the West was Won (1962) is a compendium of most of the top stars of its day and most of the clichés of its genre. After decades of honing their technique, when Hollywood decided to put the whole history of the West into one film, they did it pretty well. The script for *How the West was Won* garnered a well-deserved Academy Award. It's a "sprawling epic" set between 1839 and 1889, following four generations of the Prescotts as they move from the Erie Canal ever westward eventually to the Pacific Ocean. It's divided into five segments, each a different decade more or less, and each with its own action set piece. The first is "The River," with settlers going downriver in rafts, and then "The Plains" with a classic covered-wagon trek to the Pacific.

"The Civil War" centers on a poignant vignette that includes John Wayne straining too hard to play a character that is not John Wayne, in this case William Tecumseh Sherman. "The Railroad" is about the building of the transcontinental railroad and includes one of the most incredible scenes ever put on film: a buffalo stampede through a railroad workers' camp, and none of that is special effects, just buffalo, hundreds, though editing makes it look like thousands. The last segment is "The Outlaws" with a plot that is just a retread of the western classic *High Noon* (1952), though it does have a great shootout on a runaway train.

How the West was Won is as much myth as history of course but it provides a good overview of its period. And if the interiors are over-lit and the acting is occasionally clunky, there is plenty of what Hollywood did best: spectacle. *How the West was Won* was filmed in the curved-screen three-projector Cinerama process, which looks a little odd at times but basically good on DVD.

All the history in *How the West was Won* has been at least mentioned in this book except for the following. The development of the steamboat by Robert Fulton revolutionized water travel, as did the building of canals. The Erie Canal, where the film begins, was an artificial waterway 360 miles long, across central New York connecting the Hudson River at Albany with Lake Erie at Buffalo. Constructed from 1817 to 1825, it stimulated an economic revolution that bound the grain basket of the West to the eastern and southern markets. It also caused a spurt of canal building.

The Pony Express gets a neat encapsulation in the film. In 1860, it guaranteed mail delivery over the 1,966 miles between St. Louis and Sacramento in 11 days, requiring its skinny riders to exchange horses at top speed every 12 miles. In the movie, they are seen riding by crews working on the first transcontinental telegraph line which, when it is completed the next year, will put the Pony Express out of business.

This film is rich with significant details; for example, when Debbie Reynolds' character visits her inherited California gold mine. Notice the quick shot of Chinese panning for gold in the river. Racist laws banned them from the best areas and they were under constant threat of attack by Anglo miners, hence the noticeable skittishness of the Chinese in that shot. Note the narrator mentions Congressman Abe Lincoln's opposition to the U.S.- Mexico War.

If *Little Big Man* is art, *How the West was Won* is an exciting well-crafted Hollywood product. And if the former is the corrective for much of the latter, the latter nevertheless shows considerable sympathy for the Indians. This time it's the railroad breaking treaties and the hero takes the Indians' side. But the film also puts into the mouth of a ruthless railroad builder, played by the great Richard Widmark, a counter argument to the accusation of mistreatment. He says the Indians should have adjusted like the European peasant immigrants had to, which conveniently ignores the after-effects of devastating pandemics and war, and nearly four hundred broken treaties, and the fact that the immigrants were Europeans.

With all of Debbie Reynolds' song and dance numbers, *How the West was Won* is at least part musical, but remember: real Old West saloons were also casinos, night clubs, and brothels, and the "girls" who worked there may have been waitresses or entertainers, but they were also prostitutes.

How the West was Won is important not only for the history it tells but also for its triumphalist attitude toward that history. It premiered in 1962, when the country was still flush with its World War II victory and the unprecedented prosperity that followed, and it hadn't yet felt the social and political earthquakes of the later Sixties and the doubts that followed.

The Oscar-winning script of *How the West was Won* was written by James R. Webb (not to be confused with the politician and defender of the Confederacy of the same name). In his very next film, Webb took up the issue of Indian genocide, anticipating *Little Big Man* by six years. *Cheyenne Autumn* (1964) tells the true story of the Northern Cheyenne Exodus of 1878-9. This was another case of one of those four hundred broken treaties. The Cheyenne were tired of starving on the reservation in Oklahoma and, having been promised they could eventually return to their ancestral homeland in Wyoming, over three hundred left the reservation for Wyoming, 1500 miles away, without official permission.

Cheyenne Autumn is also the last Western by the master of the Hollywood Western, director John Ford. More than any other single individual, Ford was responsible for raising up the Western from B-grade kiddie fodder (and for creating the "anti-Western"). And more than any other single individual, it was Ford who made Indians the default villains of the formula Western. At the end of his career, he tried to make amends with *Cheyenne Autumn*.

This is an example of how important it is to have knowledge of the historical context of the production in order to fully understand a movie. The film was shot in 1963 and the script written in 1962, and that was the year that the architect of the Nazi Holocaust, Adolf Eichmann, was hanged following an internationally televised trial in Israel. In *Cheyenne Autumn,* the redoubtable Karl Malden plays a German immigrant and American army officer, Captain Oscar Wessels, who loves Indians enough to own a library of ethnographic studies in German. Yet, when ordered to, he is willing to send a group of captured Cheyenne into the certain death of a forced march in the dead of winter back to Oklahoma. And when challenged by those around him, Wessels counters with a variation on Eichmann's famous defense of his inhuman crimes: "I was just following orders." In four different scenes, Ford and Webb have Malden deliver a peroration in a thick German accent on the absolute necessity of following orders. The last time he is seen, Wessel is staggering in a daze through the strewn bodies of soldiers and Indians including mothers with wailing babies beside them.

The Russians get slammed too. Mike Mazurki, usually seen as a gangster's enforcer, plays a Polish immigrant and career soldier quitting the army in protest and complaining about Cossacks "who kill Poles just because they're Poles...just like we're tryin' to kill the Indians just because they're Indians."

These stunning accusations seem to have gotten by critics at the time and scholars since. The accusations may have seemed shrill or exaggerated or, from such a venerable source as Ford, too fantastic to be taken seriously. But what informed person today would deny that the treatment of the Indians qualifies as genocide, or a "crime against humanity," which was what the Nazis were tried for?

Cheyenne Autumn also features a drunk white mob Indian-hunting for easy glory. Plus there is deliberate distortion of the Cheyenne exodus by the press of the time. There is also a wholly irrelevant section with James Stewart as Wyatt Earp that was probably added to spice up theatrical trailers. Much of *Cheyenne Autumn* was shot in Monument Valley Tribal Park on the Arizona-Utah border, where Ford shot most of his classic Westerns. This time he used local Navajos and their faces in crowd shots add as much as the desert rock formations. He also let them use their language and they were cracking each other up by mocking the whites and telling dirty jokes in front of the cameras.

The film is stilted and preachy and clichéd in parts but it still packs a wallop. Plus, it is fun to see a formula western of the golden age in which the Indians are the good guys. However, the Indians in *Cheyenne Autumn* are still distant noble victims compared with those in *Little Big Man*, which goes so much deeper inside the Indian culture and society. Inspite of Ford and a cast of some of the biggest stars of the time, *Cheyenne Autumn* was a box office failure.

The same year that *Little Big Man* came out there was a similar film called *A Man Called Horse* (1970). Irishman Richard Harris played an English aristocrat who is captured and abused (and abused and abused) by Sioux and who then joins the tribe and becomes a warrior. It isn't very well made but it is compelling in parts as well as silly in parts, and it was successful enough to spawn two sequels. Sioux play the Sioux. Kevin Costner's *Dances with Wolves* (1990) also features a white man, in this case a Union veteran, who joins a Sioux tribe and helps them fight the Pawnee. The plot is considerably more complex and contrived than that. It was very successful at the box office and won seven Academy Awards including best picture.

Remember all those cowboy dramas on TV each week in 1959? At least six of them were connected in some way with Wyatt Earp. His own show, "The Life and Legend of Wyatt Earp" ran for six seasons. "There are so many Gunfight-at-the-OK-Corral movies that they constitute a kind of subgenre of the western," Larry McMurtry wrote. Indeed about once a decade a new generation of filmmakers has had to reinterpret the life and legend of Wyatt Earp. The best of the films have included John Ford's *My Darling Clementine* (1946) and John Sturges' *Gunfight at the O.K. Corral* (1957). Top stars such as Henry Fonda, Burt Lancaster, and James Garner have played Wyatt Earp.

Director Lawrence Kasdan's *Wyatt Earp* (1994) stars Kevin Costner and has the definitive Doc Holliday from Dennis Quaid. It is by far the most accurate, indeed it is one of those rare instances where historical accuracy trumps dramatic tension. Even so, Kasdan can't resist having the Earp Brothers and Doc Holliday walk to the O.K. Corral with their guns in their holsters. Not doing it would have been just too unchivalrous. Recent westerns may know better than to use the quickdraw showdown but nevertheless they seem to have a hard time getting away from it.

I have to mention one of the greatest Old West lawmen you never heard of: the African American, Bass Reeves (1838-1910). He was born a slave in Arkansas, fled north into the Indian Territory (now Oklahoma), and lived with the Seminole and Creek Indians. Because he knew the Indian Territory and could speak several Indian languages, he was recruited as a deputy U.S. Marshal. Reeves worked for thirty-two years as a Federal peace officer in the Indian Territory arresting over 3,000 felons including some of the most dangerous criminals of the time. Never wounded himself, Reeves admitted to having killed fourteen outlaws. He married Nellie Jennie from Texas and they had ten children and once Reeves had to arrest his own son for murder. He first came to public attention in the book *Black Profiles in Courage* (1996) by basketball great Kareem Abdul Jabbar, who has a history degree from UCLA.

For movies about Wild Bill Hickock, aside from *Little Big Man* and a few dozen before that, the best and most recent is the first season of HBO's *Deadwood* (2004-2006) in which Bill is superbly played by Keith Carradine. The first episode of that series garnered the best direction Emmy for Walter Hill. He also directed *Wild Bill* (1995) about Hickock, starring Jeff Bridges. It was based on a novel and a play, and blended myth and fact, and failed to reach the existential depths to which it aspired. Before *Wild Bill,* Hill made *Geronimo: An American Legend* (1993) starring the amazing Wes Studi. It is well-crafted with a reasonable adherence to the facts which however are buried in most of the clichés of the genre. It has the memorable plaint from Studi's Geronimo, "Why must the white man have *all* the land?"

There are literally thousands of Hollywood westerns of course, and except for the sets and the costumes, and sometimes not even those, few have much to do with the actual Old West. They're about the myth not the reality. Any list of recommendations will leave out as many favorites as it includes but here are a few of the classics, most from the Fifties, the golden era: *The Magnificent Seven* (1960) (a western version of Kurosawa's *Seven Samurai,* samurai being Japanese knights errant), *Shane* (1953) *High Noon* (1952) *The Searchers* (1956) *The Big Country* (1958) and *The Unforgiven* (1960) by John Huston, and *The Unforgiven* (2005) by Clint Eastwood.

Filmmakers have been striving in recent decades to get at the grubby actuality of the Old West, in sets and props if not always stories. A few examples are: Robert Altman's *McCabe and Mrs. Miller* (1971) (voted the eighth best western of all time in an American Film Institute poll and dubbed "perfect" by Roger Ebert), Philip Kaufman's *The Great Northfield Minnesota Raid* (1972), Phillip Borsos' *The Grey Fox* (1982) (which received the rare 100% rating from Rotten Tomatoes), Michael Winterbottom's *The Claim* (2000), and most recently, HBO's series *Deadwood* (2004-2006).

There are a number of documentaries on the West but Ken Burns' and Stephen Ives' 12 hour PBS series *The West* (1996) towers above the rest. PBS's American Experience featured an excellent documentary series on Native Americans spanning the 17th to the 20th centuries, *We Shall Remain* (2009). There are five 90-minute episodes. "After the Mayflower" deals with the Wampanoags and the Pilgrims. Then "Tecumseh's Vision" tells of the creator of the most ambitious pan-Indian resistance movement. "Trail of Tears" covers the Cherokee death march to Oklahoma. "Geronimo" tells of the legendary Apache leader. "Wounded Knee" focuses on the American Indian Movement, civil rights activists who in 1973, while demanding redress for grievances, occupied the town of Wounded Knee, site of the last large-scale massacre of Indians in the nineteenth century.

Ken Burns' very first documentary *Brooklyn Bridge* (1981) garnered an Academy Award nomination. Twenty years later, Burns took on the most American of American humorists, *Mark Twain* (2001), whose novel *The Adventures of Huckleberry Finn* (1885), according to Ernest Hemingway, is the beginning of American literature.

At www.escalloniapress.com, there are free recommendations of the best books - histories, biographies, memoirs, and even novels - related to the subjects of this chapter.

Ch. 10 – Matewan

Before

Matewan (1987) is an American classic, and it is probably the all time favorite movie of U.S. history teachers because it crams so many important topics into a single film that is also esthetically first rate.

The incident depicted will seem historically minor, a coal miners' strike in the West Virginia town of Matewan in 1920, but in fact the actual "Battle of Matewan" or "Matewan Massacre," as it is also known, was an immediate cause of the "Battle of Blair Mountain," the largest armed uprising in the U.S. since the Civil War. It involved thousands of miners and eventually thousands of army troops. The Coal Operators Association and the federal government even resorted to aerial bombardment of the coal miners' forces using bombs left over from the recently ended World War I. So, a big-budget big-cast Hollywood production would have been appropriate, but the low-budget of this independent production forced writer-director John Sayles to make a more intimate film. Low-budget maybe, but still it has a great look, for which cinematographer (and leftist activist) Haskell Wexler received an Oscar nomination.

Matewan also takes us into the twentieth century, the first twenty years to be specific. It will focus on the classic period of American immigration, one of those "important topics." From 1880 to 1914, the peak years of immigration, more than 22 million people migrated to the United States. It was called the "New Immigration." That was a term from the late 1880s referring to the influx of immigrants from southern Europe and Russia (areas that previously sent few immigrants). Many Anglo-Saxons feared the new arrivals and worried that the U.S. was no longer a "melting pot" but a "dumping ground" and there could be negative effects on the economy, politics, and culture. There emerged a second wave of organized xenophobia, the first being in the 1850s, the era of the Know-Nothings. In 1893, the Immigration Restriction League was formed and, along with other similar organizations, it began to press Congress for severe curtailment of foreign immigration.

This unprecedented wave of immigration from Southern Europe created new communities and added many new flavors (literally) to American culture, nevertheless, the immigrants faced great challenges here. Many settled in the slums of the larger northeastern cities. Often with no knowledge of English and little education, they were compelled to accept the poorest paying and least desirable jobs, and were frequently exploited. They made up the bulk of the U.S. industrial labor pool, and they made possible the emergence of such industries as steel, coal, automobiles, textiles, and garment production, and enabled the United States to leap into the front ranks of the world's economic giants.

Most of the immigrants of this period entered the U.S. at one location: Ellis Island, an island of Upper New York Bay southwest of Manhattan. From 1892 until 1924, it was the nation's main immigrant inspection station. Castle Garden Immigration Depot in lower Manhattan processed over eight million immigrants during the thirty-five years before Ellis Island. But in its tenure, Ellis Island processed twelve million immigrants, their descendants today making up a third of the nation.

For Italian immigration to the United States 1900 to 1914 marked the high point with over two million in those years, with a total of 5.3 million between 1880 and 1920. This is the immigrant group *Matewan* will focus on. Remember the anti-Catholic prejudice that the Irish faced? It was just as bad for the Italians plus they frequently had swarthy complexions. Italians have the dubious distinction of being victims of the largest mass lynching in U.S. history. In 1891, in New Orleans, nine Italian immigrants were tried and acquitted of the murder of police chief David Hennessy. Nevertheless, a mob broke into the jail where they were being held and dragged them out and lynched them, together with two other Italians who just happened to be in the jail at the time.

But the most famous example of anti-Italian bias in that era was the case of Sacco and Vanzetti. In 1920, two Italian immigrants, Nicola Sacco and Bartolomeo Vanzetti, were arrested for robbery and murder in Massachusetts. Historians agree that, whether or not they were guilty, they were given a very unfair and biased trial because of their anarchist political beliefs and their Italian immigrant status. In spite of world-wide protests, Sacco and Vanzetti were eventually executed.

Workers' efforts during this period to extend democracy into the workplace led to the often-violent rise of the labor movement in cities and mining towns. That's another of *Matewan's* important topics: unions. Our film begins with an innocent group of Italian immigrants who have literally been taken from the docks by train to a coal mining town, Matewan, in the middle of a strike.

In response to efforts by miners to organize into a labor union, the Stone Mountain Coal Company, the only employer in the company town of Matewan, announces it will cut the miners' pay. That's the significance of the opening scene in the mine when the teenage Danny tells Sephus, the miner working alone in a dark cramped corner of a mine, that the company has lowered the "tonnage rate," which is how much money the miners make per ton mined. When Danny asks, "Sephus, what're we gonna do?" the answer is a dynamite explosion in a wall of the mine.

"There's fahr in 'er hearts and fahr in 'er souls but there ain't gonna be no fahr in the hole," blue grass balladeer Hazel Dickens sings in the opening scenes. "Fire in the hole" is one of the things the miners yell to warn others that a dynamite charge is about to go off, and if there ain't gonna be none, then that means no coal is being dug and they are on strike. As she sings the second verse, look for an excellent tracking shot with a railroad hand car in the foreground (propelled along the tracks by a man pumping a handle) while behind him the miners' squalid cabins are crawling with kids.

The company has also announced that it is importing workers into Matewan to replace those who join the union. In addition to the Italians, there are African Americans from Alabama, and as they are coming in on the train, it stops outside town and the black men are told to get off. After they do, they are suddenly attacked by a screaming white mob that calls them "scabs" (replacements for striking workers). The black men defend themselves handily and manage to get back onto the train just as it is pulling away. That is another important topic: racism. In another chapter, I will deal more fully with the situation of African Americans between the end of Reconstruction and the Twenties.

While a company representative shows the black workers around, note his attitude and the list of conditions he gives for employment there. The "scrip" he mentions as their pay is company money that can only be spent at company stores. That is the great James Earl Jones as "Few Clothes" asking "What's to keep you all from jackin' up them prices at yoh stoh?" Note the answer he gets. The status for non-union laborers at this time is essentially that of an itinerant serf.

Witnessing the attack on the black workers from the train is Joe Kenehan (future Academy Award winner Chris Cooper in one of his earliest roles.). He's one of our heroes, and though he is fictional, thousands just like him did exist. Joe is an organizer for the United Mine Workers, a World War I pacifist and a former Wobbly, as members of the Industrial Workers of the World or IWW were called. On his first night in town, before he is allowed into a secret union meeting, to make sure Joe isn't a company spy, two union members interrogate him, one with a pistol in his hand. Besides setting a tone of danger and intrigue, this interrogation provides a good short roster of labor heroes of this period.

Jack London (1876 – 1916) was a journalist, social activist, and one of the first American fiction writers to earn a large fortune and gain worldwide celebrity from his fiction alone. Indeed, like Edgar Allan Poe and John Steinbeck, he may be more popular outside the U.S. than in it. He was a passionate advocate of unionization, socialism, and the rights of workers, and The Iron Heel, which Joe Kenehan is asked about, is one of London's most famous books on the subject.

Joe Hill (1879 – 1915) was a Swedish immigrant, labor activist, popular songwriter, and Wobbly. One night he was shot and wounded by his rival in a love triangle, and on that same night there was an unsolved double murder. Because of his wound, Hill was convicted and executed for the latter crime. He later became the subject of a classic American folk song, "I Dreamed I Saw Joe Hill Last Night." His ashes were placed into 600 small envelopes, and according to Wobbly folklore, sent around the world and released to the winds on May Day (Workers' Day) 1916. That's why Joe Kenehan answers that Hill is buried everywhere.

Frank Little (1879 – 1917) was a Wobbly organizing miners, lumberjacks, and oil field workers who was lynched by company thugs in Butte, Montana, for his union and anti-war activities.

"Big Bill" Haywood (1869 –1928) was involved in several important labor battles, and because of that was frequently the target of prosecutors. In 1907, he was tried and acquitted for murder in a trial that drew national attention. In 1918, he was one of 101 Wobblies convicted of violating the Espionage Act during the First Red Scare, which is yet another of our important topics. Haywood eventually fled to the Soviet Union, where he spent the remaining years of his life. Haywood's missing eye, that Joe Kenehan is asked about in the movie, was lost in a childhood accident.

Above all else, "Big Bill" Haywood was known as a founding member and leader of the Wobblies. The IWW was founded in 1905 by a group of about 30 labor radicals which also included Mary Harris "Mother" Jones (1837- 1930). She was an Irish-American schoolteacher and dressmaker who, after her husband and four children all died of yellow fever and her workshop was destroyed in a fire, became a prominent labor organizer. In 1902, at age 65, she was declared "the most dangerous woman in America" for her success in organizing mine workers and their families against the mine owners. In 1903, upset about the lax enforcement of the child labor laws in the Pennsylvania mines and silk mills, she organized a Children's March from Philadelphia to the home of then president Theodore Roosevelt in New York. Today's *Mother Jones* magazine is named for her.

Also, a founder of the Wobblies was Eugene W. Debs (1855 – 1926) who, in 1894, ran the Pullman Strike, affecting more than 250,000 workers in 27 states. President Grover Cleveland used the United States Army to break the strike and conservative courts used the Sherman Anti-Trust Act against the strikers. Debs served six months in prison. He became the nation's most prominent Socialist in the first decades of the 20th century and ran as the Socialist Party's candidate for the presidency five times. The last time, 1920, was from a prison cell, when he got 3.4% of the vote. Noted for his oratory, his speech denouncing American participation in World War I had led to his being convicted in 1918 under the Espionage Act and sentenced to 10 years.

The IWW pioneered creative tactics and organized along the lines of industrial unionism rather than craft unionism. Actually, they went even further, pursuing the goal of "One Big Union" (mentioned a couple times in our movie) and the abolition of the wage system. Most of its early members were miners, lumbermen, cannery and dock workers in the West. In 1912, the IWW organized a strike of more than twenty thousand textile workers, and by 1917, the Agricultural Workers Organization (AWO) of the IWW claimed a hundred thousand itinerant farm workers in the heartland of North America. Dedicated to workplace and economic democracy, the IWW allowed women as members and organized workers of all races and nationalities.

At its peak, the IWW had 150,000 members but it was fiercely repressed during the First Red Scare after World War I with many of its members killed, about 10,000 organizers imprisoned, and thousands more deported as foreign agitators. Then there were conflicts with other labor groups, particularly the American Federation of Labor (AFL) which regarded the IWW as too radical. The most decisive factor in the decline in IWW membership and influence, however, was a 1924 schism due to internal conflict, from which the IWW never fully recovered.

The first effective labor organization that was more than regional in membership and influence was the Knights of Labor, organized in 1869. In 1885, the Knights of Labor led railroad workers to victory against Jay Gould and his entire Southwestern Railway system. In early 1886, the Knights were trying to coordinate 1400 strikes involving over 600,000 workers spread over much of the country. Suddenly, it all collapsed, largely because the Knights were unable to handle so much at once, and because they took a smashing blow in the aftermath of the "Haymarket Riot" in May 1886 in Chicago.

In a fight between strikers and scabs, Chicago police intervened and attacked the strikers, killing four and wounding several others. As strikers were protesting the killings the next day in Haymarket Square, a group of anarchists infiltrated the striking Knights workers. As police were dispersing the peaceful rally, a bomb exploded. The police immediately opened fire. While the bomb killed seven policemen and wounded others, most of the police casualties seem to have been caused by bullets. About sixty officers were wounded along with an unknown number of civilians. The anarchists were blamed, and their spectacular trial gained international attention. The Knights of Labor were seriously injured by the false accusation that they promoted anarchistic violence. Many Knights locals transferred to the less radical unions of the more respectable American Federation of Labor.

The American Federation of Labor was formed in 1886 by the legendary Samuel Gompers. He founded it in large part because of the dissatisfaction of many trade union leaders with the Knights of Labor. The AFL was a federation of different unions and did not directly enroll workers. Its original goals were to encourage the formation of trade unions and to obtain legislation, such as prohibition of child labor, a national eight-hour work day, and exclusion of foreign contract workers. The AFL grew steadily in the late 19th century while the Knights all but disappeared. In 1955, the AFL merged with the Congress of Industrial Organizations and today the AFL-CIO represents eleven million workers.

During this period of the rise of unions, coal was the nation's main fuel, the gasoline of its day. But miners worked long hours in unsafe and dismal working conditions for low wages. Then in 1919, the United Mine Workers called a strike. They had agreed to a wage agreement to run until the end of World War I, and now that the war was over, they sought to capture some of their industry's wartime gains. Ignoring a court order, 400,000 coal workers walked out. The coal operators played the communist card, saying Lenin and Trotsky had ordered the strike and were financing it, and some of the press echoed the accusation. As the strike dragged on into its third week, supplies of the nation's main fuel were running low and the public called for stronger government action. After five weeks, the miners finally agreed to a 14% pay raise, far less than they wanted.

A few months before the strike at Matewan, union coal miners in other parts of the country went on strike, receiving a full 27 percent pay increase for their efforts. The United Mine Workers recognized that southern Appalachia, the location of the town of Matewan, was ripe for change, and sent in its top organizers, including the famous Mother Jones. Roughly 3000 out of 4000 men in the area signed the union's roster in the spring of 1920, something that they knew could cost them their jobs, and in many cases their homes. In Matewan it was unanimous, everyone signed up. And sure enough, as you will see in the movie, Stone Mountain Coal Corporation fought back with mass firings, harassment, and evictions.

Remember our friends the Robber Barons? Few of them even bothered to justify their great wealth, but many of those who did took the "survival of the fittest" doctrine from Charles Darwin's theory of evolution and applied it to human society. They argued that the wealthy were the fittest who triumphed in the jungle of the marketplace and therefore the government should not impose its regulations on them. This became known as "Social Darwinism."

Andrew Carnegie was a Social Darwinist but he also advocated what he called "the Gospel of Wealth," which held that the wealthy have a responsibility to use their wealth to benefit society. He held that "The man who dies rich... dies disgraced." To that end, after selling Carnegie Steel Company to J. P. Morgan, Carnegie devoted the remainder of his life to large-scale philanthropy, with special emphasis on local libraries, world peace, education, and scientific research. He gave away more than 350 million dollars before he died.

John D. Rockefeller, who was a devout Northern Baptist and abstained from alcohol and tobacco throughout his life, agreed with Carnegie on this issue. Rockefeller spent the last 40 years of his life in retirement and creating the modern systematic approach of targeted philanthropy. He was able to do this through the creation of foundations that had a major effect on medicine, education, and scientific research.

But all this Christian charity didn't keep the Robber Barons from hiring criminals and even murdering women and children to keep unions out of their mines and factories. If the violence the company inflicts on the strikers in *Matewan* seems extreme, it is actually mild compared to what occurred during other strikes of the period.

The Homestead Strike, for instance, was a bloody labor confrontation lasting 143 days in 1892, one of the most serious in U.S. history. The conflict was centered on Carnegie Steel's main plant in Homestead, Pennsylvania, and after a recent increase in profits by 60%, the company refused to raise worker's pay by more than 30%. Management locked the union out.

Carnegie was conveniently out of the country at the time but his associate and partner Henry Clay Frick brought in thousands of strikebreakers. On July 6, 1892 the arrival of a force of 300 Pinkerton agents (actually, thugs-for-hire, just like the Baldwin-Felts thugs in *Matewan*) from New York City and Chicago resulted in a fight in which 10 men—seven strikers and three Pinkertons—were killed and hundreds were injured. Pennsylvania Governor Robert Pattison ordered two brigades of state militia to the strike site. Then, anarchist Alexander Berkman, not directly connected to the strike, shot and wounded Frick in an attempted assassination. The company successfully resumed operations with non-union immigrant employees; however, Carnegie's reputation was permanently damaged by Homestead.

The Ludlow Massacre was an attack on a tent colony of 1,200 coal miners and their families during a United Mine Workers strike at Ludlow, Colorado in 1914. The attackers were the Colorado National Guard and guards from the Colorado Fuel & Iron Company, owned by Rockefeller. The massacre resulted in the violent deaths of possibly as many as 25 people including two women and eleven children, burned to death under a tent. In retaliation for Ludlow, the miners armed themselves and attacked dozens of mines over the next ten days, destroying property and engaging in several skirmishes with the Colorado National Guard along a 40-mile front. The entire strike would cost possibly as many as 199 lives.

The Ludlow Massacre was also a watershed moment in American labor relations. Congress responded to public outcry by directing the House Committee on Mines and Mining to investigate the incident. Its report, published in 1915, was influential in promoting child labor laws (preacher-miner Danny in the movie is barely fifteen) and an eight-hour workday.

When Joe Kenehan is finally admitted into that secret union meeting, we are treated to a tour de force of filmmaking. Director John Sayles gets some exceptional performances from colorful local nonprofessionals and script writer John Sayles provides some powerful dialogue, especially Joe Kenehan's speech in which he explains that the "coloreds" and the "dagos" aren't the workers' enemies and that a true union would include everyone. Actor John Sayles also turns in a fine performance as the evangelical preacher who considers unions the work of "Beelzebub" (the Devil). The Italian wife Rosaria, who exclaims against "Sindacatos!" when Joe and Sephus come into her home to get her husband to join the union, she is played by Maggi Renzi, Sayles' long-time life and creative partner.

Probably no one else has attained the same level of artistic achievement as both novelist and filmmaker as John Sayles. There is more on this subject in Recommendations. As both novelist and filmmaker, Sayles is something of a throwback to the literary naturalists of the late nineteenth and early twentieth centuries such as Frank Norris, Upton Sinclair, and John Dos Passos. *Matewan* is generally considered his best film and Sayles himself thinks enough of it to have written a book about it: *Thinking in Pictures: The Making of the Movie Matewan* (1987).

Sayles illuminated the process of adapting history for the screen when he said in an interview, "It seemed to me that this episode epitomized a fifteen-year period of American labor history... I incorporated things that weren't literally true of the Matewan massacre, but were true of that general fifteen-year period. I wanted to be true to the larger picture, so I crammed a certain amount of related but not strictly factual stuff into that particular story."

In *Matewan*, Sayles depicts a Wobbly vision of the white working class overcoming ethnic prejudice and all three groups, whites, blacks, and Italians, joining together against the company, which is a beautiful vision, if not an overly optimistic one for that era. This idealistic vision is illustrated in the scene in which the American workers teach the Italians baseball, but even more memorably, when musicians from all three groups finally overcome initial resistance and the Italian mandolin, country fiddle, and blues harmonica jam.

As was mentioned and as you are about to see, *Matewan* climaxes with one of the most accurate and least Hollywood of shoot out scenes.

After

The narrator, of course, is the teenage preacher Danny as an elderly man. The intertwined contending themes of *Matewan* are Joe's pacifist-socialist beliefs and Danny's Christianity. They both come together in Danny's committing his life after Joe's martyrdom to preaching the Wobbly vision of "one big union." Elderly Danny (a fictional character) tells us that, about nine months after the shoot out, heroic Police Chief Sid Hatfield (an historical character) was assassinated by Baldwin-Felts agents in broad daylight on courthouse steps and no one was arrested for it. And that was the start of what Danny calls, "The Great Coalfield War." Actually, that is the title of a book about the Ludlow Strike by 1972 Democratic presidential nominee George McGovern. What followed the Matewan shoot out is known as the "Battle of Blair Mountain."

Stories vary as to who fired the first shot in the actual Matewan shoot out, which occurred on May 19, 1920. But the ensuing gun battle left seven detectives and three townspeople dead, including Mayor Testerman and the Felts brothers. Miners hailed the battle for the number of casualties inflicted on the Baldwin-Felts detectives. Matewan, along with the Ludlow Massacre six years earlier, marked an important turning point in the battle for miners' rights.

Sid Hatfield (a descendant of half of the notorious Hatfield and McCoy Feud) became an immediate hero and symbol of hope that the coal operators and their hired guns could be defeated. Throughout the summer and into the fall of 1920, both sides were bolstering their arms, and Sid converted Mayor Testerman's jewelry store into a gun shop (and married his widow, as elderly Danny mentioned).

Acquitted for killing Albert Felts in a trial that brought national attention to the miners' cause, Hatfield's mythical stature grew even more. Then on August 1, 1921, he traveled to McDowell County to stand trial for new spurious charges: dynamiting coal company equipment. Along with him was a good friend, Ed Chambers, and as they walked up the courthouse stairs, unarmed and flanked by their wives, a group of Baldwin-Felts agents at the top of the stairs opened fire. Hatfield was killed instantly, while Chambers' bullet-riddled body rolled to the bottom of the stairs. Danny says that the company spy and traitor C.E. Lively (the traitorous store owner with glasses in the movie) shot Sid in the head but it may actually have been Chambers that he shot.

Enraged armed miners (many, like Sid, veterans of World War I) poured out of the mountains determined to march into the counties of Logan and Mingo (location of Matewan) and set up the union by force. Mother Jones tried unsuccessfully to stop them, rightly fearing a bloodbath. After four days, 13,000 had gathered in nearby Kanawha County and began marching towards Logan County. Along the way they commandeered a freight train to "Bloody Mingo," as narrator Danny called it. Meanwhile, the anti-union Sheriff of Logan County, Don Chafin, had begun to set up defenses on Blair Mountain with a private armed force of nearly 2,000 (the largest in the nation's history) paid for by the Coal Operators Association.

Republican President Warren Harding threatened to send in federal troops. Negotiators convinced the miners to return home until Chafin's men started deliberately shooting union sympathizers in a town near Blair Mountain and infuriated miners turned back towards Blair Mountain. Chafin's men, though outnumbered, had the advantage of the high ground and better weaponry. Historian Clayton D. Laurie has an article, "The United States Army and the Return to Normalcy in Labor Dispute Interventions: The Case of the West Virginia Coal Mine Wars, 1920-1921," on http://www.wvculture.org. Laurie maintains that the famous General Billy Mitchell ordered Army bombers to provide aerial surveillance for the private planes of the Coal Operators Association, which were dropping gas and bombs on the miners. To defeat unions, the federal government used air power against U.S. citizens.

Gun battles continued for a week, with the miners at one point nearly breaking through to Logan and Mingo counties. Up to 30 deaths were reported by Chafin's side and between 50 and 100 on the miners' side, with many hundreds more injured. By September 2, federal troops arrived and miners started heading home the following day. Almost a million rounds had been fired. 985 miners were indicted for murder and treason against the State of West Virginia. Though some were acquitted by sympathetic juries, many were imprisoned.

Attorneys for union leader Bill Blizzard used one of those World War I aerial bombs that didn't explode as evidence in court. It gained enough sympathy from the jury for an acquittal. In the short term, the battle was an overwhelming victory for management. Over the next several years, United Mine Workers membership plummeted from more than 50,000 miners to approximately 10,000.

There was a group of reformers during this same period who were allied with labor and were known as the Progressives. "Progressivism" is an umbrella label for a wide range of economic, political, social, and moral reforms and the Progressives were a diverse lot that included Republicans and Democrats, Protestants, Catholics, and Jews, and urban and rural reformers. But for the most part, Progressives were urban and college-educated, and included journalists, academics, teachers, doctors, and nurses, as well as business people. The Progressive Era was between the 1890s and the 1920s and almost all the notable figures of the period, whether in politics, philosophy, scholarship, or literature, were connected at least in part with this reform movement.

For Progressives, government was not the problem but the solution. They believed in using government, especially the federal government, as an instrument of reform, because only government had the power for the kinds of reforms that were called for. Leading politicians from both parties, most notably Theodore Roosevelt, Charles Evans Hughes, and Robert LaFollette on the Republican side, and William Jennings Bryan, Woodrow Wilson, and Al Smith on the Democratic side, took up the cause of progressive reform.

Progressive journalists were called "Muckrakers." They used the new mass circulation newspapers and magazines to expose political corruption, stock market manipulation, false advertising, vices, impure food and drugs, racial discrimination, and lynching. African American journalist Ida M. Tarbell's crusade against the Standard Oil Trust resulted in reforms; as did *The Jungle*, Upton Sinclair's novel exposing unsanitary conditions in the Chicago meat packing houses and the grip of the beef trust on the nation's meat supply.

A seminal event for both the Progressives and the labor movement must be mentioned: the Triangle Shirtwaist Factory fire in New York City on March 25, 1911. It was the deadliest industrial disaster in the history of the city of New

York and resulted in the fourth highest loss of life from an industrial accident in U.S. history. Because the managers had locked the doors to the stairwells and exits – a common practice at the time to prevent pilferage and unauthorized breaks – many of the workers could not escape the burning building. The fire caused the deaths of 146 garment workers and injured 71. Most of the victims were Jewish and Italian immigrant women aged sixteen to twenty-three. They died from the fire, smoke inhalation, or falling or jumping to their deaths from the eighth, ninth, and tenth floors to the streets below. The fire led to legislation requiring improved factory safety standards and helped spur the growth of the International Ladies' Garment Workers' Union, which fought for better working conditions for sweatshop workers.

Four constitutional amendments—the Sixteenth through Nineteenth—resulted from progressive activism: the federal income tax, direct election of Senators, prohibition, and women's suffrage. It will take the cataclysm of the Great Depression and the subsequent election of Franklin Roosevelt for the unions to finally get the reforms they fought for, such as unemployment insurance, old age pensions, minimum wage regulation, conservation and development of natural resources, and serious restrictions on child labor. Today, "progressive" is the self-descriptive adjective favored by most political activists on the left.

Women's organizations stood at the forefront of the social reforms and policy innovations during the Progressive era, and probably the most prominent reformer of the Progressive Era was Jane Addams (1860 – 1935). She was a pioneer social worker, public philosopher, sociologist, author, and a proponent of women's suffrage, a foe of city bosses, and an opponent of World War I. The daughter of one of the wealthiest men in Illinois, she founded Hull House in Chicago in 1889, providing social services to 9,000 per week of the city's poor, mostly immigrants. Hull House inspired more than 400 other settlement houses around the country. Addams was a key architect of what we would come to call the welfare state and helped create the role of the social worker. In 1931, she became the first American woman to be awarded the Nobel Peace Prize.

The women's suffrage movement began with the 1848 Seneca Falls Convention, organized by Elizabeth Cady Stanton and Lucretia Mott, and the Declaration of Sentiments demanding equal rights for women. Many of the activists became politically aware during the abolitionist movement. Around 1912, protests became increasingly common as suffragette Alice Paul led parades through the capital and major cities. Suffragists were arrested during their "Silent Sentinels" pickets at the White House, the first time such a tactic was used.

Across the world, grateful nations gave women the vote after their enthusiastic participation on the home front in World War I. Furthermore, most of the Western states of the U.S. had already given women the right to vote in state and national elections, and the congressional representatives from those states, including the first woman, Jeannette Rankin of Montana, demonstrated that women's suffrage was a success. The main resistance came from the South, where white leaders were worried about the threat of black women voting. Congress passed the Nineteenth Amendment in 1919 and women could vote nationally by 1920.

During the early years of the Progressive Era, there was a short-lived rural reform movement, The People's Party (1892-96), also known as the "Populists." Based among poor, white cotton farmers in the South and hard-pressed wheat farmers in the plains states, it represented a radical crusading form of agrarianism and hostility to banks, railroads, the gold standard, and elites generally. It sometimes formed coalitions with labor unions. The Populists showed impressive strength in the West and South in the 1892 elections, and their candidate for President polled more than a million votes. In 1896, the Democrats endorsed the Populist presidential nominee, William Jennings Bryan. The terms "populist" and "populism" are commonly used today to describe anti-elitism.

There is a subplot in *Matewan*, the framing of Joe Kenehan by Company spy C.E. Lively, that has some very affecting and well-done scenes but ultimately its convolutions and resolution stretch plausibility. Nevertheless, the subplot climaxes with Joe and Few Clothes alone in the woods discussing their respective wars. A couple of those important historical topics for which teachers love this film have not been mentioned yet: the Spanish-American War and World War I. The battles and diplomacy of the latter war will be covered in a later chapter so we will focus on just the home front here. World War I had been over for two years at the time of the Matewan strike and the Spanish American War for a little more than twenty.

When Joe asks if Few Clothes knows how to handle the pistol in his hand, Few Clothes replies, "Tenth Cavalry ... in Cuba ... back in '98."

Few Clothes was one of the 5000 black soldiers who participated in the Spanish–American War, a conflict in 1898 between Spain and the United States, effectively the result of American intervention in the Cuban War of Independence. In the late 1890's, American public opinion was agitated by the anti-Spanish propaganda of the "yellow journalism" of Joseph Pulitzer and William Randolph Hearst in the circulation wars of their New York City newspapers. After the mysterious sinking of the American battleship Maine in Havana harbor, politics pressured President William McKinley into a war he wanted to avoid.

"San Juan Hill ... pretty rough down there?" Joe asks Few Clothes about his war.

The Battle of San Juan Hill was the bloodiest and most famous battle of the war. It was also the location of the greatest victory for the Rough Riders as claimed by the press and their commander, Theodore Roosevelt, who became vice president on the strength of his performance in that battle. What the

American press of the time overlooked was that the "Buffalo Soldiers" (Negro Cavalry) had actually done much of the heaviest fighting.

"A splendid little war", is what Secretary of State John Hay called the Spanish–American War. He was formerly one of Lincoln's two secretaries, nearly omnipresent though silent in the movie *Lincoln*. The Spanish–American War involved a series of quick American victories on land and at sea. American attacks on Spain's Pacific possessions led to involvement in the Philippine Revolution and ultimately to the Philippine–American War. That is one of the most obscure of U.S. wars, like the equally obscure U.S.-Mexican War, and like it, the Philippine–American War was a bald-faced land grab. Instead of liberating the Filipinos from the Spanish yoke as we claimed we were doing, we simply replaced it with our own yoke. To do that we fought and defeated Filipino patriots at the cost of (estimates vary widely) possibly a million Filipino lives. At the peace conference with Spain, the United States acquired the Philippines, Puerto Rico, and Guam.

Also in 1898, after a complex series of events including an armed uprising, business interests led by Sanford Dole wrested control of Hawaii and, against the wishes of the native Hawaiians, arranged to have the U.S. annex the islands. The next year, the "Open Door Policy," created by U.S. Secretary of State John Hay, allowed the imperial powers equal access to Chinese markets, with no one of them controlling all of China (and of course the Chinese were not consulted).

All this engendered the American Anti-Imperialist League, an organization established in 1898 to battle the annexation of the Philippines. Believing imperialism violated the fundamental principles of the republic, League members were a diverse group that included Andrew Carnegie and Mark Twain, John Dewey and Samuel Gompers, and both Henry and William James. Nevertheless, the Anti-Imperialist League was ultimately defeated in the battle for public opinion.

But soon enough, Americans lost interest in an empire and turned their international attention to the building of the Panama Canal. The Canal Zone was "acquired" in 1904 after Teddy Roosevelt arranged a successful Panamanian "independence movement" from Colombia. The canal was one of the largest and most difficult engineering projects ever undertaken, one that France had already begun and abandoned when the U.S. took over. It required the resolving of formidable engineering problems and the eradication of tropical diseases that threatened the workforce. After a decade, the canal was completed, making it possible for ships (including American war ships) to travel between the Atlantic and Pacific Oceans in half the time previously required. This allowed the U.S. West Coast and the nations along the Pacific Ocean to become more integrated into the world economy.

In 1904, Theodore Roosevelt declared the "Roosevelt Corollary" to the Monroe Doctrine asserting the right of the United States to intervene in the internal affairs of Latin American countries. Between the time of the war with Spain and 1934, the United States conducted military operations and occupations in Panama, Honduras, Nicaragua, Mexico, Haiti, and the Dominican Republic. These military interventions became known as the "Banana Wars" because they were so often protecting the investments in bananas and other products of the United Fruit Company. The Banana Wars ended with Franklin Roosevelt's Good Neighbor Policy in 1934, at least until the Cold War provided a new excuse to intervene.

In 1914, U.S. troops occupied the Mexican port of Veracruz as part of Woodrow Wilson's efforts to overthrow the military dictator Victoriano Huerta, who had murdered the elected president Francisco Madero. Where Wilson failed, Pancho Villa succeeded in the Battle of Zacatecas in 1914, the bloodiest of the Mexican Revolution. But in 1916, in retaliation for U.S. support of other political enemies, Villa led 1,500 raiders in a cross-border attack against Columbus, New Mexico, killing 17 of its residents. Wilson responded by sending 12,000 troops, under General John J. Pershing, into Mexico to capture Villa, which they failed to do. Then the U.S. entered World War I.

During our involvement in that war, about 1% of the nearly half million German Americans were imprisoned. Allegations against them included spying for Germany or endorsing the German war effort. Anti-German hysteria spread throughout the country. In Collinsville, Illinois, German-born Robert Prager was dragged from jail as a suspected spy and lynched. The perpetrators were acquitted due to their patriotic motives.

The American Protective League was one of many private conservative "patriotic associations," working with the Federal Bureau of Investigation, that sprang up to support the war and at the same time fight labor unions and various left-wing and pacifist organizations. The Espionage Act of 1917 and the Sedition Act of 1918 criminalized any expression of opinion that used "disloyal, profane, scurrilous or abusive language" about the U.S. government, flag, or armed forces. Laws like those, plus government police action, the private vigilante groups, and public hysteria, threatened the civil liberties of those who disagreed with Wilson's war policies (which will be explained in a later chapter).

During World War I, conscientious objectors were permitted to serve in noncombatant military roles, but about 2000 absolute conscientious objectors refused to cooperate in any way with the military and were sent to military prisons. Joe Kenehan would have been one of those. When telling Few Clothes about his prison experiences, Joe describes the torture of Mennonites. They were a Dutch Protestant sect noted for their simplicity of living and commitment to pacifism.

But Sayles has everyone victimized by war not just Joe and the Mennonites. Few Clothes "did what I had to" in the Spanish-American War, and even Hickey, the older of those two delicious villains Hickey and Griggs, just sits in his trench and kills Germans fleeing into it, as we learn when he explains to

Danny about his World War I medal. That's another horror of war: it makes heroes of monsters like him.

The hysterical and repressive domestic political climate during World War I easily carried over into the post-war "First Red Scare." It was fueled by labor unrest and anarchist bombings and then spurred on by the Bolshevik take-over of Russia. The First Red Scare occurred during 1919–1920 and was characterized by exaggerated rhetoric, illegal search and seizures, unwarranted arrests and detentions, and the deportation of several hundred suspected radicals and anarchists. The high point was "The Palmer Raids" which occurred in November 1919 and January 1920 under the leadership of U.S. Attorney General A. Mitchell Palmer and which resulted in 500 deportations. The First Red Scare effectively ended in the middle of 1920, after Palmer forecast a massive radical uprising on May Day and the day passed without incident.

This anti-communist crusade existed outside the U.S. as well. After winning the war in Europe, the Allied powers militarily backed the pro-Tsarist, anti-Bolshevik White forces in the Russian Civil War. In what became known as the "North Russia Intervention," also as the "Northern Russian Expedition", 14 nations contributed troops, the U.S. sending 13,000. It lasted from the final months of World War I in 1918 through to 1919. Allied efforts were hampered by divided objectives, lack of an overarching strategy, war weariness, and lack of public support. The Bolsheviks were eventually victorious in the civil war and established the Soviet Union.

In 1890, American industrial production and per capita income exceeded that of any other nation. Then there was a severe nationwide depression, called the Panic of 1893 (that was the one where J.P. Morgan and the Rothschilds bailed out the U.S. government). But the country recovered, and by 1900, the U.S. again had the strongest economy in the world. Apart from two short recessions in 1907 and 1920, the economy remained prosperous and growing until the Great Depression. That was the lethal hangover after the big party of the Twenties, the subject of the next film.

Timeline for First Twenty Years of Twentieth Century

1869 Knights of Labor organized.
1886 The American Federation of Labor formed.
1892 Ellis Island opened.
1898 The USS Maine exploded in Havana harbor, a major catalyst for the Spanish-American War. That was a ten-week war fought in Cuba and the Philippines. After crushing an armed resistance, the U.S. assumed colonial control of the Philippines.
   -Republic of Hawaii annexed against the will of the Hawaiians.
   -The American Anti-Imperialist League organized.
1899 The Open Door Policy was announced.
1900 The United States helped put down the Boxer Rebellion, a popular

uprising against foreign control of China.
1901 William McKinley assassinated and Theodore Roosevelt becomes the 26th President of the United States.
1903 The movie *The Great Train Robbery* opened.
-The Ford Motor Company was formed.
-The first World Series was played.
-The Wright brothers made their first powered flight.
1904 The Roosevelt Corollary to the Monroe Doctrine was issued.
-The Panama Canal Zone was acquired.
1905 The Industrial Workers of the World was founded.
1906 The Pure Food and Drug Act and the Meat Inspection Act were passed.
-The Great San Francisco Earthquake and Fire kills about 3,000 and destroys over 80% of the city.
1908 The Ford Model T appeared on the market.
-The Federal Bureau of Investigation was established.
1909 William Howard Taft became President.
-The NAACP, or National Association for the Advancement of Colored People, was founded by a biracial group of religious leaders and humanitarians.
1910 The Fundamentals are published which spell out the basic precepts of fundamentalist religious belief.
1911 Dissident Republicans bolt the party and form the Progressive Party, which endorses anti-trust enforcement, collective bargaining, and conservation of national resources.
-Triangle Shirtwaist Company fire
-The Supreme Court broke up Standard Oil
1912 The Titanic sank.
-Teddy Roosevelt was shot, but not killed, while campaigning for the Bull Moose Party.
1913 Woodrow Wilson became President.
-The Sixteenth Amendment establishes an income tax.
-The Federal Reserve System is established controlling nation's currency and credit.
-Henry Ford developed the modern assembly line.
1914 World War I began in Europe.
-The Federal Trade Commission is established preventing monopolies and noncompetitive business practices.
1915 Margaret Sanger, who coined the term "birth control," is arrested in New York for distributing contraceptive information.
-Leo Frank, a Jew, is lynched in Atlanta, Georgia, for allegedly murdering a young female employee.
1916 Margaret Sanger opened the nation's first birth control clinic in Brooklyn.
1917 The United States entered World War I.
-First Red Scare: hysterical overreaction by law enforcement to the threat of communism.
1919 The Treaty of Versailles ended World War I.
-The Eighteenth Amendment establishes prohibition of alcohol.
-Black Sox Scandal in which gamblers "fixed" the World Series.
1920 The Nineteenth Amendment granted women the vote.
-Sacco and Vanzetti were arrested.

-The first radio broadcasts were made in Pittsburgh, Pennsylvania, and Detroit, Michigan.
  -First Red Scare ended.

Recommendations

A film that would have worked in this chapter almost as well as *Matewan* is *The Molly Maguires* (1970). It too is masterful and it too combines the labor struggle with immigration; in this case, that of the Irish. *The Molly Maguires* too has a great look thanks to multi-Academy Award winning cinematographer James Wong Howe and art direction that garnered an Academy Award nomination. It is a color film but the palate is mostly grays from the houses coated with coal dust to the slagheap mountain ranges. And most affectingly, small boys in their permanent dust cloud, doing work that required their small hands: picking stones from the coal on conveyor belts. It was filmed in a Pennsylvania coal town in which the only change from the 1870s was TV antennas. Complementing the visual imagery is a classic score by the great Henry Mancini.

This coal mining is in "Pennsylvania 1876," as a screen title tells us at the beginning, where on average ten miners per week were killed in mining accidents and many more were maimed. The original Molly Maguire may have been a poor Irish widow evicted by her English landlord. The underground Irish organization named after her exacted vengeance for the oppression of the coal companies by blowing up mines, trains, and other facilities.

The major historical discrepancies are with star Sean Connery's character, Jack Kehoe, who was indeed a leader of the Mollies but he was a pub owner and not a miner as in the film. And the villain played by Richard Harris, James McParland, judging from his long career as a union buster, probably didn't have the ambivalence and qualms of his film counterpart.

The script is by Hollywood veteran Walter Bernstein who, along with the director Martin Ritt, was blacklisted during the McCarthy Era. Indeed this movie was a labor of love and a political statement by all involved most importantly the stars. When the film was made, a topic of political debate was: is political violence ever justified (of the type then promulgated by the Black Panthers)? While the film answers in the affirmative by showing the ancestors of many white conservatives using political violence, it also points to the futility of that type of violence.

There is an unusually rich store of movies about labor and immigration and the first two decades of the twentieth century.

Martin Ritt returned to this theme in 1979 with *Norma Rae*, which tells the true story of a factory worker from a small town in North Carolina who becomes involved in union activities at the textile factory where she works. A huge box office success (which *The Molly Maguires* was not), the film also garnered the best actress award for star Sally Field from both the Academy and Cannes.

Blue Collar (1978) stars renowned comedian Richard Pryor in a dramatic role. He plays one of three Detroit autoworkers who rob a safe at the head-quarters of their union but instead of money find evidence of corruption. It's gripping and plausible and covers the grueling world of the autoworker, a job for many thousands through the twentieth century.

Hoffa (1992) is a film about Jimmy Hoffa, the notoriously corrupt president of the Teamsters' Union when it was the biggest in the country with 1.5 million members. He disappeared suddenly and inexplicably. The film stars Jack Nicholson and has a script by Pulitzer Prize-winning playwright David Mamet.

Possibly the greatest film on this subject, and one of the greatest films of all time, is *On the Waterfront* (1954). Based on a Pulitzer Prize winning newspaper series on waterfront union corruption, it won 8 Academy Awards including Best Picture, Best Actor for star Marlon Brando, Best Director for Elia Kazan, and Best Screenplay for Budd Schulberg. Leonard Bernstein's classic score was nominated but didn't win. *On the Waterfront* was shot on the docks of Hoboken, New Jersey, and it beautifully captured the gritty feel of the place and the dockworkers' lives. It is the consensus of critics and scholars that Brando in this film changed film acting forever.

For the topic of immigration, you can't do better than *The Godfather II* (1974), specifically the section about the childhood and young manhood of Vito Corleone (as played by Robert De Niro). It beautifully captures an immigrant community (in this case Italian) in the early years of the twentieth century: the street atmosphere, the celebrations, the theaters, etc.

Joan Micklin Silver's *Hester Street* (1975) tells the story of Jewish immigrants on the Lower Eastside of New York City in 1896. Star Carol Kane got an Oscar nomination in this story of the difficulties and ironies of assimilation set against an unusually accurate reconstruction of Jewish immigrant life.

Far and Away (1992) is a vehicle for the then-married stars Tom Cruise and Nicole Kidman, he the Irish peasant and she the daughter of his English landlord. There's a lot of silly formula fist fighting and romance but there is also a lot of good history starting in Ireland and the circumstances that impelled immigration. It all climaxes in the grand dramatic Oklahoma Land Rush and its prize of free farmland.

America, America (1963) is an obscure masterwork that has few scenes set in the U.S. yet as the title suggests is about an obsession with the U.S. Based upon the life of the uncle of the film's writer, director, and producer, Elia Kazan, it is set in the late 1890s and focuses on a young Greek in an impoverished Turkish village who witnesses brutal oppression of the Greek and Armenian minorities and who develops an obsession with reaching America. It's in a richly contrasting black-and-white with period and cultural details such that it won the Academy Award for Best Art Direction. The film was nominated for

Oscars for Best Director, Best Picture, and Best Screen-play. At nearly three hours, it is a torturous heart-breaking ordeal that will give you insight like nothing else into what this country has meant to so many and some of the sacrifices made to get here.

America, America ends at the Statue of Liberty and Charlie Chaplin's classic *The Immigrant* (1917) has, in the middle of a comic short, a jolting scene of solemn reverence when the poor immigrants see Lady Liberty for the first time. *The Immigrant* is pure fun start to finish and has a rare authenticity because an immigrant made it during the classic period of immigration.

Ragtime (1981) is the screen adaptation of a novel of the same name by the preeminent historical novelist E.L. Doctorow. The story takes place during the first decade of the twentieth century, and it makes brilliant use of the two nascent American art forms that would conquer the world in the twentieth century: movies and popular music. *Ragtime* recreated primitive early newsreels in which we see important historical characters of the era including financier J. P. Morgan, President Theodore Roosevelt, escape artist Harry Houdini, and African American civil rights leader Booker T. Washington. It might almost have worked in place of *Matewan*, but *Ragtime* has one big flaw for our purposes: most of it focuses on a very tiny percentage of the population, the wealthy.

Ragtime has some strong beautifully detailed scenes set in a very poor Jewish neighborhood of New York City in that era. The quality of those scenes is not surprising given the film's artistic pedigree: two-time Oscar-winning director Milos Foreman, adaptation by eminent playwright Michael Weller, and it was the last film for 1930s stars James Cagney and Pat O'Brien. But the plot strands of *Ragtime* are only loosely connected. The lurid true central story, the Stanford White high society murder, isn't interesting enough and has no protagonists that we care about. More of its screen time should have gone to the strand that followed a poor Jewish immigrant who became one of the first of that most dominant of all twentieth century artists: a movie director. Another plot strand concerns northern racism and involves a victimized black ragtime musician and a wealthy white family trying to help him. It illustrates powerfully the random racist violence, even in the North, that threatened any black man but especially a successful one.

The 1988 Emmy-winning miniseries *The Murder of Mary Phagan*, written by Larry McMurtry and starring Jack Lemmon and Kevin Spacey, is a dramatization of the true story of Leo Frank, a prominent Jewish factory manager charged and convicted with murdering a 13-year-old factory worker named Mary Phagan, in Atlanta, Georgia in 1913. After Frank's legal appeals had failed, Georgia Governor John M. Slaton in 1915, destroying his own political career in the process, commuted Frank's death sentence to life imprisonment. But then Frank was kidnapped from prison and lynched by a small group of prominent men of Marietta, Georgia, including an ex-Governor. As was the custom with lynchings of blacks, photographs were taken of the

Frank lynching, which were sold as postcards in local stores for 25 cents each, along with pieces of the rope, Frank's nightshirt, and branches from the tree. Sometimes salesmen sold lynching postcards door-to-door.

For leftist radicals of the early years of the twentieth century, we have *Reds* (1981), voted ninth best epic film of all time in an American Film Institute poll. Remember when Few Clothes asked Joe Kenehan if he was a "red"? They then shared a laugh at the cartoonish public perception of communists. *Reds* tries to repair that perception in a big-budget Hollywood epic that centers on the life and career of John Reed, a journalist and communist activist of the first two decades of the twentieth century. He is most famous for chronicling the Russian Revolution in his book *Ten Days that Shook the World* (1919). *Reds* stars Warren Beatty who also co-wrote, produced, and directed. Diane Keaton (Beatty's real life paramour during the filming) played Reed's paramour, feminist Louise Bryant, and Jack Nicholson played playwright Eugene O'Neill, long before his Nobel Prize.

Reed, Bryant, O'Neill, and their cohorts initially came together in opposition to American involvement in World War I — a war whose motive Reed succinctly identifies in the film as "profit." Or as Joe Kenehan put it to Danny during a game of catch, it was a case of "workers recruited to kill workers." The irony is that twenty years later, almost everybody agreed that the U.S. should not have entered World War I. Indeed, that very attitude caused an isolationism that hindered preparation for World War II.

Germane to our purposes, *Reds* also features "witnesses," elderly Americans who either knew Reed and Bryant or were contemporaneous with them. The film is punctuated with short pieces of interviews with the witnesses, the most famous of whom is classic modernist writer Henry Miller (1891–1980). The "witnesses" also give documentary heft to a film that is over half romance. *Reds* was nominated for 12 Oscars, winning three, including best cinematography and best director. This film about the only American buried in the Kremlin came out in 1981 at the beginning of the presidency of the most notoriously anti-communist of presidents, Ronald Reagan, who screened the film in the White House.

Iron-Jawed Angels (2004) is an HBO production and a true story about the radical young suffragettes Alice Paul (Oscar-winner Hilary Swank) and Lucy Burns (Frances O'Conor) during the early years of the Twentieth Century as they revolutionize the movement to get women the right to vote. They picket outside the White House and draw the ire of President Woodrow Wilson. Then they get arrested and serve 60-day sentences where they suffer under unsanitary and inhumane conditions. Then Paul and other women undertake a hunger strike during which guards force-feed them milk and raw eggs.

For the home front during World War I, there is *East of Eden*, a 1955 classic directed by Elia Kazan and based on the last quarter of the novel of the same name by John Steinbeck, which he considered his magnum opus. It is about a wayward young man (the iconic James Dean in his first major screen role) seeking his own identity and vying for the affection of his deeply religious father against a favored brother, paralleling the story of Cain and Abel. Set in the central California coastal towns of Monterey and Salinas, it touches most of the bases of the World War I homefront: jingoism, war profiteering, the draft, and anti-German rioting. This is another case of the movie improving on the book.

For Asian foreign policy during the early years of the twentieth century, there is *55 Days at Peking* (1963). Inspite of the star power of Charlton Heston, Ava Gardener, and David Niven, plus the requisite spectacle and romance of a big budget epic of the time, it was a box office catastrophe. It is a dramatization of the siege of the foreign legations in Peking (now Beijing) during the Boxer Rebellion of 1900. Fed up with foreign domination (Remember the "Open Door Policy"?), the Dowager Empress used the Boxer secret societies to attack foreigners within China. There is a lot of silliness in this movie, such as Caucasian actors in the principle Chinese roles, and of course it's full of imperialist heroics, but over all it's fair to the Chinese perspective. The filmmakers were thinking of the distant future when they quoted Napoleon in the dialogue, "Let China sleep, for when she wakes the world will tremble." She has long been awake. Every informed American needs to know the history in this movie. The Chinese do.

Also, there is *The Sand Pebbles* (1966) starring Steve McQueen as a rebellious machinist's mate in 1920s China aboard a fictional gunboat. It represents the Western gunboats that for decades patrolled the Yangtze River enforcing unfair trading privileges and asserting political influence in China.

Barack Obama is not only the first black president, he is also the first Hawaiian president. There have been a number of films on the history of that isolated Pacific one of these United States. The most recent, *Princess Kaiulani* (2009), stars Q'orianka Kilcher, the magnetic young actress who played Pocahontas in *The New World*. Here she is again a heathen princess in love with an Englishman but there is fortunately much more to this film, though it got mostly bad reviews. Roger Ebert called it an "interesting but creaky biopic." Fair enough, but it is also gorgeous looking, uses Q'orianka Kilcher well, and it gets right the politics that lead to the blatant and indisputable theft of Hawaii from the Hawaiians by a U.S. government lead by business interests and their bought politicians.

Hawaii (1966) was based on part of James Michener's best-selling novel of the same name and is about the first American missionaries there. It's a familiar Puritans in the tropics affair with a predictable romantic subplot between Julie Andrew's missionary wife and Richard Harris' reappeared ex-lover. It does devote a lot of time to the Hawaiians and their customs.

The Hawaiians (1970) was from the same Michener novel and has Charlton Heston playing a fictionalized amalgam of Lorrin Thurston, Sanford Dole and other leaders of the business insurgency (some of whom were children and grandchildren of the missionaries). Heston's swaggering capitalist conquistador is unintentionally comical and even offensive. It was one of the last serious attempts by Hollywood to find anything admirable in the type. Forty years later in *Princess Kaiulani,* Lorrin Thurston is a grasping schemer and Sanford Dole is the weak voice of reason among the conspiring businessmen. *The Hawaiians* is not a good film but it does give a good feel for nineteenth century Hawaii and it has a subplot that focuses on Chinese immigrants.

Amigo (2010), also written and directed by John Sayles, is a big sprawling nineteenth century novel of a movie set in 1900 during the Philippine–American War. This is history illustrated but not altered. It is accurate in almost every detail, beautifully written, and convincing and gripping right to the end. Featuring a large Filipino cast and shot by a mainly Filipino crew, it uses four languages, Spanish, Tagalog, Chinese, and English, and looks from the perspective of each. It is dominated by a grizzled Chris Cooper chewing-the-scenery as some Patton of the Pacific. Nevertheless, even minor characters get shading; that is, personally revealing dialogue.

The Philippine–American War was a template for later ideological expeditions in Central America, Iraq, and, most importantly for Sayles and his fellow boomers, Vietnam. "We're here to win hearts and minds," says Colonel Hardacre (Chris Cooper). The same phrase was used for the same policy in the Vietnam War. The racist term "gook" used by some Americans to describe the Vietnamese originated in the Philippine–American War.

The majority of critics praised *Amigo.* Peter Travers wrote in Rolling Stone: "*Amigo* is combustible filmmaking, something that stays with you long after the final credits. In an entertainment universe of escapism and short attention spans, Amigo is a rousing antidote and a cause for celebration." J. Hoberman wrote in the Village Voice, "*Amigo* is intelligently rip-roaring, a thoughtful action film, a teachable moment." In the New York Times, A.O. Scott wrote, "*Amigo* is a well-carpentered narrative, fast-moving and emphatic, stepping nimbly from gravity to good humor...It is politically aware, occasionally melodramatic and maintains a certain intimacy despite sprawling across multiple characters and stories ... All in all, he is a pretty good history teacher, the kind who knows how to make even difficult lessons entertaining and relevant."

The Philippine–American War is in the PBS documentary *Crucible of Empire: the Spanish-American War* (2007), the best available on the subject. Tellingly, there are no documentaries on the history of labor in the U.S. by either PBS or the History Channel. That says something about the sensitivity of the subject, even today, and especially for organizations, like PBS and the History Channel, dependent on corporations.

Which is not to say there isn't a great documentary about organized labor in the U.S. More than half a century after the events in *Matewan, Harlan County U.S.A.* shows striking West Virginia coal miners' living in conditions in the 1970s little changed from those of the '20s, including lethal violence from company thugs. There are also a number of old timers featured who recall the upheaval of the early decades of the twentieth century. *Harlan County U.S.A.* won the 1976 Oscar for Best Documentary. It was by Barbara Kopple who won a second Oscar in 1991 for *American Dream* about a strike by Hormel meat packers.

For immigration, there is Ken Burns' PBS doc *Statue of Liberty* (2004). For more than a century, it has been a symbol of hope and refuge for generations of immigrants. In this doc, it gets the Burns treatment, which is, in his words, "the story of the making of a remarkable work of art ... but also the story of the idea of liberty." *Not For Ourselves Alone: Elizabeth Cady Stanton and Susan B. Anthony* (1999) is also a Ken Burns doc about those two leaders of the women's suffrage movement.

PBS's *American Experience* series is especially rich in docs about our period. *America 1900* (2005) presents a comprehensive picture of American life in that year, themes include the impact of technology, the rise of racism, immigration, and the search for a national identity, and the rise of America as a world power. There is also: *Emma Goldman* (2004), about the brilliant and out-spoken leftist activist; *Triangle Fire* (2011) is about the Triangle Shirtwaist Factory fire; *The Great San Francisco Earthquake* (2006) and fire of 1906 that killed about 3,000 and destroyed over 80% of the city; *Panama Canal* (2011); and *Influenza 1918* (2006) about the worst epidemic in American history that killed over 600,000 during World War I. Nicknamed "Spanish influenza," it killed 50 to 100 million world wide—3 to 5 percent of the world's population.

At www.escalloniapress.com, there are free recommendations of the best books - histories, biographies, memoirs, and even novels - related to the subjects of this chapter.

Index

If you've enjoyed *A History of the U.S. in 20* Movies, you might also enjoy these other books by M.W.Jacobs. *San Fran '60s* and *More San Fran '60s* are short story collections set in Sixties San Francisco. Plus, there is *Choicest Rock Band Names as Tiny Poems*. From thousands collected over decades throughout the Anglophone world, these are the choicest few hundred. All these books are all available in paperback and ebook edition on Amazon. There are excerpts and rave reviews of all these books at escalloniapress.com.

San Fran '60s

The Street – A present-tense, stream-of-expanded-consciousness stroll the length of Haight Street on an afternoon at the height of the Summer of Love.

Unlivable With - A college love affair beset by a jealous husband and a predatory junkie culminates in a night of sex on LSD.

Bernie's Big Secret – A well known underground journalist was abandoning his wife and infant son, his career and country, and he wouldn't tell his best friend why.

Amateur Insanity - A nineteen year old, damaged by an upbringing among rednecks, and his roommate, an older scarred veteran of the civil rights movement, experience the gamut of the Summer of Love culminating in mental hospitals and murders.

Junkie Love - Three linked stories about addicts of various types during various phases of the drug culture. There's a legendary junkie burn-artist and there's armed robbery between dealers. And it all culminates in a meeting with William Burroughs.

Gilroy – Three dealers are driving from San Francisco to LA in the middle of the night on LSD and transporting LSD during the summer of 1967. They must contend with rednecks at a truck stop as well as demons of their own in their hurtling steal cage.

Summer of '66 – Four roommates in an illegal basement apartment in the Haight-Ashbury, plus those who crash there, in the gestational summer before the Summer of Love.

More San Fran '60s

Oaxaca - A long letter to a best friend during and about hitchhiking across Mexico immediately after the collapse of the Haight-Ashbury. It goes from stuck-in-the-desert to port city brothels to hippie prison hell against the mystery and magnificence of Mexico.

Long Hair - She was *summa cum laude* and a groupie, and though she admitted they would be an ideal couple, he didn't have long enough hair.

Satori – The whopper of all acid trips and a peek at ultimate reality … maybe.

The Magic Mountain Music Festival and Fantasy Fun Faire – It was the first hip rock festival (a week before Monterey Pop), headlined by the Doors, and the chick he didn't even dare fantasize about has picked him, or has she?

The Neocon - A character study spanning four decades from Sixties San Francisco through atrocity-ravaged Guatemala to the Iraq War.

Night of the Synchronized Paranoias – Two gorgeous chicks picked up on Haight Street are in the pad waiting to have fun while the two hosts are having simultaneous attacks of crippling drug paranoia.

There Is Only One Misfortune - Two men, a brilliant mystic who is also a successful businessman, and a hippie philosophy major, try to reach an ultimate understanding of the universe in a single, brutal eight hour argument.

Be-in – It was the first time the hippies were all together in one place and it was the founding event of the Counter Culture.

Summer of Love, Chicks - Four separate but interlocked stories trace a knot of sex, love, and psychosis through the Summer of Love.

Humanity's Tail - Various attacks by rednecks in the Haight, from murder to brandished rifles to attacks at night in the park during acid trips.

The Beatles' Last Concert Ever – It was in San Francisco six months before the coalescence of the Haight-Ashbury Counter Culture. The Beatles' influence is traced through various lives, plus, of course, there is the concert itself.

Choicest Rock Band Names as Tiny Poems

A Darwinian welter of tens of thousands of rock bands desperate for attention has created some remarkable names, a tiny percentage of which qualify as "found poetry." Indeed this may be a form of anonymous folk poetry like graffiti, bumper stickers, advertising catch phrases, and especially idiom. The choicest rock band name may even be the culmination of literary historical trends and may be pointing the way to a new poetic form for the age of texting, tweeting, the six-word memoir, and haiku reviews. An essay in the book makes the case.

Two-word Band Names

Corner laughers

Cupid's alley

Lightning riders

Reigning echoes

Guns debating

Liquid Picasso

Surreal Two-word Band Names

Cat spin

Colostomy pinata

Rutabaga paradox

Giddyup Einstein

The thes

Boxing Gandhis

Three-Word Band Names

Dying heart smile

Reasons in amber

One star sky

End begins again

Murals in metaphors

Deaf to silence

Surreal Three-Word Band Names

Pass the cat

Sonic fuzz monkey

Deputy hate angel

Smell the music

One-Word Band Names

Pretaliation

McJesus

Idiocracy

Techstacy

Bubbabarian

Drunkenstein

Othercide

Siolence

Nonsense One-Word Band Names

Scruffynurfherder

Schlafunkmotron

McRamahamasham

Tallulalunabella